LABOR IN THE TIME
OF TRUMP

LABOR IN THE TIME OF TRUMP

Edited by Jasmine Kerrissey,
Eve Weinbaum, Clare Hammonds,
Tom Juravich, and Dan Clawson

ILR PRESS

AN IMPRINT OF CORNELL UNIVERSITY PRESS   ITHACA AND LONDON

First published 2019 by Cornell University Press

Library of Congress Cataloging-in-Publication Data

Names: Kerrissey, Jasmine, 1977– editor. | MacLean, Nancy. Koch network's long game and its import for progressive organizing.
Title: Labor in the time of Trump / edited by Jasmine Kerrissey, Eve Weinbaum, Clare Hammonds, Tom Juravich, and Dan Clawson.
Description: Ithaca : ILR Press, an imprint of Cornell University Press, 2019. | Includes bibliographical references and index.
Identifiers: LCCN 2019013357 (print) | LCCN 2019017124 (ebook) | ISBN 9781501746611 (pdf) | ISBN 9781501746628 (epub/mobi) | ISBN 9781501746598 | ISBN 9781501746598 (cloth) | ISBN 9781501746604 (pbk.)
Subjects: LCSH: Labor movement—United States—History—21st century. | Labor Unions—Political activity—United States—History—21st century. | Working class—United States—History—21st century. | United States—Politics and government—2017-
Classification: LCC HD6510 (ebook) | LCC HD6510 .L33 2019 (print) | DDC 322/.20973—dc23
LC record available at https://lccn.loc.gov/2019013357

This book is dedicated to Dan Clawson, who never stopped laying the groundwork for the next upsurge.

Contents

LABOR IN THE TIME
OF TRUMP

INTRODUCTION

Jasmine Kerrissey, Eve Weinbaum, Clare Hammonds,
Tom Juravich, and Dan Clawson

After being dismissed as irrelevant for a decade, the labor movement has featured prominently in news headlines as this volume goes to press. There has been plenty of bad news. Right-to-work legislation was passed in Michigan, Indiana, West Virginia, Wisconsin, and Kentucky. The Supreme Court's decision in *Janus v. AFSCME* threatens to undermine public-sector unions. In the private sector, union density continued its long decline from 35 percent in the mid-1950s to under 7 percent in 2018 (Bureau of Labor Statistics 2019). The 2010 *Citizens United* decision, permitting unlimited corporate contributions to political campaigns, has crippled unions' political clout.

At the same time, there has been a wave of good news for working people and their movements. Teachers in West Virginia, Kentucky, Oklahoma, North Carolina, Arizona, Colorado, Los Angeles, Oakland, and beyond went on strike and won, defying the law and pundits. More than twenty million workers have received raises as a result of the Fight for $15 movement. The largest gains in union membership have been among young workers (Schmitt 2018). Worker centers have continued to push innovative strategies to organize workers in their communities outside of the National Labor Relations Act (NLRA) framework.

The 2018 midterm elections created some checks on the right-wing agenda, with Democrats winning the House of Representatives and many governorships. Labor was particularly thrilled to dethrone Scott Walker, the poster child of anti-union politics, although not before he signed legislation severely limiting the powers of the incoming Democratic governor and legislature. While these electoral outcomes were mostly good news for workers and unions, it remains to be seen whether the newly elected officials will pursue a pro-worker agenda. In the 2010s, pro-worker ballot initiatives prevailed in red and blue states alike. Voters are showing their support for sick days, family leave, and minimum wage increases, indicating broad support for improving the lives of workers.

The election of Donald Trump, and the increasing pushback against the right wing agenda, calls on us to reflect on the larger forces that threaten workers' rights, as well as the ways that workers, unions, and community-based organizations are fighting back. Scholars and activists alike must step back to analyze the attack on labor unions in the larger context of US politics and movements and to understand the roots of the right wing agenda, along with the multiple forms of resistance that unions and working-class communities have created in response.

This book provides that opportunity for rethinking and strategizing the most effective ways to move forward. We focus on two broad themes: how the right wing has organized, and unions' emerging challenges and strategies. We hope that this volume sparks a continued conversation about the context in which labor is fighting back and the strategies that are proving most effective in furthering an agenda of economic and social justice.

Does Trump Matter?

Trump's election in 2016 may have provided a wake-up call for labor and the Left, but the underlying processes behind this rightward shift had been building for at least forty years. Analysts continue to argue over the reasons for his victory, including the Electoral College system, reduced turnout by key Democratic constituencies, and voter suppression. Although the election was unusual in many ways, it did not represent a true political realignment. The people who supported Trump, for the most part, were the same people who supported previous Republican candidates Mitt Romney, John McCain, and George W. Bush. Some Republican voters may have been disturbed by Trump's open racism, the multiple accusations of sexual harassment against him, or his career as a billionaire exploiting workers, but they voted for him anyway. Trump voters were overwhelmingly white, and, contrary to popular assumptions, their median income was above average. Union voters were slightly more likely to vote for Trump than for previous Republican candidates. Still, union members and their families went for Hillary Clinton overall, giving her an eight percent advantage in union households.

The Trump campaign was not a traditional Republican campaign. Trump appealed to workers by denouncing globalization, insisting he would pull the United States out of bad trade deals and thereby defend working-class manufacturing and mining jobs. He promised a massive plan to rebuild America's infrastructure, generating millions of jobs. He promised to protect Social Security and Medicare, and to fix the tax code to help working families. Alongside this populist economic platform, the Trump campaign appealed directly to nationalist, nativist, and racist ideologies, some of these appeals being open and explicit.

Trump's promises resonated with many working people, including some building trades unions, who saw new pipelines and infrastructure as a boon to their members, and some industrial unions, who saw Trump's Buy American focus and promise to impose tariffs as a way to stabilize their industries. Despite Trump's clear antiunion record, a number of union leaders met with him soon after his inauguration and promised to work with him. Progressives, in unions and elsewhere, saw Trump's invitation to some unions as an explicit attempt to divide the labor movement and viewed the agreement to work with Trump as a betrayal.

Once in office, Trump's economic agenda has looked more like a traditional neoliberal corporate platform. With both houses of Congress controlled by Republicans in Trump's first two years, the administration was very successful at controlling appointments to the courts, including lower courts as well as the Supreme Court, and moving the judiciary in an explicitly right-wing political direction. The Republican-appointed National Labor Relations Board is considering reversing rules that aim to level the playing field in union elections, including access to the names and contact information for all eligible workers in a bargaining unit. The Republican administration has also worked to dismantle regulatory systems, most notably environmental policies. These efforts—stacking courts, attacking unions, and gutting regulatory systems—have serious long-term implications for workers. There are also crises that are more immediate for working people. Immigrant workers face threats of workplace raids and deportations, and workers of color face a Trump-sanctioned climate of racism and xenophobia.

In other ways, however, the election of 2016 did not represent a sea change for working people. Privatization, charter schools, education "reform," mass incarceration, policing borders and deporting immigrants, replacing strikers with scabs, preventing nontraditional workers from forming unions, signing on to unfair trade agreements, and increasing defense spending at the expense of social programs were all policies and practices that began long before Trump and likely would have continued if Hillary Clinton had become president. States with Republican governors and legislatures would continue passing right-to-work laws and other legislation aimed at undermining labor and progressive groups. State and local budgets would still be underfunded and public services would still be starved, while a small number of people amassed obscene amounts of money. Right-wing policy groups and think tanks would still be flourishing.

Trump's election did trigger one crucial change for the labor movement, however: millions of people turned out for marches, protests, and other forms of political activism. This new energy and spirit of activism began before Trump—arguably with the Occupy movement, the protests in Wisconsin, the Bernie Sanders campaign, and the critiques of the economic system in movements focused on climate change, immigrants' rights, #MeToo, and Black Lives Matter—but the resistance deepened and spread across the country following the election.

This Political Moment

If not Trump, what defines this political moment? We have seen a sharp increase in inequality, weakened labor and left movements, and the resulting dominance of the corporate agenda. Despite a lot of talk about Trump and American exceptionalism, the United States does not look very different from the rest of the world. In 2016, British voters opted for "Brexit"—withdrawal from the European Union—leading to political turmoil in England. Right-wing populist governments are in power in Austria, Hungary, India, Italy, the Netherlands, Poland, the Philippines, Argentina, Brazil, Colombia, and Chile, and are contesting for power in other liberal democracies, often based in significant part on nativist anti-immigrant sentiment, as well as an antielite message similar to Trump's. Unions and workers' movements are on the defensive in many countries.

Several trends have converged to define this moment, and understanding these forces is essential to the chapters in this volume. First, neoliberalism dominates the global economy. The neoliberal approach rejects the historical role of the government in overseeing the economy, which had been in place since the New Deal. Instead, markets are sacrosanct, and any constraints on capitalist prerogatives should be minimized. For the neoliberals, government, democracy, and unions are problematic. In place of public schools, for example, neoliberals argue that we should have vouchers or charter schools, all in competition with each other. Neoliberals push to privatize traditional government functions, including schools, prisons, the welfare state, roads, and even the military, with private contractors taking over duties once reserved for soldiers.

The second trend is the process of globalization. Markets, finance, and production chains are not national but rather international, with capital and resources originating in different countries and crossing national borders. For example, small-scale Mexican farmers are pressured by US agribusiness, and unionized US autoworkers with good wages and benefits must compete with low-wage Mexican auto workers who lack independent unions. Right-wing opposition to immigration is not only economic but also racial. Immigrants from the Global South are racialized and criminalized accordingly. Financial capital flows freely across borders, uncontested, while people trying to follow the jobs are scrutinized and controlled by legal restrictions, walls, and deployment of troops.

The third force is financialization. Financial interests increasingly dominate manufacturing and service industries. Manufacturing is disappearing from the United States, and profits are made not by producing goods or services but rather by investing capital, repackaging assets, taking on debt, and selling off pieces of the restructured asset. Profits come not only from producing a better product at a cheaper price but also from trading currencies and other financial instruments.

Neoliberalism creates winners and losers; globalization strengthens and expands markets; and financialization rewards those with large amounts of capital to invest. Market mechanisms are increasingly replacing governments as the way to distribute public goods, and neoliberal governments exist to expand and reinforce markets through privatization. Gone is our shared understanding that people have a right to education, health care, public libraries, and pensions—not to mention the right to get together at work and advocate for their interests, if necessary by withholding their labor. Instead of a strong public sector whose activities are democratically controlled and equally accessible to all—despite the flaws with the actual functioning of that democracy—the conservative ideal is to abolish public schools and instead support privately run or for-profit charter schools and/or vouchers, replace collective pensions with individual financial investments in 401(k) plans, drastically restrict public libraries and other services, and cut health insurance and transfer the costs and risks to individuals.

All these trends are closely related to increases in inequality. In the United States, in much of the era after World War II, workers' wages rose as productivity increased. This pattern had been broken by the 1980s—only the top 10 percent continued to see their wages rise, while other workers' wages stagnated (Bivens, Gould, Mishel, and Shierholz 2014). This pattern has persisted in the 2010s despite record-high stock prices and low unemployment rates. Meanwhile, the average CEO-to-worker pay ratio skyrocketed from 20 to 1 in 1965 to 312 to 1 in 2017 (Mishel and Schieder 2018). The three richest men in America (Jeff Bezos, Bill Gates, and Warren Buffett) own more wealth than 160 million Americans combined (Collins and Hoxie 2017).

Inequality is even worse for women and people of color. For instance, black workers earn 75 percent as much as white workers and women earn 83 percent as much as men. The issue is magnified for women of color, who are overrepresented in low-wage jobs in retail, fast food, and home health care (Pew Research Institute 2016). Black women, for example, are only 6 percent of the workforce but account for ten percent of workers in low-wage occupations (National Women's Law Center 2017). These income and wealth gaps impact almost every aspect of life: educational achievement, life expectancy, infant mortality, incarceration rates, and life outcomes. US communities are facing the corollaries of inequality, including concentrated poverty, disease, alcoholism, drug overdoses, and suicides. Rising inequality also has political consequences, creating distrust of government and elites, contributing to resentment and insecurity, and laying the groundwork for right-wing populism.

Labor and Unions

Decades ago, unions were an essential piece of the liberal order, defining workers' rights and power in the workplace. They were major drivers of economic equality and fairness in workplaces and important to shaping public policy that supported working people. Not only did unions bring benefits to their own members, but the labor movement was also a force for equity and power for the working class as a whole. The union "threat effect" compelled nonunion employers to offer the same benefits to their workers as union employers did—lest their employees try to unionize as well—improving life for millions of workers and their families. The equalizing effects of unions have been particularly important for women and workers of color, since transparent union wages and grievance procedures help to fight discriminatory employment practices.

Today, unions represent less than 7 percent of the private sector workforce, the union threat effect still exists but is drastically reduced, and a hostile legal climate and business community make it extraordinarily difficult to mount a successful strike or organizing campaign. The 2016 elections of Trump and Republican governors in states such as Michigan, Wisconsin, and Illinois were possible in part because unions' power and membership had been decimated.

Initially, unions in the public sector faced a less hostile environment than those in the private sector. This climate took a sharp turn after the 2008 recession, when the narrative of the overpaid public-sector worker gained traction—despite the evidence that the consolidation of income was occurring among the rich, not public-sector workers. States began to gut public-sector union rights, and well-funded right-wing networks began to aggressively use the court system to weaken public-sector unions, who were the largest organized opposition to the right wing's political agenda. The 2018 Supreme Court ruling in *Janus v. AFSCME* sent the message that the attack on public-sector workers was now in full swing.

The erosion of unions does not mean the absence of activism, however. Unions have built aggressive organizing campaigns in health care, media, food services, hotels, and education, among other areas. In 2018, there was a dramatic increase in strikes, led by teachers and other educators. Workers continued to organize in a variety of organizations, including "alt-labor," representing workers in nontraditional jobs or contingent positions, such as domestic workers, restaurant workers, and taxi drivers, among others. Worker centers across the United States continued to play a critical role at the community level, assisting those working in the informal economy and fighting wage theft, especially for undocumented workers and those not protected by standard labor laws. The Fight for $15 campaign, initially driven by the Service Employees International Union (SEIU), created a national movement to raise wages for some of the most poorly paid workers in the United States. Labor-backed coalitions, including Jobs with Justice and an array of local coalitions, have been central not only to organizing campaigns but also to advocating for policy initiatives that support workers, from a higher minimum wage to paid family leave. Even in states that elected Republicans, ballot initiatives supporting workers have won in nearly every state where they have been attempted, indicating possibilities for issue-based campaigns by labor movements and their allies.

Three Theories about the Attack on Workers

What created our current political situation? In chapters 1–3 of this book, Nancy MacLean, Gordon Lafer, and Bill Fletcher and José La Luz, respectively, offer contrasting explanations for the development and upsurge of the right wing.

In chapter 1, Nancy MacLean takes a long view of the emergence of libertarian ideology and the development of the Far Right. Based on her discovery of the archive of public choice economist James Buchanan, MacLean argues that it is these ideas, promoted through a deep, broad, densely connected network of right-wing think tanks, foundations, and sponsored academics, that have driven an ideological agenda. In this way, these parties weaponized these ideas and deployed a series of policy initiatives at the state level. The Koch brothers and a host of others fund this movement, and a wide range of academics, commentators, media personalities, and politicians are true believers. MacLean argues that the right knew early on that voters would reject their policy agenda, which would benefit only a minority of citizens. Consequently, right-wing activists pushed a stealth campaign of incremental changes that obscured the true motives of their radical agenda. Their goal, MacLean suggests, was to turn America back to the way it looked in 1900—a nation without workers' rights, without public regulation, run by business-dominated government institutions free of democratic accountability. Beginning at the state level, through gerrymandering and model legislation, they have attacked Social Security, Planned Parenthood, and unions, while pushing through massive tax cuts and privatization to permanently undercut state power. Conservatives have attacked government itself; this coalition has already lined up twenty-eight of the thirty-four states required for a constitutional convention that could fundamentally change democracy as we know it. MacLean explains how a war of ideas has provided the underpinnings of contemporary right-wing populism.

Gordon Lafer, by contrast, argues in chapter 2 that the problem is a corporate assault, driven not by ideology but rather by business's self-interest. The actions and policy interventions he describes are not limited to a set of committed ideologues—rather, business as a whole participates, especially mainstream business associations like the US Chamber of Commerce and the American Legislative Exchange Council (ALEC). Lafer shows that the most dangerous antidemocratic actions and policies are supported by a large majority of corporate actors. When so-called ideologues like the Koch brothers encounter a conflict between their ideology and their self-interest, self-interest wins: in the 2008 recession, the Kochs supported the government bailout of banks, which violated their ideological commitments but was essential to their business interests. ALEC drafts model legislation and spreads it across all fifty states, including narrow bills that benefit individual firms as well as sweeping legislation that supports the business community overall. Lafer argues that this corporate assault has transformed the political process at the state level and restricted the scope of democratic deliberation. Like MacLean, Lafer underscores how the corporate agenda is at odds with what a majority of voters want. Even in states that voted for Trump, evidence shows that the right has been unable to convince voters to support its policy agenda. For Lafer, this working-class resistance and support for progressive issues provides hope that organized opposition based on issues can defeat the corporate agenda.

In chapter 3, Bill Fletcher Jr. and José La Luz argue that the core problem is not ideology or corporate self-interest but rather the rise of a right-wing populism that feeds on racism and xenophobia. When workers suffer from stagnating or declining incomes, loss of benefits and pensions, declining health and health care coverage, and increased job insecurity, the right gives them an answer: blame black people, Latinxs, immigrants, Jews, or Muslims; blame the media elites, academics, or experts, not your employer; embrace the rich in the hope that someday you can be one of them; and condemn powerless people as the cause of your problems. Fletcher and La Luz describe how populism draws its energy from a racist, sexist, and xenophobic framing of the impact of the economic crisis on working-class Americans while also rejecting the postwar global order in favor of a return to American isolationism. They lament the Left's failure to offer plausible solutions and to create lasting solidarity across gender, race, ethnicity, and sexuality. Fletcher and La Luz write that no revival of labor will be possible without engaging union members about race, gender, immigration, and the true nature of right-wing populism.

How the Right Wing Advances Its Agenda

In Part II of this volume, Jon Shelton, Sarah Jaffe, and Donald Cohen each detail mechanisms by which the right wing has pursued its goals.

In chapter 4, Jon Shelton outlines the rise of Scott Walker in Wisconsin, which foreshadowed contemporary attacks on public-sector workers and the election of Trump. As the industrial economy collapsed and Wisconsin workers' resentment intensified, Walker won the governor's seat in 2010 by blaming public workers and the special privileges they enjoyed and by promising to restore employment for industrial workers. Shelton details how Walker forced through Act 10, a legislative attack on unions in what had been one of the most progressive states. Act 10 required unions to demonstrate annual recertification with 51 percent support of the entire bargaining unit, and unions could only bargain over wages that were capped at the rate of inflation. Not surprisingly, union membership declined by 40 percent, and public services were slashed, including public school and university systems. Despite Walker's promises, Wisconsin lags far behind projected job growth and employment levels in neighboring Minnesota, with its progressive agenda. The Walker agenda, and the coalitions that arose to resist it, presaged the Trump moment; it is an open question whether Walker's 2018 ouster itself is a precursor to future elections.

In chapter 5, Sarah Jaffe unpacks myths about the white working class and its support for Donald Trump in the 2016 election. Popular media wrongly suggest that millions of white, economically disadvantaged, uneducated blue-collar workers were responsible for Trump's victory. Jaffe examines the evidence, showing that two-thirds of Trump voters made more than the median income but more than half of those without college degrees were in the top half of the income distribution. Jaffe suggests that these voters were not motivated by enthusiasm about Trump's priorities but rather were protesting a system that had left them behind. The myth of the struggling white working-class voter, clamoring for Trump to make America great again, ignores the millions of working-class workers who are people of color and misunderstands racism. Jaffe shows how important it is to listen to Trump voters, to understand why working-class people are angry, and to question the media's narrative of the white working class.

In chapter 6, Donald Cohen focuses on the right wing's astonishingly successful efforts to privatize public goods and services. Privatization has been one of the highest priorities of the right wing for many years, and Cohen shows how it threatens both labor and democracy. Intentionally blurring the lines between public and private institutions, private companies and market forces undermine the common good. Cohen documents the history of privatization in the United States, from President Reagan's early efforts to Clinton and Gore's belief in private markets. Showing how privatization undermines democratic government, Cohen describes complex contracts that are difficult to understand, poorly negotiated "public-private partnership" deals, and contracts that provide incentives to deny public services. With huge amounts of money at stake, privateers are increasingly weighing in on policy debates—not based on the public interest but rather in pursuit of avenues that increase their revenues, profits, and market share. Privatization not only destroys union jobs but also aims to cripple union political involvement so that the corporate agenda can spread unfettered. Nevertheless, community-based battles against privatization have succeeded in many localities, demonstrating the power of fighting back to defend public services, public jobs, and democratic processes.

Challenges and Coalition Opportunities

In Part III, Lara Skinner, Shannon Gleeson, and Cedric Johnson tackle key issues confronting unions today: climate change, immigration, Black Lives Matter, policing, and mass incarceration.

In chapter 7, Lara Skinner outlines tensions among unions in the energy sector and debates about a pro-climate, pro-worker agenda. Proposals for "green jobs" that protect the environment do not ensure good, union jobs. Energy-sector unions have often been wary of such proposals, arguing correctly that green jobs are rarely available in the same quality or quantity as jobs in fossil-fuel industries. Drawing on cases from climate initiatives in New York State, Skinner argues that unions must be at the table when proposals to expand green jobs are designed and implemented. Skinner outlines a practical plan for unions to work with politicians and communities to ensure "just transition." Skinner argues that while climate change issues have often pitted labor unions against the environmental movement and its progressive allies, there are also examples of successful "blue-green" alliances. These coalitions strengthen the labor movement by forging new ties with important allies and allowing workers to proactively shape the role of unions and workers in the emerging green economy.

In chapter 8, Shannon Gleeson tackles one of the most controversial issues of the Trump regime: immigration. Trump aggressively and unapologetically embraces an anti-immigrant agenda—focusing on Mexicans crossing the border, "chain migration" of families, and those arriving from what he calls "shithole" or Muslim-majority countries. Gleeson examines how various union bodies have responded to the "immigration question." She describes the labor movement's complicated history on this issue, including complex and sometimes inconsistent positions on undocumented workers, guest workers, and paths to citizenship. In the past decade, however, the AFL-CIO has evolved to be strongly in favor of immigrants' rights, linking the fate of immigrants to rights for all working people. Not every union is on board, and many working people worry that immigrants threaten their jobs, but many progressive unions—as well as worker centers and alt-labor groups—have been at the forefront of organizing for immigrant rights. Gleeson finds that unions in locations that receive large numbers of immigrants have been leading the charge, forging sanctuary unions, advocating for inclusive policies, and negotiating fair contract language. At the national level, labor groups have been active in efforts to save the DREAM Act, Deferred Action for Childhood Arrivals (DACA), and Temporary Protected Status. Unions have worked against the Muslim ban and Islamophobia, and in support of refugees, often through involvement with interfaith coalitions. Despite the challenges and despite working people's complicated views, Gleeson's research demonstrates that unions must adopt an intersectional lens and collaborate with community-based and advocacy organizations to build a progressive agenda in the age of Trump.

In chapter 9, Cedric Johnson tackles the issues of mass incarceration and aggressive policing, and their impact on low-income communities and people of color. Johnson places Trump's defense of police and denigration of Black Lives Matter into historical context. He connects the rise of the carceral state with an ideology that pathologizes poverty, blames working-class and unemployed people for their failure to get rich, and defines an urban "underclass" as the problem. In this context, Johnson analyzes Trump's reverence for police as the "thin blue line" that separates civilization from chaos. Focusing our attention on the intersection between class and race, Johnson unpacks the logic that has motivated a long-standing effort to shift power and resources away from the working class and toward the corporate elite. Blaming the most vulnerable groups has effectively absolved elites of their responsibility for worsening labor conditions, disappearing jobs, and falling real wages for workers, while the profits of CEOs and owners are higher than ever. Blaming minorities, the poor, and immigrants also serves to persuade the anxious middle class that they would be doing well in the neoliberal order if it were not for these "other" groups stealing what was rightfully theirs, thereby convincing the white middle class that capitalism is not the problem.

Johnson argues that liberal antiracist arguments misunderstand the class relations that underlie our current system of policing. The postwar transformation of cities and the rise of suburbs created a push to aggressively protect property values and opportunities for growth and profit. Liberal solutions that ignore this history risk making exploitation and repression more politically tolerable. Johnson concludes that labor groups have a crucial role to play in fighting police abuse and mass incarceration. Working with civil rights organizations and local community-based campaigns, unions can mobilize the working class and challenge the enforcement regime that protects inequality.

Labor Strategies and Responses

How do unions build power in an increasingly right-wing climate? MaryBe McMillan, Jennifer Klein, and Kyla Walters explore union strategies in different settings.

In chapter 10, MaryBe McMillan, president of North Carolina's state AFL-CIO, reflects on the challenges and opportunities of building workers' power in North Carolina. To change the political balance of the nation, McMillan argues, we must change the South, which is gaining in jobs, population, and political influence. Home to more than a third of the US population, the region is larger than the Northeast and Midwest combined. Political representatives from the South disproportionately contribute to right-wing agendas, including right-to-work, low wages, and voter suppression—although the competitive campaigns of progressive candidates in Florida, Georgia, and Texas in 2018 suggested that there are cracks an organized Left can pry open. McMillan outlines essential strategies for organizing in the South, or in any right-to-work states with hostile political climates. First, she argues, start small and dream big. In North Carolina, Moral Mondays brought together unions and allies to protest legislative attacks on public education and voting rights, contributing to a Democratic takeover of the state Supreme Court, ousting the incumbent Republican governor, and creating the national Poor People's Campaign. Second, we must address issues of race and gender equality. The labor movement is in a unique position to change attitudes and long-standing structures of inequity. Third, unions must build strong locals and unite with community allies. This requires internal worksite organizing where stewards and rank-and-file members lead the efforts. Finally, the labor movement, including central labor councils and state federations, must build political power. Lasting political change will depend on building a bigger, bolder labor movement.

Chapter 11, by Jennifer Klein, also tackles how to build power under challenging conditions. Klein analyzes the case of home health care, which stands outside

New Deal labor laws and is one of the largest and fastest-growing low-wage occupations. Building on decades of organizing, persistent political action, and mobilization with clients, home-care workers' unions won legislative battles enabling states to take on the role of employer and winning the right to engage in collective bargaining. By 2010, these unions had gained 400,000 members—at a time when many unions saw membership losses. The right fought back through the courts, culminating in the 2014 *Harris v. Quinn* decision to reject these arrangements. Anti-union groups are now aggressively encouraging union disaffiliation through door-to-door campaigns, but home-care unions are fighting back. A critical component is deep member training and education, including "leadership academies" to cultivate workers' political education and skills. Klein's chapter reminds us that members make the union—with or without state recognition. A strong, mobilized rank and file, along with active coalition partners, has made substantial gains.

Chapter 12, by Kyla Walters, examines the dynamics behind a high-profile campaign led by the Massachusetts Teachers Association (MTA). In 2016, right-wing forces sought to expand charter schools through a ballot initiative. Initially, all signs suggested that the charter expansion would easily pass, with a huge early lead in polls, enormous financial backing from business and financial interests, and support from the popular Republican governor. The MTA mobilized, and the ballot measure was defeated in a landslide. Walters identifies several mechanisms that contributed to the teachers' success. Most important, the MTA committed to fighting. A progressive caucus within the MTA won the union presidency in 2014. While the previous union administration had a record of compromising, the new leadership focused on challenging corporate-backed education policies and organizing the fight from the bottom up. Trusting, educating, and training rank-and-file members, the union mobilized thousands of teachers to go out into their communities to be "everyday spokespeople" for public schools. The MTA committed millions of dollars to trainings, campaign materials, and public events, building a broad, interracial coalition. Together with the NAACP, Jobs with Justice, and others, this grassroots coalition defeated Wall Street's money and showed the power of social justice organizing. Fifteen months later, in spring 2018, a string of strikes in red states showed that educators in many places have both the inclination and the capacity to fight, even where teacher strikes are prohibited.

What Next?

How should labor respond to the conditions we now face? These chapters provide many answers. Too often, labor leaders, academics, and activists, all in different ways, focus on immediate and urgent issues that demand our attention. We all need to step back, to think about how we got here, to understand where we are now—to consider, from a longer-term perspective, what it would take not just to win today's battles but also to transform the current framework.

The chapters in this volume address the fundamental shifts that have occurred in the last two generations and provide examples of building power under today's conditions. One lesson is the need to see the big picture, to understand the many-faceted nature of the right-wing attack and the multiple sources of its power: a war of ideas; systematic efforts to mobilize corporate self-interest; the building of a voting base through an appeal to racism, nativism, and emotions; structural changes that remove democratic decision making; and attacks on all fronts. To have a reasonable hope of success, a left response has to be aware of those dimensions and more and has to develop sources of power that do not attempt to mirror the right but rather are adapted to the very different structural circumstances of the left.

Many of the chapters emphasize the need for internal organizing and education, to combat racism and xenophobia, and to develop deeper understandings of inequalities of money and power. Education needs to be internal, among workers and union members, but labor's success will also depend on educating the broader public. Deep internal organizing is necessary to develop committed and talented union activists. Organizing among low-wage women, immigrants, and people of color shows what many know to be true: workers can and will fight for themselves.

The chapters also demonstrate that unions' political orientations and commitments matter, and that progressive leadership within unions can build power, even against tough odds, to take on controversial but crucial issues. Struggles within unions matter as much as struggles between labor and capital. Internal union movements or caucuses with an antiracist agenda, a deep bench of leaders, and a willingness to involve members in struggles with employers are much more likely to result in unions that build and exercise power. Strong leadership understands where members are and moves them to realize an agenda that addresses their core commitments and needs.

The authors highlight the labor movement's crucial role in politics and policy. Labor's electoral strategy is hotly contested; while some unions continue to endorse the mainstream Democratic candidates, others support left-wing populists from Bernie Sanders to Alexandria Ocasio-Cortez. Many unions advocate, organize, and engage in policy debates around legislation and governmental regulations and promote open democratic processes, fighting privatization and neoliberal reforms. While many unions defer to the Democratic Party agenda, others call on labor to create its own agenda, identifying specific ballot initiatives that serve the interests of unions and working people, collecting signatures to qualify those measures for the ballot, and campaigning to get them passed. Many labor issues—a higher minimum wage, paid sick time, and paid family and medical leave—have very high levels of support, not only from Democrats and independents but from Republican voters as well.

Broad engagement with the community is essential to fighting back, as so many of the authors of this volume demonstrate. If the labor movement is to have an impact on the most serious issues of our time—economic inequality, climate change, immigration, mass incarceration, voter suppression, the right to organize, and the protection of democracy itself—unions will have to work with as many allies as they can muster. The working class is more than just traditional unions, and only a broad movement has the potential to achieve the most far-reaching goals.

Building corporate lobbies and the right-wing ideology surrounding them is fundamental to capitalism—as is the impulse to generate wealth at the top and eliminate unions. How the labor movement responds, however, is generating fierce debates within the labor movement. The right-wing agenda is at odds with what most people want, and it is up to the labor movement and its allies to expose and counter that contradiction.

The challenge for labor and the left is to marshal the forces that believe another world is possible.

References

Bivens, Josh, Elise Gould, Lawrence Mishel, and Heidi Shierholz. 2014. "Raising America's Pay: Why It's Our Central Economic Policy Challenge" *Economic Policy Institute*, paper #378.

Bureau of Labor Statistics. 2019. "Union Members Summary." *Economic News Release*, January 18. https://www.bls.gov/news.release/union2.nr0.htm.

Collins, Chuck, and Josh Hoxie. 2017. "Billionaire Bonanza: The Forbes 400 and the Rest of Us." *Institute for Policy Studies*, accessed April 9, 2019. https://inequality.org/wp-content/uploads/2017/11/BILLIONAIRE-BONANZA-2017-Embargoed.pdf.

Mishel, Lawrence, and Jessica Schieder. 2018. "CEO Compensation Surged in 2017." *Economic Policy Institute*, August 16. https://www.epi.org/publication/ceo-compensation-surged-in-2017.

National Women's Law Center. 2017. "Low Wage Jobs are Women's Jobs." Accessed April 9, 2019. https://nwlc.org/wp-content/uploads/2017/08/Low-Wage-Jobs-are-Womens-Jobs.pdf.

Pew Research Institute. 2016. "Racial and Gender Wage Gaps Persist in US Despite Some Progress." Accessed April 9, 2019. https://www.pewresearch.org/fact-tank/2016/07/01/racial-gender-wage-gaps-persist-in-u-s-despite-some-progress/.

Schmitt, John. January 25, 2018. "Biggest gains in union membership in 2017 were for younger workers." *Economic Policy Institute*, January 25. https://www.epi.org/publication/biggest-gains-in-union-membership-in-2017-were-for-younger-workers.

Part I

THREE THEORIES ABOUT THE ATTACK ON WORKERS

1

THE KOCH NETWORK'S LONG GAME AND ITS IMPLICATIONS FOR PROGRESSIVE ORGANIZING

Nancy MacLean

When historians look back on this moment fifty years from now and try to make sense of it, I do not think they will be focusing on Donald Trump. I think they will be more interested in a quiet yet radical transformation now under way. In fact, Trump's conduct has distracted attention from an ingenious slow takeover, led by brothers Charles and David Koch of the radical right, of core branches of our government, beginning at the state level, moving on to the federal courts and Congress, and then extending into federal departments and agencies. This takeover has advanced with assistance from hundreds of well-funded organizations and campus outposts funded by the Koch donor network. This infrastructure consists of national bodies such as the Cato Institute, the Heritage Foundation, the American Legislative Exchange Council (ALEC), and the Federalist Society; more than 150 state-level organizations, whose work is aligned through the State Policy Network; organizing enterprises, including Americans for Liberty, Concerned Veterans for America, the LIBRE Initiative, and Generation Opportunity; international affiliates of the Atlas Network, with operations in close to a hundred countries; and campus-based centers of allied faculty. Their campus presence has expanded exponentially over the last decade, with over 300 colleges and universities now receiving funding from the Charles Koch Foundation, which is "leveraging" them, to use its language, to move its radical transformation driven by dark money.

My research has found that the right wing has been winning because the Koch network has effectively weaponized the ideas of a figure who is little known to the mainstream or the Left but who supplied the crucial ideas in play today, much as Milton Friedman supplied those of an earlier era. His name is James McGill Buchanan, and he was the first US southerner to win the Nobel Prize in economics, which he was awarded for developing the fields of public choice political economy and constitutional economics. (For fuller treatment and documentation not cited here, see MacLean 2017).

The Koch Network's Driving Ideas

I believe that knowing about these ideas—and how the Koch network's operations have weaponized them—is important not just in its own right, to see more clearly what is happening, why, and how. It is also important because having that knowledge may equip concerned citizens to lead the way out of the current crisis of our democracy before it is too late. A public-health nurse who read my book on the subject used this analogy: you need to get the diagnosis right before you can determine the best treatment plan.

So what are these ideas? Here are six key elements of the radical right's overarching vision:

1. Market forces alone should determine social outcomes, with no interference from government. Government has only three legitimate roles: enforce the law, ensure social order, and defend us from foreign enemies (the easily recalled summary is courts, cops, and armies). Everything else should in time be eliminated because it interferes with property rights, economic liberty, and personal responsibility. That is why the Koch network fought the Affordable Care Act and why it attacks labor union rights and worker protections, backs school voucher programs and unlimited charter school expansion, blocks action on climate change, and works to dismantle regulations of all kinds.

2. Any attempt by the people to use their numbers to modify markets, as unions and government policies such as minimum wages do, is illegitimate and akin to gangsterism. The Koch team believes that we should only have the right to act as individuals, not to muster any collective countervailing power to that of corporations, as Americans have been accustomed to doing for generations. That is the core belief behind the *Janus v. AFSCME* case, which abolished "fair share" or "agency" fees for public-sector unions nationally, enabling workers to get the benefits of the union without paying for them in hopes of mortally wounding them. It is also why organizations in the Koch-allied State Policy Network are now using the Freedom of Information Act to identify union members and going door to door to try to

convince them to stop paying dues. Free speech is not the true ultimate goal here, despite its role in persuading the Supreme Court's right-wing majority; the goal is to break down the collective power of the people to block implementation of the radical libertarian program, including the privatization of public education, Social Security, and Medicare, the end of Medicaid, and more.

3. Democracy does not require majority rule; in fact, democracy is not even an especially desirable form of decision making. The radically antidemocratic libertarian cause believes in a unanimity standard: only if everyone (above all, the very wealthiest among us) supports a particular policy and voluntarily agrees to pay for it can it be said to truly represent the common good. That is why the logic of the *Janus* anticoercion argument is likely to be applied to taxation now that there is precedent. It is also why Koch-allied organizations and elected officials are working so hard to limit voting by those most likely to oppose their agenda, including African Americans, Latinos, and young people.

4. Elected officials do not really care about the common good; they only care about getting reelected, using other people's money to dole out favors to ensure that. That is why we have deficits even in times of prosperity. That is also why even the most conservative of Republican presidents, Ronald Reagan and George W. Bush, disappointed the radical libertarians, because they did not go nearly far enough to end what the latter routinely deride as the "dependency" of the people on government. They proved too deferential to the voters, allowing the "takers" to continue to prey on the "makers," hence the need for this more radical gambit (MacLean 2017).

5. Because the people cannot be trusted to restrain their claims on the wealthy, and elected officials cannot be trusted with the power to tax and spend, iron-clad binding restraints must be put on both. Buchanan urged changes so significant that they would amount to a "constitutional revolution" (Buchanan 1973). That revolution would put shackles on what government could do, including such measures as making balanced budgets mandatory, limiting the right to vote, placing permanent caps on tax rates, imposing congressional term limits, and requiring vast supermajorities for any change of substance after their constitutional revolution. (MacLean, 2017b).

6. The only way to achieve such radical and unpopular changes is by stealth, spreading misinformation (such as climate science denial and the myth of mass voter fraud) and relying, initially, on the branch of government that is easiest for corporations to capture and deploy. That is state government, as shown by Wisconsin under Scott Walker and my own home state of North Carolina, two prime laboratories for this approach.

How could serious intellectuals justify these six propositions? To a libertarian like Buchanan, there is no common good. Any such notion of shared purpose will lead government to coerce those who do not agree with the majority. Democracy, Buchanan and his colleagues came to argue, violates the individual liberty of the minority. The minority he was concerned with was wealthy taxpayers who do not share the majority's view of the public interest. Buchanan and his colleagues argued that government all but steals their property if it taxes them for purposes they do not agree with.

Thus, when in 2012 Republican presidential candidate Mitt Romney spoke disdainfully to donors regarding "the 47 percent" of Americans he said would never vote for him because they were too "dependent" on government, millions of Americans were shocked. Romney was not offering a new idea, however. By then, the Heritage Foundation was maintaining an "annual index of dependency," derived from public choice economics, to stigmatize net tax recipients and devise strategies for ending tax transfers (Whiteside 2012; MacLean, 2017).

Buchanan was the figure who gave scholarly imprimatur to such thinking, and he did not hold back, showing an animus that reflected his southern white conservative commitments. He spoke of net tax recipients as "parasites" on the "productive" and warned of "predators" and "prey" (MacLean 2017). His very vocabulary made fellow citizens appear as a menace, not even truly human. It is a vocabulary that is disinhibiting, that licenses hostility. And it, too, is rife on the Right today. Trump's language of "us and them" gains legitimacy from Buchanan's theories, as does his definition of the Washington, D.C., political environment as "the swamp" (BBC News, 2016).

What would a world guided by Buchanan's ideas—as weaponized by the Koch network's power—look like? More stark and cruel than most of us can imagine: each of us wholly on our own (actually, each family, since the libertarians depend on women's unpaid labor for their households), with no help from government. If circumstances prevent us from providing for ourselves, then all we can hope for is private charity, should the wealthier choose to give it. Think of the world of Charles Dickens as the desideratum of this cause.

The libertarian morality thus deems it better to have people die from lack of health care than receive it from government, from taxes paid by others. Commenting on the Affordable Care Act, which brought health care to millions who lacked it, Michael S. Greve, then chairman of the Competitive Enterprise Institute (a Koch-funded "do tank," by its own depiction), said, "This bastard has to be killed as a matter of political hygiene. . . . I do not care how it is done, whether it's dismembered, whether we drive a stake through its heart, whether we tar and feather it and drive it out of town, [or] whether we strangle it" (Lichtblau 2015). The Competitive Enterprise Institute had devised and funded the case against the

Affordable Care Act. Greve was also the strategist behind the *Janus* case and its predecessor (Lichtblau 2015). He has since been rewarded with a professorship at the Koch-funded Scalia School of Law, a key base of the network's legal operations (MacLean 2017).

What did Greve mean by political hygiene? That for citizens to receive any new reason to value government would be for the libertarian cause a hazard so perilous that only violent imagery could convey the urgency of its extinction. So this is what the radical right means, ultimately, by personal responsibility: you should be on your own for all your needs, and if you fail to anticipate and save for those future needs, you deserve your fate. Not only that, but your suffering will have instructive value for others in the new world the libertarians are ushering into being: watching what befalls you, as government no longer helps you, will teach others that they must work hard and save. What libertarians seek, in short, is a world in which ironclad new rules—constitutional rules—keep us from using government to help ourselves and one another.

So what kind of country would the libertarian dream constitution usher in? It would look a lot like America in 1900: a place where workers had no legal right to organize for a collective voice; where corporations were free of democratic accountability, whether for discrimination, pollution, or consumer protection; a place of mass voter suppression; and, needless to say, a place with no Social Security, Medicaid, or Medicare.

Consider two concrete examples: education and health care. In the Buchanan-Koch long-term vision, parents will have to pay out of pocket the cost of their children's schooling, as they pay for food and shelter. That is what the insiders mean by personal responsibility. To most of us, the idea of taking health insurance away from people who cannot afford to pay for it is cruel, but for backers of this cause, it is a necessary step toward their vision of pure liberty. As one long-time Koch grantee, Robert W. Poole of the Reason Foundation, put it, the economic liberty nirvana is a "full liability society." That is, you make the choice to have children? Fine, but do not expect other taxpayers to help you in any way. If you make a choice, then you bear full liability for its outcome (Poole, TK).

Ideas into Policy

Of course, ideas by themselves do not change the course of history. They need sponsors, organizers, and infrastructure to take hold among significant numbers. Then, to prevail, they must be embedded in policy, ideally in policies that are not easy to change. What is needed to make this happen? Buchanan began his work in the mid-1950s, a time of pervasive belief in government and trust that it could fix market failures for the common good. Buchanan made the case that government could not do what people looked to it to do, because politicians were not really seeking to advance the public interest as they claimed. Instead, they were just trying to get elected, or reelected, by promising benefits from taxes levied on others. Buchanan theorized that the same was true of all public actors: agency officials, union leaders, activists, and advocates were all out for their own advantage, takers seeking to exploit makers.

Such ideas appealed to the then-marginal radical right elite, so Buchanan's program had sponsors from the very outset. Among them was the era's leading backer of free-market fundamentalism: the William Volker Fund (the lineal progenitor of the Institute for Humane Studies, Charles Koch's pet academic operation, which today is handing out a small fortune to attract faculty and students to the cause). The organizers and infrastructure came with time, with investments by arch-right corporate backers that came to include the likes of Richard Scaife, General Electric, several fossil-fuel corporations—and Charles Koch, among others.

They began to build this supportive apparatus in earnest in the 1970s. Buchanan's ideas again guided the long game. One of his greatest gifts to the right was this advice: if you do not like the outcome of the political process over a long period of time, stop focusing on changing *who* rules and instead focus on *the* rules—in particular, on how to change them to get the outcomes you want. This mattered because the smartest architects of today's right wing—Buchanan and Koch foremost among them—were well aware that the society and government they desired would never gain the backing of a majority of voters. Repeated historical experience had taught them this, beginning with the crushing defeat of Barry Goldwater in the 1964 presidential election everywhere but in his home state of Arizona and states of the Deep South that practiced voter suppression.

Therefore, the only way to achieve the radical transformation they sought would be, in effect, behind the backs of the people. The Koch network has fed bromides about limited government and lower taxes to the voters they need while quietly pursuing an integrated strategy that requires elements of stealth to succeed—and will hurt those same voters. With input from Buchanan and the team of scholars he cultivated, the architects identified incremental changes that could build on one another in a cumulative manner, so that this cause never has to inform the people of the true endgame—or even be honest about the purpose of each play that moves the overall project closer to its destination. As Charles Koch himself said when he launched this effort in earnest in 1997: "Since we are greatly outnumbered, the failure to use our superior technology ensures failure" (MacLean 2017).

From that point forward over the ensuing two decades, Koch's team used Buchanan's "technology" to devise a road map for a radical transformation that could be carried out largely below the radar of the people, yet legally. The plan was (and is) to act on so many separate fronts at once, in what insider Tyler Cowen urged "big-bang clustered bursts," that others outside the movement would not realize the slow-motion revolution under way until it was too late to undo it (MacLean 2017). Examples include laws to destroy unions without saying that this is the true purpose (like Wisconsin governor Scott Walker's Act 10); spreading misinformation, such as denial of climate science and promotion of the myth of mass voter fraud; suppressing the votes of those most likely to resist the corporate libertarians' measures; and using privatization to alter power relations in a lasting manner (see Cohen, chapter 6, this volume). In each case, the change reduces democracy, not least by undercutting the ability of organized people to resist the transformation.

As an example of what this means in practice, consider the attempt to end Social Security, which would be perhaps the Koch team's biggest policy victory. Buchanan laid out a plan to do it in a way that would avoid what happened when President Reagan's first proposed budget called for stark cuts. Buchanan began by reiterating what he and Koch both understood: "There is no widespread support for basic structural reform, among any membership group" in the American polity, "among the old or the young, the black, the brown, or the white, the female or the male, the rich or the poor, the Frost Belt or the Sunbelt" (MacLean 2017, 178) He therefore warned against an honest, frontal strategy, calling instead for what I call a crab-walking approach, one that would become the model for other stealth assaults. He advised the Cato Institute that "those who seek to undermine the existing structure" must proceed along the following lines:

- Step one: Sow doubt in the minds of voters about Social Security's viability, because, Buchanan said, that will "make abandonment of the system look more attractive."
- Step two: Divide and conquer, in careful sequence. Recipients were to be split apart as follows. Buchanan defined the first group as those already receiving social security benefits. These current recipients and those close to retirement should be reassured that their benefits would not be cut. Buchanan referred to this tactic as "paying off" existing claims. He pointed out that as the citizens most attentive to any change in the system, those close to retirement or in retirement were the ones who would fight the hardest to preserve it. Getting them out of the struggle would greatly enfeeble the remaining coalition.

- Step three: Focus on high earners. Tell them that for the system to survive they would have to be taxed at higher rates in order to receive benefits. This would sully the image of Social Security as an insurance program in the minds of the wealthy by making it look more like means-tested programs. And if the message were repeated enough, such that the wealthy began to believe that others were not paying their fair share, they in turn would also become less opposed to altering the program—and might even relish its end.
- Step four: Aim a lot of propaganda at younger workers. They would need to be constantly reminded that their payroll deductions were, in Buchanan's words, providing "a tremendous welfare subsidy" to the aged (MacLean 2017, 179). Thus, at the time of Occupy Wall Street, Charles Koch's top scholar ally, Tyler Cowen, and Veronique de Rugy, a colleague from the Koch-funded Mercatus Center at George Mason University, proclaimed: "The Occupiers should not be occupying Wall Street. They should be occupying AARP" (Norquist 2008; Cowen and de Rugy 2012). The Koch network funds an organization called Generation Opportunity that targets young people with that diversionary case.

This "patchwork pattern of 'reforms'" (Buchanan himself put quotation marks around the word "reforms" to make sure the message was clear that reform was not the real endgame) could tear asunder groups that hitherto had been united in their support of Social Security (MacLean 2017, 180). Better still, Buchanan noted, the member groups of the once unified coalition that protected it might be induced to fight one another. When that happened, the broad phalanx that had upheld the system for generations might finally fracture.

How, then, will people support themselves in old age in the world the Koch network seeks to bring into being? The answer to that is, again, through "personal responsibility" (translation: "You are on your own"), but that is just the beginning. In order to encourage everyone to save, early and without government help—and to put all this money back in the hands of capitalists—they push for legislation to make private retirement saving easier. That, Koch strategists saw, could pull Wall Street financial corporations into the fight against Social Security, as they would profit from the replacement of social insurance with private individual savings accounts.

For the libertarian Right, then, Social Security privatization means a savvy triple win, in which ideological triumph over the most successful and popular federal program would be the least of the gains. First, it would break down citizens' lived connection to government—our habit of believing it offers us something of value in navigating our lives. Second, it would weaken collective organization by splitting apart groups that had looked to government for solutions to their common problems. Third, and just as important, by putting a vast pool of money into the hands of corporations, enriching them, it would make them eager to lobby for further change and willing to fund the advocacy groups in the vanguard of the libertarian revolution. It is a testament to the continued power of the majority that the Right has not managed to secure the privatization of Social Security, despite how much thought, money, and effort has been invested in that quest.

Still, in other arenas today, the Koch network is pleased with the impact it is having, including what it has won since the election of Donald Trump. Their project was advancing rapidly before his election, and his administration, in turn, has accelerated its gains. At a donor summit in spring 2018, Charles Koch stated, "We have made more progress in the last five years than I had in the previous 50" (Hayden 2018). Indeed, at an earlier donor summit, Mark Holden, a top Koch operative, said this: "We're close to winning . . . [and the critics] don't have the real path" (MacLean 2017, 244).

I found that "real path" in my research. It starts with gaining control over an ever-growing number of states: at this writing, thirty of fifty, no small achievement for a minority cause. It then moves through those states' legislatures to alter the rules of the political process in each one, in a manner that will ultimately choke progressive national policy, too. Among the pivotal changes are extreme redistricting to enable minority rule—to a degree never seen before; hamstringing labor unions, especially public-sector unions, teachers' unions in particular as the most powerful and progressive in today's America; and undermining other strong liberal lobbies, such as Planned Parenthood. Then, with these core power bases of "the enemy" (as they define it) enfeebled, the strategy moves on to the next phase, with voter suppression, preemption by state legislatures of local progressive wins, and, again, privatization of public resources to alter power relations in a lasting way.

The Supreme Court decision in the *Janus* case is one important example of such strategic rules changes and alteration of incentives, hallmarks of Buchanan's school of political economy. Many Americans have interpreted *Janus* as a pure and simple case of union busting. However, the case was a pivotal piece of the radical Right's stealth plan to take power out of the hands of citizens and public officials alike—and make sure that this power never returns by radically altering the rules of our democracy as enshrined in the Constitution.

Recall that their ultimate endgame is an incredibly radical transformation of our governing institutions, legal system, and ethical norms—one that would force total personal liability by undercutting our government's capacity to do the kinds of things that citizens have looked to government to help with. The Koch donor network, in short, seeks to enchain democracy. The plan is, over time, to bind our political process in such a way as to make government unable to comply with the will of the people—at least where that majority will would involve tax transfers or regulation. This is a messianic plan, now decades in the making, to fundamentally change the relationship between the government and the people—and to do so permanently. The ever-strategic Grover Norquist, a longtime Koch grantee, equates the anticipated transformation with a Roman pilum—a spear powerful enough to penetrate any shield, and barbed, so it "could not be pulled out" (Norquist 2008, 217, 222).

As incremental change builds on incremental change, from "right-to-work" laws, to voter suppression, to redistricting in order to misrepresent the will of the remaining voters, these libertarians seek the ultimate rules change: altering the US Constitution—at the first and only state-convened constitutional convention. The goal is to amend the Constitution in a manner that would rule out in advance most of what progressive social movements have accomplished—not since the 1960s but since the 1900s.

Although that goal may sound far-fetched, it may be close to fruition. Article V of the Constitution provides two routes to amendment: through Congress or through a convention called by two-thirds of the states. A constitutional convention would face no preset limitations: as numerous legal authorities including Laurence Tribe note, it could consider any and all revisions to the Constitution (Riestenberg 2019). And while lately the eyes of journalists and citizens have been fixated almost exclusively on Donald Trump, organizations and elected officials funded by Charles Koch and his donor network—with ALEC in the lead—have been lining up the authorizations needed for a convention. They now have the backing of twenty-eight of the thirty-four states required. It gets worse. Here is a stunning fact: until the 2018 midterm elections, there were six states in which Koch allies controlled both houses of the legislature but that had not yet authorized a convention: Idaho, Kentucky, Minnesota, Montana, South Carolina, and Virginia. The Koch team believed that all six could line up within the next few years, especially as the deficit surged from Trump's vast tax cuts for the wealthy and profligate military spending. Now, thanks to Minnesota's blue turn, there are five, buying us all more time to organize.

In short, through its hundreds of ostensibly separate national organizations, the Koch network is working to radically alter government and society, to bring unfettered capitalism into being—without being honest with the people. The question this stealth plan presents us with, once we know it, is at one level quite simple: is the kind of world they seek one that we want to live in and bequeath to our children and future generations? That is the real public choice.

What Is to Be Done?

In light of all this, what should be the goal of those who believe in government of, by, and for the people? Inform, inform, inform: do not let the Koch network operate in the dark, as it seeks to, without letting the people know what it is actually aiming for. Beyond that work of sounding the alarm far and wide, what else should we be doing?

If we have the Koch battle plan, if we now know where it is all coming from and why the ultimate prize is rewriting the Constitution, what other implications for organizing are there? For one, taking stands just on issues like jobs, health care, or reproductive rights will not work as it once did, because the Koch network has so transformed the working of our political system. The Left has had great success at winning public opinion on issue after issue, and in local campaign after local campaign, while steadily losing power because of what the other side has wrought. To escape this trap, we have to learn to think as strategically as the Right has—and that means getting out of our silos, developing our own long-term integrated game plan, and aligning with the allies needed to achieve it.

The first step is to recognize that democracy itself must become a key focus of work and reform—and that the public must be alerted to the profound danger it is in. And not just from Donald Trump, as so many seem to imagine. Trump's administration is the tumor, not the cancer, as one observant activist I spoke with put it. The cancer is the chronic condition of American politics that has allowed the Koch strategy to get as far as it has: escalating and unmatched inequality, dark corporate money in politics, obstacles to voting, partisan gerrymandering, loss of accountability, and more.

As a historian who has studied this, I simply do not see any way to get out of the acute crisis we face from the Koch network, and the Trump presidency it enabled, without deep reform of the rules of government to empower the voters and rebuild countervailing power to the sway of extreme wealth like that of the Kochs. They rigged the rules to serve their ends, and the first order of business must now be to fix those rules—and not with a few modest tweaks. The challenge we face from the property supremacists is historic, akin to those our ancestors faced in the 1860s and the 1930s. We cannot succeed without serious reconstruction—no more than the Union could be saved without Emancipation or the people protected from the ravages of the Great Depression without mass organizing and the New Deal. People in every issue and constituency silo need to understand that you cannot achieve what you most care about with a broken democracy.

We need to realize that today's Right is coming not for any one group but in fact for all who depend on organizing to affect government policy: every labor

union, and every civil rights, feminist, consumer, environmental, good government, people with disabilities, and retirees' group, is at risk. The strategic architects of all this are doing it for a coldly calculated reason, not simply from atavis-
tic prejudices (though they have shown, again and again, that they are willing to
exploit and exacerbate prejudices to achieve their ends). The overarching reason
is that all their targets rely on the twentieth-century model of government that
the radical Right deplores: government with the capacity to carry out the will of
the people using progressive taxation and corporate regulation. In other words,
the Koch-led Right wants to take away the very tools that enabled all the popular
successes of the twentieth and early twenty-first centuries, from consumer protection and public health to labor rights and standards, retirement security, workplace diversity, clean air and water, and marriage equality.

There is the kind of fun irony that history is full of in all this, however, in that
in trying to take away that shared toolkit, the radical Right may be doing for the
progressive side what we have been so unable to do for ourselves: get us to realize
how much we actually have in common in our values and goals, and how deeply
we need one another to preserve our shared methods and achievements—and
indeed our common planet.

What does knowing this history do for us? How can this information inform
action? We can start to insist that those on the Right tell the truth—and that journalists know enough to ensure this. When Koch allies say they are going to "reform" something to "save" it, ask if they support the principle of whatever is at
stake: public education; social insurance; graduated taxation so that those who
gain more pay more; tax-funded scholarship assistance for those who otherwise
cannot afford college; federally owned parks and public lands; majority rule on
fiscal matters; and so on. Demand that they define their terms and argue con-
cretely for their values. People need to know that in the Right's definition of liberty, it is better to let people starve, go without shelter, or even die than to have
them "dependent" on government.

We need to expect and prepare for efforts to amend state and federal constitutions. These will be designed to replace checks and balances with locks and bolts,
such as by imposing permanent tax and spending caps with requirements for a
supermajority vote to lift them at any time in the future. This is already happening in some states, with proposals for a "Taxpayer Bill of Rights" and efforts to
amend state constitutions to include right-to-work protections and strict voter
ID laws to make it all but impossible for voters to get rid of them. As Clint Bolick, a Koch-funded legal strategist since the 1970s and and now Arizona Supreme
Court justice, has explained: "state constitutions . . . can be amended more easily than the U.S. Constitution"—and pave the way to that (Bolick 2012). We must
especially block the effort to hold a federal constitutional convention.

We must anticipate efforts to divide previous coalition partners in order to weaken opposition to the Right's agenda. It is vital for all believers in democracy, not just those in the labor movement, to defend unions' and workers' rights to organize free of employer retaliation. The Koch-libertarian cause pushes right-to-work laws, because they know these will weaken and in time debilitate the strongest organizational barrier to achieving their agenda. But also any group not harmed in the near term should understand that it will be eventually, and that any perks it is awarded are temporary and strategic, to weaken others first and to come after its own members later, as in the case of building trades unions lured by the prospect of pipeline jobs or mass incarceration activists enticed by the money and power the Koch network has brought to that cause in hopes of reducing penalties for white-collar crime.

We should also be alert to the major push under way to transform higher education, particularly public universities, by using control of red-state legislatures to push through radical cuts in public funding and changes in governance while redirecting resources to implant base camps for the cause akin to, if not as extensive as, the flagship enterprise at George Mason University, which encompasses the economics department, the Mercatus Center, and the Scalia School of Law. To protect academic integrity and shared governance in our colleges and universities, faculty should consider joining the American Association of University Professors and assisting the work of UnKoch My Campus, the two organizations that are leading this fight, often working together. We must also be aware that every time a right-wing speaker is shouted down, it helps this cause make its case for why universities must be radically reconstructed, using claims of violated "free speech" to persuade boards of trustees and administrators to grant their Trojan horses entry. Do not take the bait. Instead, change the terms of the conversation.

Take action to limit the Right's ill-gotten power in other ways. For example, do everything possible to remove dark, untraceable money from politics—they could not have achieved what they have without it. Rigorously enforce tax laws on nonprofits—this is where this cause is closest to breaking the law, which is likely why they pushed back so aggressively on Obama-era Internal Revenue Service audits and have been trying to discredit the agency ever since.

Turn near-term victories into lasting power shifts. When Democrats are elected, as many were in 2018, hold them to a "must-have" agenda of robust pro-democracy reforms to unrig the rules. If some balk, mount opposition to them in primary elections so they learn how nonnegotiable commitment to this agenda is.

While enlisting new power to win deep structural reforms, also think creatively about how to widen fissures on the Right with wedge issues that could inform and peel away sections of constituencies its strategists counting on keeping in the dark and at odds with progressives. Examples include retirees who are dependent on Social Security and Medicare; parents concerned with saving public education; veterans and active-duty military personnel whose health care is at risk from the Koch-backed push to privatize the Veterans Administration; hunters, fishers, and other outdoor enthusiasts who care about land, water, and species protection; and those people of all faiths who do not now realize that the libertarian ethical system is at odds with the best in every major religious tradition but who responded with horror and anger to the caging of children on the US-Mexico border.

Above all, help our fellow Americans to understand that democracy is not something we can just assume will survive. It has to be fought for time and again. Let them know, too, that the Koch cause, in its infinite cynicism, is counting us out, betting that we will not fight, because we will not understand the full importance of what is being done to us without our knowledge or assent. They honestly believe we are more devoted to our electronic toys than to our shared world; it is up to us to prove them wrong.

Reflections on the Importance of the 2018 Midterm Elections

In the 2018 midterm elections, intense state-level organizing secured stunning wins that collectively constituted a promissory note toward stopping the Koch network's agenda by winning the power to fix our democracy. The state-level wins were as impressive as gaining the majority in the House of Representatives. Democrats netted about 300 new state legislative seats. They also gained seven governorships—not only in the Midwest and on both coasts but even in states in deep red regions: New Mexico, Colorado, and Kansas. Seven legislative chambers in five states also flipped from red to blue, giving Democrats seven new trifecta states (i.e., control of both legislative houses and the governorship): Connecticut, Colorado, Maine, Minnesota, New Mexico, New York, and Washington. That narrowed the three-to-one Republican advantage in this arena to less than two to one.

Critically, these state victories will put restraints on Republican Party plans to use the congressional redistricting process after the 2020 census to extend the antidemocratic operation it carried out in 2010 in a secretive project called Redmap. The most audacious and technically sophisticated gerrymander in US history, Redmap enabled state Republican officials to use vast reams of detailed voter data to manipulate district lines to rob Democratic voters of their fair share of political representation (Daley 2016).

Perhaps most important, the citizen groups that did so much to secure these victories also won critical ballot initiatives to begin fixing our broken political system, including new state measures that will provide independent redistricting, automatic voter registration, rights restoration for former felons (won in Florida this cycle), public financing of elections, and other kinds of measures to promote government of, by, and for the people rather than just those in the wealthiest 1 percent of the population.

What should be done between now and 2020 to win that crucial election—and those following it? Starting now, put money and effort into grassroots state-level organizing, anchored in local communities, to shift red to purple, purple to blue, and blue to bluer. With a geographically based Senate and Electoral College, any approach that fails to invest in every state amounts to slow suicide.

The lesson from 2018 should be clear: keep investing in *all* states and in ongoing intensive year-round organizing programs, so the map of possibility at every level once again expands and the power is built to secure lasting structural reforms that prevent the rules from being rigged as the Right has managed to do for so long.

References

Anon. 2016. "How Might Trump 'Drain the Swamp'?" BBC News, October 18.

Bolick, Clint. 2010. *Two-Fer: Electing a President and a Supreme Court.* Hoover Institution Press.

Buchanan, James M. "America's Third Century." *Atlantic Economic Review* 1 (November 1973), 9–12.

Cowen, Tyler, and Veronique de Rugy. 2012. "Reframing the Debate." In *The Occupy Handbook*, edited by Janet Byrne. New York: Little, Brown.

Daley, David. 2016. *Ratf**ked: The True Story behind the Secret Plan to Steal America's Democracy.* New York: Liveright.

Fang, Lee. 2013. "Generation Opportunity, New Koch-Funded Front, Says Youth Are Better Off Uninsured." *The Nation*, September 19.

Hayden, Jen. 2018. "Koch Brothers Reward GOP for Massive Tax Break, Will Flood $400 Million into Midterm Elections." *Daily Kos*, January 29.

Lichtblau, Eric. 2015. "Challenge to Health Overhaul Puts Obscure Think Tank in Spotlight." *New York Times*, March 5.

MacLean, Nancy. 2017. *Democracy in Chains: The Deep History of the Radical Right's Stealth Plan for America.* New York: Viking Press.

MacLean, Nancy. 2017b. "The GOP tax bill could kill two birds with one stone." *The Hill*, December 26.

Norquist, Grover G. 2008. *Leave Us Alone: Getting the Government's Hands Off Our Money, Our Guns, and Our Lives.* New York: HarperCollins.

Poole, Robert W., Jr. 1972. "Reason and Ecology." In *Outside, Looking In: Critiques of American Policies and Institutions, Left and Right.* New York: Harper & Row, 253.

Reistenberg, Jay. 2019. "U.S. Constitution Threatened as Article V Constitution Nears Success." *Common Cause website.* https://www.commoncause.org/resource/u-s-constitution-threatened-as-article-v-convention-movement-nears-success/.

Whiteside, John. "Romney Struggles to Steady Campaign after Secret Videos." Reuters, September 18.

2

RIGHT-WING POPULISM, THE CORPORATE ATTACK ON WORKING AMERICANS, AND THE LABOR MOVEMENT'S RESPONSE

Gordon Lafer

This chapter will analyze the politics of the Trump period by using economic class relations as a lens to understand President Trump's election, to make sense of his administration's policies, and to assess how the labor movement should respond to this challenge.

To start, given the rise of right-wing populism across much of the developed world (including both Eastern and Western Europe, Turkey, India, and Israel), Trump's victory cannot be explained solely by factors unique to American political culture. The simultaneous rise of conservative populism in multiple countries suggests that there is something particular about the time we are living in that cannot be explained simply by domestic conditions. Rather, it is the exhaustion of neoliberalism that has destabilized politics in many countries and that has created an opening both for a bolder Left (seen in Syriza, Podemos, Jeremy Corbyn, and Bernie Sanders) and for a nationalist right. The experience of long-term economic decline has led to widespread anxiety, rage, and resentment and has in turn created a politics that is combustible and unstable. The 2016 election marked the end of neoliberal hegemony in American politics—for both Democrats and Republicans. After forty years of neoliberalism, life in the United States has simply gotten too rough for voters to be satisfied with moderate platforms. It is telling that the appeal of both Donald Trump and Bernie Sanders rests partly in the fact that they had been saying the same thing for decades rather than constantly revising talking points based on the latest polls. The question, then, is why these candidates, who had long been consigned to the political margins, suddenly became viable in 2016.

The Trump candidacy was made possible by the long-term deterioration in living standards for working- and middle-class Americans. The essential promise of his campaign was to provide decently paying jobs for the two-thirds of American workers who do not have a college degree and who work in jobs that do not require higher education. Yet this promise is directly at odds with the agenda of the nation's premier corporate lobbies, which have long dominated the Republican Party. These organizations—from the more "radical" Koch brothers to the more "mainstream" US Chamber of Commerce—unanimously opposed the Trump candidacy, based in equal parts on discomfort with his populist rhetoric and fear that his racist, antigay, misogynist, and anti-immigrant positions would doom their party to defeat.

Both political parties are centrally defined by the contradictions between their donors and their base. For several decades, the GOP operated on an implicit agreement that the corporate lobbies would get the tax breaks and economic goods they sought, while the base would organize around antiabortion, antigay, and anti-immigrant crusades. Following the two Obama election victories, both the GOP leadership and premier corporate lobbies concluded that this formula could no longer work—the issues that had previously galvanized their base had come to alienate so many voters that it was no longer possible to win national elections on this basis. Following the 2012 election, the GOP established a blue-ribbon commission to chart its path forward. Its report called for a softer stance on social issues, warning that "we need to campaign among Hispanic, black, Asian, and gay Americans and demonstrate we care about them, too" (Barbour et al. 2013).

The actual economic agenda of the corporate lobbies is broadly unpopular, and thus the party that promotes their agenda must organize its base around other issues. Thus, the central political challenge facing the corporate lobbies is how to advance an agenda that will make life materially harder for most Americans without provoking a political backlash. The collapse of its thirty-year formula for uniting donors and the base has produced a fundamental crisis for the Republican Party, which remains unresolved. The 2009–2011 Tea Party meant many different things to its supporters, but to the corporate donors who gave this movement life it was an experiment in creating an activist conservative base that would be galvanized only around antitax and small-government sentiments, without the baggage of social conservatism. Thus, the Tea Party's manifesto—the Contract with America, which candidates were required to endorse in order to receive the movement's backing—focused exclusively on economic liberty, with no mention of abortion, marriage equality, immigration, or religion (New York Times/CBS News 2010). For the Koch brothers' Americans for Prosperity and other corporate donors behind the Tea Party, this was an attempt to maintain base conservatives' support for the corporate agenda without alienating the growing number of young, female, and Latino voters. The strategy seemed to work for a year or two, but then it fizzled. Finally, candidate Trump blew up the Tea Party strategy and offered an alternative, which doubled down on racist, sexist, and anti-immigrant appeals, coupling them with economic populism.

Since taking office, Trump has promoted a narrowly nationalist populism—championing the plight of American workers where it conflicts with "foreigners" (on questions of trade and immigration) but siding with employers and investors on all questions of domestic economic policy. In every area except free trade, the Trump administration has been a loyal soldier for the corporate interests that have traditionally dominated the GOP. This includes the 2018 tax cut, rolling back environmental and banking regulations, antiunionism in the National Labor Relations Board, defunding public services, privatizing education, loosening regulations on payday loans, and denying employees' right to sue for wrongful termination.

The contradiction between Trump's populist rhetoric and his elitist policies serves to heighten the tensions within the GOP coalition. To the extent that his policies make economic life worse for working-class conservatives, the president must rely on whipping up ever more intense nationalist sentiment in order to maintain the loyalty of his base. This is a worrisome strategy for the corporate lobbies, but following the failure of the Tea Party, they have no better alternative. Thus they are watching, month by month, to determine whether the sentiment of nationalist populism and the benefits provided to the evangelical right can serve to maintain majority support while corporations continue to pursue tax cuts, deregulation, and shrinking wages and public services—all to the detriment of the party's base voters. The corporate lobbies worry that the coalition cannot win another election or that the intensity of nationalist sentiment will spill over into uncontrollable social chaos. For now, they are riding this train, seeing how far it can take them, even while nervously eyeing the exits.

It is critical to see the relationship between the corporate lobbies and Trump's right-wing populism. Without the support of the corporate lobbies, the Trump administration would be unable to carry out any of its agenda, particularly given that the Republican Congress is entirely dominated by politicians who are products of and remain reliant on corporate backing. Perhaps for this reason, Trump has appointed figures allied with the Kochs, the US Chamber of Commerce, and Wall Street—all of whom opposed him in the Republican primaries—to top administrative positions. For the corporate lobbies, Trumpism is a solution to their central political challenge. It may not be their ideal solution, but it is the best they have at the moment, and with unified Republican control of the federal government, the alliance with Trumpism is too good an opportunity to pass up. Thus, the skittish but enduring alliance between right-wing populism and corporate elites must be understood above all as a solution to the corporations' defining problem: how to manage the politics of accelerating inequality and economic hardship.

The Central Role of the Corporate Lobbies

In the swirl of news coverage and social media debates, contemporary politics is marked by myriad heartfelt and crosscutting arguments, polarizing participants around questions of race, gender, ethnicity, religion, immigration, patriotism, militarism, environmentalism, and more. All these issues are obviously real, and millions of Americans are driven to activism over these concerns. Yet, in the midst of this complex politics, there is a set of political actors that clearly wield the greatest power to shape American law: the nation's premier corporate lobbies. The US Chamber of Commerce, the National Association of Manufacturers, and the National Federation of Independent Business, together with the Koch brothers' Americans for Prosperity, constitute the largest and best-funded corporate lobbies in the nation. As of 2009, the political and advocacy budget of the US Chamber of Commerce alone was larger than that of either the national Democratic or Republican parties. Behind the politicians and the parties, these are the most powerful forces determining who is elected to office and what ideas are adopted into law. Normally a closely guarded secret, the corporate agenda was revealed in detail in 2011 when a whistleblower made public thousands of internal documents from the American Legislative Exchange Council (ALEC), the premier coordinating body for corporate lobbying in the state legislatures.

Why Look to the States?

Examining the record of state legislation provides a particularly illuminating window into the corporate agenda. For most of the Obama administration, the federal government was deadlocked, and battles over tax, employment, and labor policy instead played out in state legislatures. Because so many federal responsibilities have been transferred to the states, and because most state legislatures have no filibuster rule, state politics offers fertile ground for rewriting the rules of the economy.

Furthermore, corporate political influence is at its greatest at the state level, in part because so few people pay attention to state government. Political scientist Martin Gilens notes that only when policy debates attract widespread public attention are politicians even modestly responsive to the bottom 90 percent of the population (Gilens 2010). Yet, if such attention is rare at the federal level, it is even rarer in the states. Fewer than one-quarter of adults are able to name their state senator or representative, and fewer than half even know which party is in the majority (Center for the Study of Democratic Institutions 2012). Thus, not only are state legislative races cheaper to buy, but with state lawmakers generally lacking name recognition or organized bases of support, there is little counter-weight to the power of money in politics.

For all these reasons, the record of state legislation provides by far the most comprehensive picture of the corporate lobbies' policy priorities. During this period, America's most powerful lobbies have been pursuing an ambitious agenda that aims to fundamentally reshape the balance of power between employers and employees.

The Supreme Court's 2010 *Citizens United* decision ushered in a new era in state legislation, shaped by the impact of unlimited corporate spending on politics. From 2008 to 2012—the election cycles immediately preceding and following the *Citizens United* ruling—the US Chamber of Commerce more than doubled its political spending. In addition, a slew of new corporate-funded advocacy organizations appeared during this period. Taken together, spending by the major corporate-funded groups was more than six times higher in 2012 than in 2008 (Center for Responsive Politics n.d.).

The 2010 elections were the first conducted under the new rules, and they brought dramatic change. Eleven state governments switched from Democratic or divided control to Republican control of the governorship and both houses of the legislature. Since these lawmakers took office in early 2011, the United States has seen an unprecedented wave of legislation aimed at lowering labor standards and slashing public services.

The best-known effort came in Wisconsin, where the newly elected Republi-can governor, Scott Walker, pushed through legislation that effectively eliminated the right to collective bargaining for his state's 175,000 public employees (see By-bee 2011). Yet, what happened in Wisconsin was part of a much broader pattern. In the five years following *Citizens United*, bills restricting public employees' collective-bargaining rights were adopted in fifteen states. In the same period, twelve states passed laws restricting the minimum wage, four eased limits on child labor, and nineteen imposed new caps on unemployment benefits.

While the corporate lobbies primarily work in tandem with GOP leaders, they should not be understood simply as a component of the Republican Party. The corporate lobbies have not hesitated to pursue their own interests when they con-flict with those of party leaders, even when doing so jeopardizes Republican legislative seats. Likewise, their agenda sometimes confounds party lines—most importantly on education reform, where traditional Democratic supporters in the technology and finance industries work in concert with Republican legislators and conservative corporate groups.

The American Legislative Exchange Council (ALEC), the most important national organization advancing the corporate agenda at the state level, brings thousands of state lawmakers together with Fortune 500 lobbyists in order to promote business-friendly legislation. ALEC convenes bill-drafting committees, with half the committee members elected legislators and the other half corporate lobbyists, which together produce model legislation that is then introduced in states across the country. The organization claims to introduce 800–1,000 bills each year in the fifty state legislatures, with 20 percent becoming law.

Ultimately, the "exchange" that ALEC facilitates is between corporate donors and state legislators. The corporations pay ALEC's expenses and contribute to legislators' campaigns, and in return, legislators carry the corporate agenda into their statehouses. Through this network, corporate lobbyists have established a well-funded, highly effective operation that combines legislative drafting, electoral politics, lobbying, grassroots activism, and policy promotion.

What Is the Corporate Agenda?

Both the US Chamber of Commerce and ALEC often pursue initiatives that directly benefit the bottom line of particular corporate members. In 2009–2010, for example, the health insurance industry provided more than $100 million to the Chamber to advocate against health-care reform (Frates 2012). All three of the world's leading emitters of greenhouse gases—Chevron, ExxonMobil, and BP—are affiliated with the Chamber, which in turn lobbies against regulation of coal mining, fracking, and CO_2 emissions (Bridge Project 2015; Chamber Watch n.d.). The Chamber has also received significant funding from tobacco companies and is engaged in an international effort to defeat antismoking laws (Hakim 2015).

At the state level, much of ALEC's activity is similarly targeted at issues of direct financial concern to member companies. In one outreach message to potential members, ALEC trumpeted its operation as "a good investment" for corporate partners, boasting that "nowhere else can you get a return that high" (Kuhner 2014). When drug companies invest, ALEC lobbies to prohibit imports of lower-cost drugs from Canada. When Coca-Cola invests, it lobbies against taxes on sugary soft drinks. When private prison operators invest, it advocates for policies that would raise occupancy rates, such as the detention of undocumented immigrants and the restriction of parole eligibility. And when "payday loan" companies invest, it opposes a law prohibiting such firms from charging more than 36 percent interest (Laffer, Moore, and Williams 2011; People for the American Way 2011; Sullivan 2010).

But both ALEC and the Chamber also promote a broader economic and de-regulatory agenda that is not directly tied to the profitability of specific donors. They support cuts to "entitlements" such as social security, unemployment insurance, and food stamps; push for more trade agreements on the NAFTA model; seek to shrink public funding for schools; oppose paid sick leave and workplace safety regulations; and work to undermine labor unions and restrict their participation in political debates (Laffer, Moore, and Williams 2011). A wide range of initiatives aimed at shifting economic power from workers to owners—including forced privatization, "right-to-work" laws, and the abolition of minimum-wage and prevailing-wage laws—reflect model statutes developed by ALEC and promoted through its network. Some of ALEC's most powerful corporate members are also active in the Chamber, and the Chamber itself is an active member of ALEC, as are Koch Industries, the National Federation of Independent Business, and Americans for Prosperity. For all of them, this part of the legislative agenda is aimed not at immediately enhancing specific companies' revenues but at re-shaping the underlying balance of power between workers and employers.

The corporate legislative agenda has contributed significantly to the crisis of inequality and economic hardship. Corporate lobbies' success simply in preventing the minimum wage from being adjusted for inflation has resulted in an estimated $100 billion per year being transferred from workers to owners (Economic Policy Institute 2015). For waitstaff and other tipped employees, the corporate lobbies have successfully kept the federal minimum wage frozen for decades—at $2.13 per hour—and ALEC lobbies state legislators to avoid raising state rates above the federal threshold. The degree of ALEC's success dramatically impacts living standards: in the states where tipped employees make only $2.13 per hour, the poverty rate for waiters and waitresses is 80 percent higher than in states where waitstaff make the regular minimum wage (Allegretto and Cooper 2015, 14). The legislative battles over wage theft also have dramatic impacts. The most comprehensive survey suggests that nearly two-thirds of low-wage workers have some amount of money stolen out of their paychecks when employers violate wage and hour laws, fail to pay overtime or minimum wage, or understate workers' hours (Bernhardt et al. 2009). Yet ALEC, the US Chamber of Commerce, and allied corporate lobbies have in multiple states succeeded in prohibiting the creation of effective mechanisms for recovering stolen wages.

Hypocrisy and Consistency in the Corporate Agenda

When one brings all of its components together, it is apparent that the corporate agenda is rife with contradictions. For example, ALEC's model legislation opposing minimum-wage increases argues that "increasing starting wages lures high school students into the full-time work force, resulting in an increase in high school drop-out rates" and therefore that the minimum wage should be kept low in order to prevent students from working more and studying less (ALEC 2009). Yet, in Michigan, Wisconsin, and Maine, ALEC and other business lobbies worked to lift restrictions on the number of hours high school students are permitted to work during the school week. The ALEC-affiliated Restaurant Association argued that they should be able to work more because "employment teaches teenagers [valuable] skills such as . . . responsibility, problem-solving, and customer service" (Deloney 2011).

Even some of the principles that seem closest to genuine conservative ideology turn out to be mere conveniences. Corporate contortions around the principle of local rule can sometimes be dizzying. In Kentucky, the state Chamber of Commerce has suggested that local governments have the legal right to adopt their own "right-to-work" laws but not to raise the minimum wage (Kocher 2015; Greer 2014). Similarly, ALEC has promoted legislation in multiple states that bans localities from using project labor agreements (PLAs) for public construction, but when California mandated that cities seeking state construction funds retain the option of PLAs—not requiring that they be used but simply that the possibility remain on the table—the ALEC-affiliated Associated Builders and Contractors denounced the measure as a potentially unconstitutional "interfer[ence] with local control" (Associated Builders and Contractors 2012).

Such contradictions are so glaring and numerous that they seem to indicate hypocrisy or an absence of belief. In fact, they throw into sharp relief the unity of interests and goals underlying the corporate lobbies' agenda—the coherence and logic that reconcile seemingly contradictory positions. All of them aim, most fundamentally, at shifting the balance of power between the economic elite and the rest of the country toward even greater inequality. This means weakening or eliminating whatever legal or institutional mechanisms enable working people to exercise control over their terms of employment—including unions; minimum, prevailing, or living-wage laws; procedures for suing employers to recover stolen wages; rights to paid sick leave or overtime; and even licensing standards that provide employees a measure of leverage in the labor market. At the same time, it means efforts to maximize American companies' ability to transfer jobs to the world's lowest-wage and most politically repressive countries while permitting immobile service industries to import "guest workers" from those same countries. Combined, the catalog of corporate-backed bills amounts to a formula not only for decreasing American workers' wage standards but also for structurally undermining nonprofessional workers' ability to improve their lot.

What Is Particular about This Time in History?

To understand contemporary corporate political strategy, we must take account of the differences between our time and what came before. The struggle between employers and employees—and the outsized influence of business lobbies—is hardly new. Chambers of Commerce fought against the eight-hour day, social security, and the minimum wage (Fay in New York Times 1936; Riddle 2007; New Republic Staff 2009). An impressive body of scholarship has shown that the country's big business lobbies have consistently sought to minimize or reverse the accomplishments of the New Deal, starting shortly after it began (see, e.g., Weir 1993; Phillips-Fein 2009; Domhoff 2013; Waterhouse 2013). Yet the shape of the struggle changes, and we cannot understand corporate lobbies' aims in the twenty-first century simply by examining their behavior in the 1940s or 1970s. Today's corporate agenda is framed, in particular, by rising inequality, a shrunken economic left, and the impact of globalization and financialization on corporations' strategic plans.

One of the current US economy's distinguishing features is the degree of globalization to which it is subject relative to earlier periods. For the first time, many of the country's most powerful political actors are companies whose headquarters may be located in America but whose profitability does not primarily depend on the fortunes of American society. Foreign sales now account for 48 percent of the S&P 500's total corporate revenues (Pollard 2015). Among ALEC member corporations, Exxon Mobil, Caterpillar, Procter & Gamble, Pfizer, Dow Chemical, and IBM all earn more than 60 percent of their revenue outside the United States (Silverblatt 2015). This marks a new departure in American politics; some of the most influential actors in the legislative process have political interests that are increasingly disconnected from the fate of the country's citizens.

These interests have also been influenced by the dramatic growth of the financial sector relative to the economy as a whole—a process that has fundamentally reshaped corporate priorities. Beginning in the 1970s, a series of legal and regulatory changes gradually allowed pension funds to invest in stocks and higher-risk financial instruments; permitted savings and loans, commercial banks, insurance companies, and investment banks to merge their operations; and created a large market of unregulated investment instruments. Together, these changes triggered a wave of hostile takeovers and leveraged buyouts and led nearly all publicly traded companies to reorient their operations in order to maximize short-term returns to shareholders. In the late 1960s, nearly 60 percent of corporate profits were treated as retained earnings and reinvested in firms' operations (Bakir and Campbell 2010). Today, that figure is under 10 percent, with the bulk of the rest devoted to shareholder dividends and share buybacks (Lazonick 2014).

The combination of globalization and financialization has increasingly led American executives to disengage from the fate of the country's people. Every year since 2011, Harvard Business School has surveyed its alumni—among the elite of US business leaders—on their views of the American economy. The responses suggest, above all, a divorce between corporate and public interests. These executives are simultaneously optimistic about the ability of American firms to compete in global markets and strongly pessimistic about what awaits American workers. The first survey revealed a flood of jobs going overseas. That year, alumni reported fifty-six cases in which their companies moved at least 1,000 American jobs overseas, overwhelmingly motivated by cheaper labor abroad. For the remaining US employees, a large plurality of survey respondents agreed that their firms would continue to outsource work and reduce wages and benefits in the coming years (Tankersley 2014; Porter and Rivkin 2012, 2014).

Thus, the view of those at the top of the economy confirms what those at the bottom have been experiencing. Understanding the political agenda of twenty-first-century corporate leaders means taking seriously that actions that enrich investors while undermining the American job market are not accidental or mistaken but represent the rational self-interest of shareholders. This again underlines the fundamental contradiction at the heart of the Right: it is driven by a corporate political machine that is ceaselessly attacking the living standards of its base.

Populist Public Opinion: Corporate Headache, Progressive Hope

While corporate power may be more impressive than ever, there is one key battle that the country's business elites have failed to win: they have not been able to convince the voting public that their platform makes sense. On the contrary, polling shows that the public is deeply suspicious of the corporate project and on specific issues is often in sharp disagreement with it. A majority of the country in 2015 favored capping the incomes of corporate executives, and two-thirds called for raising taxes on the very rich (Scheiber and Sussman 2015). More than two-thirds support eliminating the carried-interest loophole in order to tax hedge-fund managers at the same rates as everyone else (Jones 2013).

The list of what people think the government should do must read like a nightmare script for the corporate lobbies. Nearly three-quarters of the country—including a majority of Republicans—support immediately raising the minimum wage to $10.10 (Pew Research 2014). A strong majority supports expanding unemployment insurance for the long-term jobless (Pew Research 2014). Eighty percent of voters support requiring employers to provide a minimum number of paid sick days to all workers (Mermin and Stalsburg 2015).

There is also strong support for public services and social insurance. Eighty-four percent of the public supports making universal prekindergarten available to all children (Halpin and Agne 2014). Not only do nearly 90 percent of Americans want to protect Social Security and Medicare from any budget cuts, but three-quarters think we should consider increasing Social Security benefits (Pugh 2014). Nearly 80 percent believe that the federal government should ensure that everyone who wants to go to college can, and nearly 90 percent believe "the federal government should spend whatever is necessary to ensure that all children have really good public schools" (Pugh 2014).

When asked about principles rather than specific programs, public opinion is diametrically opposed to that of economic elites. Policy prescriptions long since written off by elected officials are common sense to the American public. Just over half the country, for example, supports the view that "our government should redistribute wealth by heavy taxes on the rich," and six in ten favor "national health insurance, which would be financed by tax money" (Pugh 2014). More than half believe "the federal government should provide jobs for everyone willing to work who cannot find a job in private employment," and nearly 80 percent say the "minimum wage should be high enough so that no family with a full-time worker falls below the official poverty line" (Pugh 2014).

People have a wide variety of motives for voting for candidates, including their positions on many issues unrelated to economic policy. When given a chance to vote on specific policies, however—most commonly through ballot initiatives—many conservative voters break with the corporate agenda.

In 2014, for instance, voters in Arkansas, Nebraska, and South Dakota—all deeply red states where Republicans control all three branches of government—approved ballot initiatives to raise their state's minimum wage (Levine and Noah 2014), and while Arizona supported Trump over Clinton in 2016, this same electorate also voted to raise the state's minimum wage and create a right to paid sick leave.

A Progressive Strategy in the Face of Corporate Political Power

Issue-Focused Politics

The labor wing of the Democratic Party faces three simultaneous challenges: it needs to win elections against better-funded opponents; it needs to organize a critical mass of Trump voters onto a more progressive platform; and it needs to pursue a political vision that will unite rather than divide union memberships— all the more critical following the decision in *Janus v. AFSCME*. The experience with ballot initiatives points to the most promising way forward for progressives in this era: organizing around issues rather than candidates or parties. This is most easily done in states and cities that permit ballot initiatives on specific laws. In places where this is not possible, progressives must work to convert candidate campaigns into issue campaigns—for instance, declaring that a group or party will back all candidates who support three key issues in order to focus the race on those policies rather than the personal attributes of individual candidates. In the Congress as well as in state and local votes, progressives must focus on issues that expose the contradictions between the corporate donors and the working-class base of the conservative movement. There are multiple such issues, at both the federal and local levels. For example, the Trump administration's promotion of mandatory tip pooling—effectively allowing restaurant owners to take billions of dollars each year out of the pockets of waitstaff—could easily be the subject of a campaign that combined legislative action in Washington, DC, with field organizing in target states. Similar campaigns could be mounted to focus on threats to Medicaid, interest rates on payday loans, the minimum wage, paid family leave, Buy American provisions in infrastructure projects, and the prevailing wage in the construction industry. All these are issues in which the interests of ALEC or US Chamber of Commerce member corporations are being carried out by corporate-funded politicians against the wishes of working-class voters in both parties. By focusing repeatedly on these issues, campaigns will serve to educate voters as to the economic agenda of GOP officials and will help organize a cross-party consensus for a more progressive economic policy.

An issues-focused politics is equally critical for forging internal cohesion within labor unions. In most unions, an estimated 30–40 percent of members are Republican voters, many of whom are politically alienated from their union's leadership. Elected union leaders are understandably nervous about engaging this large minority within the membership. While that fear is reasonable, it may, however, also prove fatal. Organizing around progressive policy issues, rather than a simple allegiance to candidates or parties, is the only way for unions to restitch the bonds of membership and re-create political solidarity within the union.

A Labor Strategy within the Democratic Party

Carrying out such a political program also entails confronting barriers within the Democratic Party. No less than the GOP, the Democrats have long been defined by the tension between big-money backers in the financial, technology, and entertainment industries and the party's grassroots, particularly the labor movement. The moneyed wing of the party may support diversity, environmentalism, marriage equality, and even a modestly higher minimum wage, but it will oppose the type of bold and ambitious economic proposals that alone provide hope for driving up voter turnout among normally nonvoting poor people or swaying working-class conservatives away from right-wing nationalist populism.

The two wings of the Democratic Party are operating on contradictory political strategies. The corporate wing aims to capture the votes of moderate Republicans and independents by emphasizing the social outrages of the Trump administration. The party's economic left wing aims to capture the votes of working-class conservatives by emphasizing the elitist corporate agenda at the heart of both the GOP and the Trump administration. Neither camp can prove, at this point, that its strategy is the more effective path to power, but this fact marks a dramatic break from past decades, when it was accepted wisdom that only neoliberal Democrats could win national office. The evidence now suggests that a Sanders-type candidate is as likely as a corporate Democrat to win.

The split within the Democratic Party—and the argument over which strategy is the surer path to victory—is unlikely to be resolved anytime soon. For the labor movement, however, only the Sanders/Left strategy offers a viable path forward. Only a bold, issues-based campaign holds the possibility of winning truly meaningful advances for working people; of organizing significant numbers of Trump voters onto a more progressive program; of building a high degree of unity among union members; and of forging a strategic response to the class interests that lie at the heart of both parties' actions.

References

Allegretto, Sylvia, and David Cooper. 2014. "Twenty-Three Years and Still Waiting for Change: Why It's Time to Give Tipped Workers the Regular Minimum Wage." Economic Policy Institute, July 10. https://www.epi.org/publication/waiting-for-change-tipped-minimum-wage/.

American Legislative Exchange Council (ALEC). 1996. "Resolution in Opposition to any Increase in the Starting (Minimum) Wage." https://www.alec.org/model-policy/resolution-in-opposition-to-any-increase-in-the-starting-minimum-wage/.

Associated Builders and Contractors. 2012. "California Lawmakers Pay Back Their Big Labor Allies, Take Steps to Deprive Charter Cities of Local Control." The Truth about PLAs, May 1. http://thetruthaboutplas.com/2012/05/01/california -lawmakers-pay-back-their-big-labor-allies-take-steps-to-deprive-charter-cities -of-local-control.

Bakir, Erdogan, and Al Campbell. 2010. "Neoliberalism, the Rate of Profit, and the Rate of Accumulation." *Science and Society* 74:323–342. http://guilfordjournals.com /doi/abs/10.1521/siso.2010.74.3.323.

Barbour, Henry, Sally Bradshaw, Ari Fleischer, Zori Fonalledas, and Glenn McCall. 2013. *Growth and Opportunity Project, Republican National Committee*, 6. http:// goproject.gop.com.

Bernhardt, Annette, Ruth Milkman, Nik Theodore, Douglas Heckathorn, Mirabai Auer, James DeFilippis, Ana Luz González, Victor Narro, Jason Perelshteyn, Diana Polson, and Michael Spiller. 2009. *Broken Laws, Unprotected Workers: Violations of Employment and Labor Laws in America's Cities*. National Employment Law Project. https://www.nelp.org/wp-content/uploads/2015/03 /BrokenLawsReport2009.pdf.

Bridge Project. 2015. *The U.S. Chamber of Commerce: Backing Corporate Greed at the Expense of Working Families and Small Businesses*. http://bridgeproject.com/app /uploads/US-Chamber-Of-Commerce-Report.pdf.

Bybee, Roger. 2011. "After Proposing Draconian Anti-union Laws, Wisconsin Governor Walker Invokes National Guard." *In These Times*, February 15.

Center for Media and Democracy. "Corporations That Have Cut Ties to ALEC." http:// www.sourcewatch.org/index.php/Corporations_that_Have_Cut_Ties_to_ALEC.

Center for Responsive Politics. n.d. *Outside Spending*. https://www.opensecrets.org /outsidespending/index.php?type=Y.

Center for the Study of Democratic Institutions. 2012. Vanderbilt Poll, May. http://www .vanderbilt.edu/csdi/tl2012.pdf.

Chamber Watch. n.d. "The U.S. Chamber and BP." Accessed October 18, 2015. https://www.chamberofcommercewatch.org/challengingthechamber/energy/.

Deloney, Andy. 2011. *Statement of the Michigan Restaurant Association in Support of House Bill 4732*, House Commerce Committee, June 21. http://house.michigan .gov/SessionDocs/2011–2012/Testimony/Committee4-6-21-2011-4.pdf.

Domhoff, William. 2013. *The Myth of Liberal Ascendancy: Corporate Dominance from the Great Depression to the Great Recession*. Boulder, CO: Paradigm.

Economic Policy Institute. 2015. *It's Time to Raise the Minimum Wage*, April 30. http://www.epi.org/publication/its-time-to-raise-the-minimum-wage/#data -tables-characteristics-by-state6.

Frates, Chris. 2012. "Exclusive: AHIP Gave More Than $100 Million to Chamber's Efforts to Derail Health Care Reform." *National Journal*, June 13. http://www .modernhealthcare.com/article/20120613/INFO/306139980.

Gilens, Martin. 2010. *Affluence and Influence: Economic Inequality and Political Power in America*. Princeton, NJ: Princeton University Press.

Greer, Carolyn Tribble. 2014. "Business Groups Urge Metro Council to Reject Minimum Wage Increase." *Louisville Business First*, September 29.

Hakim, Danny. 2015. "U.S. Chamber Fights Smoking Laws While Hospitals and Insurers Sit on Its Board." *New York Times*, July 1. https://nyti.ms/1NuXr0f.

Halpin, John, and Karl Agne. 2014. *50 Years after LBJ's War on Poverty: A Study of American Attitudes about Work, Economic Opportunity, and the Social Safety Net*. Report. Center for American Progress, January. https://www.americanprogress .org/wp-content/uploads/2014/01/WOP-PollReport2.pdf.

Jones, Jeffrey M. 2013. "Fewer Americans Now View Their Income Taxes as Fair," *Gallup*, April 15. http://www.gallup.com/poll/161780/fewer-americans-view -income-taxes-fair.aspx.

Kocher, Greg. 2015. "Several Kentucky Counties Passing or Considering 'Right to Work' Laws." *Lexington Herald Leader*, January 17. http://www.kentucky.com/news/local /counties/scott-county/article44547798.html.

Kuhner, Timothy. 2014. *Capitalism v. Democracy: Money in Politics and the Free Market Constitution*. Palo Alto, CA: Stanford University Press.

Laffer, Arthur, Stephen Moore, and Jonathan Williams. 2011. *Rich States, Poor States: ALEC-Laffer State Economic Competitiveness Index*, 4th edition. American Legislative Exchange Council. http://washingtonpolicywatch.files.wordpress.com /2012/08/ rsps_4thedition.pdf.

Lazonick, William. 2014. "Profits without Prosperity." *Harvard Business Review*, September. https://hbr.org/2014/09/profits-without-prosperity/ar/1.

Levine, Marianne, and Timothy Noah. 2014. "Minimum Wage Hikes Win." *Politico*, November 5. http://www.politico.com/story/2014/11/minimum-wage-increase -wins-in-four-red-states-112565.

Mermin, David, and Britany Stalsburg. 2015. *Recent Survey Findings*. Lake Research Partners, January 16.

New Republic Staff. 2009. "Women's Suffrage and Other Visions of Right-Wing Apocalypse." *New Republic*, December 21. http://www.newrepublic.com/article /womens-suffrage-and-other-visions-right-wing-apocalypse.

New York Times. 1936. "Fay Denounces Spread of Federal Power: Declares Trade Groups Must Form Solid Front to Preserve Freedom." April 28. https:// timesmachine.nytimes.com/timesmachine/1936/04/28/87933275.html ?pageNumber=15.

New York Times/CBS News. "2010 National Survey of Tea Party Supporters," April 5–12. http://s3.amazonaws.com/nytdocs/docs/312/312.pdf.

People for the American Way. 2011. *ALEC: The Voice of Corporate Special Interests in State Legislature*. http://www.pfaw.org/ rww-in-focus/alec-the-voice-of-corporate- special-interests-state-legislatures.

Pew Research Center. 2014. *Most See Inequality Growing, but Partisans Differ Over Solutions*. Report, January 23. http://www.people-press.org/2014/01/23/most-see -inequality-growing-but-partisans-differ-over-solutions/.

Phillips-Fein, Kim. 2009. *Invisible Hands: The Businessmen's Crusade against the New Deal*. New York: W. W. Norton.

Pollard, Timothy. 2015. "S&P 500 Foreign Sales Up in 2014." *Pensions and Investments*, July 14. http://www.pionline.com/article/20150714/INTERACTIVE/150719950 /sampp-500-foreign-sales-up-in-2014.

Porter, Michael, and Jan Rivkin. 2012. *Prosperity at Risk: Findings of Harvard Business School's 2011–12 Survey on U.S. Competitiveness*. Harvard Business School, January. http://www.hbs.edu/competitiveness/Documents/hbscompsurvey.pdf.

Porter, Michael, and Jan Rivkin. 2014. *An Economy Doing Half Its Job: Findings of Harvard Business School's 2013–14 Survey on U.S. Competitiveness*. Harvard Business School, 2014. http://www.hbs.edu/competitiveness/Documents/an -economy-doing-half-its-job.pdf.

Pugh, Derek. 2014. "The American Majority Is a Populist Majority." Campaign for America's Future, Populist Majority Memorandum, June. https://www.scribd.com /fullscreen/225509828?access_key=key-16Fj3fcbzItt5bATtVMg&allow_share =true&escape=false&show_recommendations=false&view_mode=scroll.

Riddle, Margaret. 2007. "Washington State Senate Approves Eight-Hour Workday for Women on March 2, 1911." History Link, October 8. http://www.historylink.org /File/8315.Scheiber, Naomi, and Dalia Sussman. 2015. "Inequality Troubles Americans across Party Lines, Times/CBS Poll Finds." *New York Times*, June 3. http://nyti.ms/1IiuMwi.

Silverblatt, Howard. 2015. *S&P 500 2014: Global Sales*, S&P Dow Jones Indices LLC, July. https://us.spindices.com/documents/research/research-sp-500-2014-global-sales .pdf.

Sullivan, Laura. 2010. "Prison Economics Help Drive Ariz. Immigration Law," *NPR Morning Edition*, October 28. http://www.npr.org/2010/10/28/130833741/prison -economics-help-drive-ariz- immigration-law.

Tankersley, Jim. 2014. "America's Execs Seem Ready to Give Up on U.S. Workers." *Washington Post*, September 11. http://www.washingtonpost.com/news/storyline /wp/2014/09/11/americas-top-execs-seem-ready-to-give-up-on-u-s-workers.

Waterhouse, Benjamin C. 2013. *Lobbying America: The Politics of Business from Nixon to NAFTA*. Princeton, NJ: Princeton University Press.

Weir, Margaret. 1993. *Politics and Jobs: The Boundaries of Employment Policy in the United States*. Princeton, NJ: Princeton University Press.

3

TRUMP, RIGHT-WING POPULISM, AND THE FUTURE OF ORGANIZED LABOR

Bill Fletcher Jr. and José Alejandro La Luz

The Moment

Donald Trump is a symptom of an underlying disease: the development of right-wing populism in the United States as a nationalist and irrationalist response to the confluence of multiple crises. To the extent that organized labor has refused to address the rising tide of right-wing populism specifically, and larger issues of race, gender, the environment, and the economy more generally, it has lacked the capacity to confront this existential threat to its own existence. This chapter makes this argument and then delineates approaches that we believe can and must be undertaken in order to not only combat right-wing populism but lay the foundations for a renaissance of organized labor.

The election of Donald Trump as president in November 2016 took place in the context of an almost palpable sense of anxiety within the United States. It was an anxiety brought about by the convergence of three major, and interrelated, crises.

The first, which gained the greatest amount of attention in the November 2016 elections, was the deepening economic crisis. In the Western capitalist world, the result was the slow but steady jettisoning of so-called Keynesian economics, to be replaced by what we now understand to be neoliberal economics. Neoliberal economics has emphasized the removal of all obstacles to the accumulation of profit, and the elimination of the public space in favor of greater privatization.

It is noteworthy that the totality of neoliberal economics was not addressed in the 2016 election cycle. The focus was primarily on one part of it: free trade. The historic failure of most of organized labor to develop an appropriate analysis of neoliberal globalization, and their narrow focus on trade instead, opened up a tremendous space for Trump and the right-wing populists to drive through.

The second major crisis is one of mass migrations and demographic changes. The United Nations estimates that there are 244 million migrants globally, roughly 3 percent of the world's population (United Nations 2016). In the United States, demographic changes—including but not limited to migration—are expected to alter the population from majority white to no one group in the majority by the middle of the twenty-first century. This reality challenges the foundation myth of the United States and has become a rallying cry for that element of the political Right that frets about what they see as the coming "white genocide." Third and finally, the environmental crisis poses the question of whether humanity can make it out of the twenty-first century in civilized fashion or at all.

In sum, the collision of these three crises has resulted in anxiety about the capacity of the established so-called democratic capitalist states to operate. Though the nation-state remains essential to capitalism, it is not focused on the needs of the nation but rather serves principally as the enforcement mechanism for global capitalism. To the extent that the capitalist nation-state serves the interests of global capitalism, it loses credibility in the eyes of the population, opening up terrain for challenges from both the Right and the Left. The capitalist nation-state can no longer deliver on the social contract that supposedly existed, thereby laying the foundation for frustration and anger, and possibly much more. It is on that terrain that right-wing populism is able to grow, particularly when not challenged by a dynamic Left.

Coming to Grips with Right-Wing Populism

Populism is a political movement without a firm ideology but nevertheless counterpoises "the people" versus "the elites." Establishment ideologues frequently disparage populism and associate it with demagoguery. Populism in general is better understood to be a framework or an impulse rather than an ideology. Our focus will be on right-wing populism.

Right-wing populism generally has certain defining characteristics:

- It is a systemic problem that rises to the surface during periods of sharp crisis. Particularly in periods of financial crisis in Western capitalism, right-wing populism frequently contains an anti-Semitic edge (if not outright posture).

- It constitutes a revolt against the future. Right-wing populism is founded on myth and fears the future. Instead, it wishes a return to a past that never existed or that has been mythologized. For groups like al-Qaeda, it is a legendary caliphate. In the United States, it is frequently the Confederate States of America (see Fletcher 2015). Especially, in the case of the United States, the key to understanding right-wing populism is to grasp the concept of the United States as a white republic.
- It is revanchist. It is a movement focused on revenge and taking back what was allegedly stolen from "the people."
- It draws its power from identifying "the people" in terms that are racist, sexist, and/or xenophobic. It is critical to understand this, since the platform of right-wing populist movements can sometimes appear to be left-wing. But the object of their interest is always a segment of the actual population.
- In the current moment, it is a movement that is based among displaced and anxious "natives" (i.e., nonmigrant populations, not "native" as used in reference to the indigenous). It has a strong sexist/patriarchal current, particularly in populations where men believe that they have been displaced—economically and, in some cases, socially or politically—by women.

In order to appreciate the question of right-wing populism and the current crisis, one must situate it in the specific unsettling that resulted from neoliberal globalization. In the United States, discussion of the growing economic divide—which received a great deal of attention first with the Occupy movement and more recently with the 2016 election—focused largely on the impact of neoliberal globalization on the white worker specifically or the white workforce more generally. What this fails to appreciate is that the reconstruction of capitalism originated in the late 1950s and early 1960s and fell principally on African American and Latino workers (MacLean 2008), but for whites as a whole, there was little perception of a crisis until it hit them. By the mid-1970s, this is precisely what transpired, in what was then the worst recession to have hit the United States since the Great Depression. When the shock waves of the reconstruction of global capitalism began to be felt more broadly in the United States, a far-right movement began to gain traction, guided by theorists who referred to themselves as the New Right, such as Richard Viguerie and Paul Weyrich. This right-wing movement was multifaceted and included both secular and religious conservatives as well as right-wing populists (Berlet and Lyons 2000). Sometimes these forces collaborated, whereas in other cases they were in competition. But they became very visible with the rise of several reactionary mass movements, including those that were antitax; antiabortion; focused on gun rights; antibusing; anti–Panama Canal treaty; and, increasingly, anti–racialized immigrant— racialized because there is no mass movement in the United States, for example, mobilized against immigrants from Ireland or Russia. The term "immigrant," when used in a derogatory fashion, is almost exclusively reserved for those from the Global South (e.g., Latin America, the Caribbean, Africa, and Asia). What often goes by the name "anti-immigrant" in the contemporary United States is actually opposed to immigrants from the Global South. These right-wing populists' objections to the welfare state were rooted in racial and ideological objections to the provision of services to the so-called undeserving. Right-wing populism has been a movement that bases itself largely among whites who feel that they are losing out on the so-called American Dream and are being eclipsed by people of color.

The other contributing factor to the right-wing movements has been neoliberal economics. Neoliberals saw the welfare state as an obstacle to the accumulation of profits. The interests of these two sections of the right—neoliberal capitalists and right-wing populists—could and did converge. That was true even when those representing neoliberal capital did not see themselves on the right (e.g., Democrats in New York City during its infamous 1975 fiscal crisis).

As neoliberal economics spread from the Republican Party into the Democratic Party—ultimately becoming the dominant framework—it had a significant impact on the base of the Democratic Party. The Democratic Party went through a monumental change, experiencing demographic expansion, especially bringing in more women and people of color, while embracing neoliberal economics and distancing itself from many of the basic demands of the trade union movement. This has been—incorrectly—described as the rise of "identity politics." It was more a reflection of contradictory tendencies rooted in very different struggles. The Democratic Party's ultimate embrace of civil rights and expansion of the social safety net to include people of color was itself considered a betrayal by many whites, who saw this as providing services and benefits to illegitimate and undeserving populations. Identity politics was a major point of contention within the Democratic Party in the aftermath of Trump's 2016 victory. Senator Bernie Sanders saw the 2016 election as a white worker populist revolt rather than understanding that what had unfolded was a white nationalist revolt driven by right-wing populism. In fact, one can argue that the Trump victory *was* a victory for identity politics, though in this case meaning a *white identity*.

Complementing the transformation of the Democratic Party is the ambiguous role of the mainstream of organized labor when it came to these changes in the Democratic Party specifically and civil rights in general. With the advent of the Cold War, unions, which tended to have the best records on civil rights, were subject to allegations of being communists and, in many cases, expulsion from the Congress of Industrial Organizations (CIO) and, after 1955, exclusion from the AFL-CIO, the organization that resulted from the merger of the CIO with the American Federation of Labor (AFL). Those unions that remained held a broad spectrum of views on race, gender, and civil rights. Though there were unions that addressed race, such as the Packinghouse Workers, 1199: the National Health Care Workers' Union, the Distributive Workers of America, and, in contradictory fashion, the United Auto Workers, there were also unions that had white-male-only clauses as a condition of membership, and an even broader assortment that were otherwise blind and intransigent on matters of race, gender, and civil rights (Spero and Harris 1968). In some cases, there were local unions that served as "base areas" for reactionary activities, a phenomenon not just reserved for the South but also found in such places as Boston in the 1970s during the height of the school desegregation battle. Thus, white union members often saw no contradiction between militant trade unionism on the one hand and racism and sexism on the other.

Furthermore, neoliberalism introduced a growing authoritarianism at the level of the democratic capitalist state, creating what Nicos Poulantzas (2014) called the "neoliberal authoritarian state." The parameters of democracy have been shrinking since the 1970s. The acceptable discourse has become increasingly limited, while the so-called national security state has been strengthened. This is not fascism. There are various forms of right-wing authoritarianism, including fascism, coup regimes, and conservative dictatorships. Neoliberal authoritarianism appears to be a preemptive assault on the popular classes in anticipation of resistance to the continued impact of global capitalist restructuring and the global environmental crisis. At the risk of speculation, we suggest that this authoritarianism may extend beyond neoliberalism, particularly if neoliberalism itself collapses. The transnational capitalist class would face a challenge with regard to methods of accumulation if neoliberalism were abandoned, but in either case, the pressures of the environment, along with the overaccumulation crisis within capitalism, may continue the tendency toward authoritarian solutions.

The fact that neoliberalism and forms of the neoliberal authoritarian state have been introduced by both politically conservative *and* politically liberal administrations should not lead one to the conclusion that this is all a grand conspiracy or that all these politicians are the same. If anything, this process appears to be driven by the strengthening of the transnational capitalist class, though in each case the specific features of the development of neoliberalism and the neoliberal authoritarian state are unique to the given nation-state. It should be added that there continue to be struggles between the domestic capitalist class and the representatives of the transnational capitalist class that play out in the political arena.

To some extent, one sees this in the contradictory signals sent by the Trump administration when it comes to economic policy, as in debates concerning tariffs and over which segments of capital benefit and which are harmed, but it can also be seen in struggles in connection with free-trade agreements.

Right-Wing Populism versus Neoliberal Globalization?

Right-wing populism poses a challenge, but to what? It quite ironically has emerged as an inconsistent, disingenuous, and nationalist opponent of neoliberal globalization. It is true that neoliberalism has destroyed the dream of white Americans, but discussions of the alleged "white working class" and the November 2016 election frequently miss the point. If November 2016 was a revolt against neoliberal globalization, why did workers of color not jump in? Indeed, why were they not recognized as its first victims? Right-wing populism builds itself on populations that are feeling displaced by neoliberal globalization, but it does not necessarily challenge neoliberalism. Authoritarian at its core, though right-wing populism may rhetorically challenge both neoliberalism and globalization, it does so on the basis of an authoritarian nationalist welfare statism that privileges the so-called native population over the "outsider," whether the outsider is an immigrant or a member of a domestic "enemy" population. Although much of white America has reacted with a vengeance, this has led to a bizarre, ahistorical scenario in which right-wing populism suggests that the white working population has been the principal victim of neoliberalism (however defined) rather than recognizing that the domestic effects of neoliberal globalization have fallen disproportionately on African Americans and Latinos. Similarly, the current regime in Poland is taking an extreme right-wing nationalist, though welfarist, approach. Thus, one cannot look for consistency on economics within right-wing populist movements. The critical question revolves much more around who the right-wing populists define as the legitimate population.

It is here that matters relative to race generally and to the Obama era in particular become relevant. The central feature of the Republican assault on the Obama administration revolved around race and the racialization by the political Right of what remains of the welfare state. Obama's victory in 2008, and to a lesser extent his reelection in 2012, seemed to be—for many people—the harbinger of a new era. Too many liberal and progressive people saw in Obama what they wanted to see. Obama, however, was a neoliberal when taking office and remained committed to that vision, albeit with elements of a more progressive stance on certain basic social issues and in favor of a social safety net, but he was not committed to the old Rooseveltian welfare state or to Keynesian economics. He was committed to stabilizing capitalism, which his administration largely did in the context of the 2008 financial collapse. Examples of this include the failure to penalize Wall Street for the collapse, the insufficient funds put into the stabilization process (for fear of a political backlash), and the anemic support for the Employee Free Choice Act (which would have opened up new paths for the growth of organized labor).

Most progressive social movements misread the Obama administration and made a series of mistakes—some strategic, others tactical. The most basic mistake was strategic.

In November 2008, a hole was blown in the defense system of the conservative forces led by the Republican Party. The explosion was devastating and led to a massive retreat by Republicans, in part because they could not explain what had happened, but the retreating conservatives were not pursued; the pro-Obama forces did not follow through on their initial victory.

The Obama administration promoted the demobilization of the progressive base and in doing so laid the foundation for the reemergence of right-wing populist movements, including the Tea Party and, later, the Trump presidential campaign. This demobilization began almost immediately after the 2008 election, when Obama collapsed "Obama for America" into the Democratic Party, thereby undermining the possibility of an independent progressive organization that could have embraced a much broader agenda. The Obama administration did just enough in its policies—and in its very existence—to infuriate the right wing but at the same time not enough to inspire progressive social movements. At every turn, it seemed prepared to compromise with the forces of evil, as if doing so proved it was a mature political actor or prove again and again that this was not the administration of an "angry black man."

The Tea Party and the birther movement filled the void. Organized labor did little but complain about what the Obama administration was not doing, and the black freedom movement was badly divided over how to respond, in part because masses of African Americans saw hope in Obama and saw in his attackers the faces of evil.

The leadership of organized labor expected that the Obama administration would deliver on promises in connection with the Employee Free Choice Act (EFCA), legislation aimed at making it easier for workers to join or form labor unions. Major divisions in the Democratic Party, along with a central focus on health care reform, tabled this for the Obama administration, but more importantly, organized labor treated its concerns, including the EFCA, as matters that were to be the focus of lobbying rather than a focus of mass organizing. This monumental error by the leaders of organized labor took place in the middle of the greatest recession since the Great Depression, when the trade union movement was well positioned to link the demand for the EFCA with the demand for comprehensive economic justice. Instead, the leaders just groused.

Trump as the Personification of White Nationalism and Right-Wing Populism

Anyone who claims to have expected Trump to win is being less than honest. That said, there were sufficient historical and contemporary reasons to believe that it was at least possible. Trump tapped into a sentiment among many white Americans that had rarely—at least in the past three decades—been so openly expressed by mainstream politicians. Until Trump, political racism played out through what many people called "dog whistle politics." With Trump, however, we had the full emergence of what one might call "bugle politics." This bugle politics reflected a sense within much of white America that Trump was needed in order to correct what they believed to have been the greatest mistake in the history of the United States: the election of a black president.

The white rage went deep. It was expressed in a wave of revanchism. This anger, which was organized within right-wing populism, served as one wing of what one might call a "united right front," whose principal objective has been and remains the overturning of the progressive victories of the twentieth century. Despite Trump's protests to the contrary, his movement fit well within the framework set by the united right front.

So, why did Trump win? It is urgent that we step away from many of the myths that were elaborated almost from the moment that Trump was declared the victor on November 8. The main factors were (1) that this was an Electoral College victory, since Clinton won the majority of the popular vote; (2) the Republican base "returned home" and did not splinter; (3) voter suppression, particularly against the African American and Latino electorate; (4) a small but significant voter reversal in key states (in part influenced by a major strategic miscalculation by the Clinton campaign that simply assumed she would win in the Rust Belt); (5) that race and gender were key motivators for the Trump voter, much more than concerns about the economy (or, to put it differently, race and gender were the lenses through which the economy was viewed); (6) and the demobilization of the Obama base, in part resulting from an uninspiring Democratic candidate and disappointment with the Obama administration.

To this list we must add the failure of organized labor to educate its base against right-wing populism. This problem existed on many levels, including a fear of addressing race and gender, and a manner of presenting the challenges facing working people as largely grounded in onerous trade agreements. The failure to offer a comprehensive analysis of neoliberal globalization came back to bite organized labor in the rear when Trump made opposition to free-trade agreements one of his central rhetorical points. For many union members, it all sounded familiar. This was equally a challenge for the Sanders campaign. Its economic message sometimes sounded as if it were Trump's right-wing populist message. The absence of a racial justice analysis and an antixenophobic framework allowed many voters to perceive *incorrectly* that Sanders and Trump were speaking to the same issue.

In reviewing this list, there are two points that we wish to highlight. The first is that there was no mandate for Trump. In losing the popular vote, in effect he lost the election. The second point concerns the Russians. While we are absolutely convinced of Russian meddling, just as there has been US meddling in many foreign elections, and we believe that the influence of "black propaganda," or "fake news," is important, it would be incorrect to look at those points as game changers. They were contributing factors that might not have been in place had the Clinton campaign had a better strategy; had Clinton herself been a convincing populist candidate; had FBI director James Comey not issued his statement two weeks prior to the election on e-mails supposedly pertinent to an investigation into Clinton's use of a private e-mail server; and had the other factors noted not been in play, with voter suppression probably the most underrated factor.

The Crisis of Organized Labor and the Challenge of Right-Wing Populism

So, what has all of this meant for organized labor in the United States? It is first important to situate the crisis facing organized labor (Fletcher and Gapasin 2009). This crisis started in the late 1940s with Cold War witch hunts against leftists within union ranks and the impact that these had on everything from organizing strategy to member education, leading to a collapse of any semblance of progressive internationalism and an abandonment of the antiracist struggle. Organized labor, with certain exceptions, missed the emergence of key social movements, including the black freedom movement, the women's movement, the Chicano and the Puerto Rican freedom movements, and the anti–Vietnam War movement.

Missing these movements was not simply a matter of corrupted morals and politics but also one of missing the strategic opportunity to create the sort of social and economic justice bloc that could very well have transformed politics in the United States. This failure meant that organized labor evolved in the direction of a so-called special interest rather than as a broad and inclusive social movement.

A second factor in understanding the crisis of organized labor is to appreciate the failure of the reform movement that swept much of organized labor in the 1990s. This movement, which emerged slowly out of the late 1980s, was an effort at altering the practices of the existing trade union movement in the absence of fundamental restructuring and reorientation. The focus of the reform effort was largely on organizing the unorganized and by October 1995 had led to the victory of a reform slate in the national AFL-CIO election, headed by then Service Employees International Union (SEIU) president John Sweeney, United Mine Workers of America president Richard Trumka, and American Federation of State, County and Municipal Employees leader Linda Chavez-Thompson and known as the New Voices slate.

Despite the cautious optimism of the moment, the reform effort, largely directed from the top, was unable to exercise its potential. Significant accomplishments took place, including the massive victory of public-sector organizing in Puerto Rico; the large-scale organizing of new sectors, such as home care; invigorated central labor councils; and the campaign in defense of the Charleston Five, when five longshore workers in South Carolina were arrested for a peaceful protest against nonunion labor on the docks.

Yet, there were real constraints within which the reform movement operated, some of which were self-imposed. In some cases, this harkened back to the Cold War and the fear of left-wing unionism. The main challenge remained the ideological paradigm within which most of organized labor operated (i.e., the framework developed by Samuel Gompers, founding president of the American Federation of Labor). This paradigm of so-called pure and simple trade unionism restricted the ability of organized labor to see itself as truly part of a classwide movement. Though the reformers of the 1990s emphasized member mobilizations and new organizing efforts, as well as building coalitions, they limited the extent and depth of member education and, at the end of the day, continued to assert the possibility of a return to the so-called Golden Age of Capitalism, during which many of the leaders of organized labor believed that peaceful coexistence had reigned supreme. This misassessment was grounded in a fundamental misreading of the labor movement's actual history (particularly the virulent racism and antiunionism in the South and Southwest during this Golden Age), of neoliberal globalization, and of the growing authoritarian tendency within so-called democratic capitalism. These factors contributed to blindness to the danger inherent in right-wing populism and to its potential to have an impact on labor union members.

We noted earlier the impact of the Cold War. Worker education specifically was both marginalized and minimized (in form and content). Touching on issues of race, class, and a basic framework for understanding the political economy, including the corporate-driven US foreign policy, was deemed dangerous in that it might lead one to be branded as a communist. The "safer" route was to avoid these issues entirely and instead become cheerleaders for the so-called American Dream and focus primarily on training union leaders to develop the skills and knowledge to perform their duties more efficiently. Among other things, such an approach weakened the ability of organized labor to correctly identify the right-wing populism and prepare its own members to resist it.

A third factor in the crisis was the failure of Richard Trumka's administration of the AFL-CIO to build a governing, transformative coalition after his election in 2009. Trumka, an outstanding leader out of the United Mine Workers of America, had been the AFL-CIO's secretary-treasurer under its president John Sweeney. In ways that have never been revealed, he was caught up in a scandal that brought down the reform administration of Ron Carey in the Teamsters Union. For several years after that, Trumka was virtually out of sight; he reemerged slowly to become heir apparent to Sweeney.

Trumka is a visionary himself, but he failed to create a governing coalition that supported not only his agenda but also the transformation of organized labor. Instead, there has been more of an atmosphere of tolerance of his administration on the part of the organization's affiliates. One of his boldest ventures was the creation of the AFL-CIO Labor Commission on Racial and Economic Justice in the aftermath of a rash of police killings of African Americans. Though this commission had the endorsement of others in the leadership of the AFL-CIO, it was highly controversial in that it explicitly examined the question of race and the role of organized labor in economic and racial disparities and institutional biases. (Important as this commission was, there were limitations, including focusing more on the black/white racial binary rather than expanding to examine the construction of race in a broader framework.) Unfortunately, after the November 2016 election, the commission's work largely came to a halt.

Trumka's elevation to the presidency contrasted with the October 1995 victory of the New Voices slate in the AFL-CIO, in which there was a formidable coalition of unions that backed the platform of the New Voices ticket. Though their support was ultimately ephemeral, their existence as a bloc did have an impact on the profile of organized labor.

By contrast, Trumka's election was not viewed as a fundamental shift, though many progressives expected or hoped that he would deepen reform efforts. To a great extent, his administration did not depart dramatically from his predecessor's. The Trumka administration seemed to be, more than anything else, Trumka.

A fourth factor in the current situation has been seen in splits within organized labor on both the environment and trade. With regard to trade, beginning during the Sweeney administration, there was rising discontent with what some of the unions based in manufacturing believed had been relative silence in the face of industry relocation and so-called deindustrialization. This anger was focused on matters of trade agreements, including the expansion of free-trade agreements after the passage of the North American Free Trade Agreement (NAFTA).

As we noted earlier, the deeper problem was a narrow analysis of the economic crisis facing the US working class specifically and the global working classes generally. While free-trade agreements contributed to the situation, the larger factor was the comprehensive nature of neoliberal globalization. Neoliberal globalization is not the result of an evolutionary process but rather has been orchestrated through political and economic agreements and expedited by developments in technology. Free-trade agreements are the component that reflects the need of global capitalism for economic integration.

To the extent that organized labor focused almost exclusively on trade agreements, it advanced a narrow, nationalist framework that could be—and was—taken advantage of by right-wing populists, including Donald Trump. The desperation of much of organized labor in the face of the economic crisis seems to have led many in the union movement to see the overturning of free-trade agreements as the whole solution rather than as one part of the answer. Furthermore, the elimination of free trade raises the question of what sort of trade needs to be proposed by the trade union movement in the United States. It also raises the question of the relationship of the US working class to working classes in other parts of the world, which are regularly crushed not only by trade agreements but also by the practice of predatory capitalist penetration in their countries.

The trade union movement has also been torn by conflicting approaches to the environmental crisis. This became evident in the context of the battles over oil pipelines, including the Keystone and Dakota pipelines. Organized labor was split, with several building trades unions, such as the Laborers' International Union of North America (LIUNA) and the United Brotherhood of Carpenters and Joiners of America (UBC), adamantly supporting pipeline construction while others, such as the Communications Workers of America (CWA) and National Nurses United (NNU), spoke out in opposition to it—frequently in alliance with community-based organizations. The extent of this tension was displayed in heated exchanges between LIUNA and the CWA, but the split was much deeper.

In the aftermath of the November 2016 presidential election, several building trades unions welcomed Trump's commitment to move forward with environmentally threatening projects. The AFL-CIO found itself unable or unwilling to develop a coherent pro-worker, pro-environment policy, apparently concluding that the building trades unions, or some segment of them, might split off on their own if it did.

The divide on the environment was a display of the narrowness of the trade unionism practiced by much of organized labor. While the progressive segments of organized labor recognized that attention must be focused on reorganizing the economy in an environmentally friendly manner—in which quite literally millions of jobs could be produced—those forces that are more conservative appear to believe that the jobs that the fossil-fuel industry promises should be grabbed, in a case of better the devil you know than the devil you do not. Such a view, which we would argue is a capitulation, is consistent with the notion of labor as a special interest rather than a representative of the broad interests of working-class people.

A fifth factor in the current moment is the emergence of left/progressive leadership in some key unions, including the American Postal Workers Union, the Amalgamated Transit Union, the CWA, NNU, and, in a different location, the SEIU and the United Steel Workers of America. The first four of these unions backed the presidential candidacy of Senator Bernie Sanders and have positioned themselves to conceptualize a legacy for this movement within organized labor. It is too early to ascertain the longevity of this effort. The question, however, is whether this left/progressive leadership grouping is prepared to push the envelope on the limits of trade unionism. Specifically, it is one thing to endorse a progressive presidential candidate but another thing to transform the very nature of trade unionism.

The final development was referenced earlier but should be identified explicitly: the rise of an openly collaborationist wing within organized labor. Meeting with Trump immediately after his inauguration, this element, which included the presidents of the UBC and the LIUNA, went far beyond the already unacceptable argument of finding common ground with conservatives. These leaders offered praise to Trump, including with regard to his "America First" platform. Rather than recognizing the danger presented by Trump and his right-wing populist movement, they have been prepared to view Trump as someone advancing the interests of US workers. The racial blindness of these leaders has been nothing short of spectacular.

Is There a Place for Organized Labor in the "Resistance"?

In the aftermath of the November 2016 election, the AFL-CIO issued a statement attempting to explain the results (Trumka 2016; Hiatt 2016). Though preliminary, it was still anemic. In fact, one of the striking features of the postelection environment was the lack of a comprehensive analysis of the election results by organized labor. In fact, the relative silence has been deafening.

What are we to make of this? Among other things, the failure of most of organized labor to engage in open internal debate has come back at the unions. Many union leaders are fearful of their own members, not really knowing which of them voted for Trump. As a result, we are witnessing paralysis, and part of that paralysis is a failure of analysis.

The existence of Trump supporters within the ranks of organized labor should not have come as a surprise to labor's leadership. In general, somewhere between 30 percent and 40 percent of union households tend to vote Republican. This is a significant minority. The difference in 2016 was that this minority was quite vocal, and their anger with the Democrats overlapped with the frustration that many non-Republicans had with the neoliberal policies advanced by most Democratic Party politicians, including Hillary Clinton.

If organized labor is to be a full component of the resistance, it must rethink its relationship to electoral politics, but more importantly, its relationship to its own membership. Our suggestions are as follows. In order to defeat right-wing populism, the leadership of organized labor must engage in a discussion with its own membership about right-wing populism but also about race, gender, and the role of the United States in international politics and economics. This is far from a new conclusion. In 1995, the AFL-CIO commissioned a study by Peter Hart Research that indicated, among other things, that "most members have no ideological framework for organizing information about politics and public policy . . . and some even have a rough economic analysis that includes the global economy, trade, weakened unions, and growing inequality. . . . [H]owever, these members generally have little or no ideological orientation that would link economics, government, and politics . . . and few can articulate any explanation for what has gone wrong, who is responsible, or what should be done about it. . . . [L]acking such an orientation, *their substantial economic grievances do not lead them to the progressive political conclusions we might expect*" (Garin and Molyneux 1995, emphasis added). The study also concluded that "labor's long-term strategic mission is to develop an ideological framework among the membership" in order to "tell a compelling story about the economy, corporate irresponsibility, and the conservative policies *that have helped shift even more bargaining power to capital over labor*" (Garin and Molyneux 1995, emphasis added). The nature of this engagement must be such that it encourages the kind of education and debate that would allow union members to grasp the complexity of the changing political economy and how the rise of right-wing populism is fueled not only by economic insecurity but also by racism and xenophobia. The efforts promoted by the national AFL-CIO, for instance, through its Race Commission, or the work of the

Washington State Labor Council to advance a racial justice education project, are positive cases in point of what is desperately needed.

Anti–right-wing populist education in the trade union movement must be democratic and centered on workers. Historically, worker education in certain of the more progressive and Left-led CIO unions included the study of democracy and the meaning of democratic values and democratic rights, as well as the role of social movements. A lot of that took place in collaboration with labor education centers such as the Brookwood Labor College and the Highlander Center.

Now more than ever, unions need to reshape their leadership development programs to engage leaders at all levels in discussions and reflection about the political economy. Such discussions need to address the meaning and implications of neoliberalism for their standard of living and their rights not only as workers but also as citizens and residents of the larger society. In our view, this also must include a discussion of the ascendancy of populism, most specifically of right-wing populism, and of its appeal to certain groups of workers and union members, including the role that racism and xenophobia play in this whole process.

We must think about an all-around education process. In union apprenticeship programs, for instance, it is not enough to teach basic union history; it is also critical to have an examination of capitalism as a system, as well as discussions of the nature and shape of various reactionary social movements. In stewards' training, participants should be encouraged to come forward with challenges that they receive from conservative and ultraright members that they may have found difficult to answer. This can become part of the learning process. New educational materials should be offered, ranging from illustrated books to online programs, that encourage deeper education and provide the opportunity to explore matters in greater scope. Education that challenges right-wing populism, racism, sexism, xenophobia, and other views is not a one-shot experience. Union institutions should make this a regular part of their programs.

In addressing right-wing populism, not only educational campaigns are necessary at all levels but so are organizing and mobilizing campaigns that are explicitly targeted at institutions and issues that are utilized by right-wing populists and other enemies of workers. Thus, unions must advance campaigns that challenge the economic devastation carried out by multinational corporations—both in the United States and overseas—with regard to everything from the environment to the implications of corporate abandonment of geographic areas (such as plant closures). The union must be seen as the entity that is fighting for consistent democracy and consistent economic justice, and not fighting only for the interests of its current members.

It is important that we note the question of internationalism, or the lack thereof. Organized labor has paid precious little attention to educating its mem-

bership regarding international affairs, the role of the United States in foreign regimes, and the global class struggle. As we mentioned earlier, the approach of
much of the US trade union movement in its opposition to trade agreements has
been protectionist and, in the worst cases, has demonized foreign workers as
though they are the source of the problem rather than being victims of neoliberal
capitalism along with US workers. Opposition to NAFTA, for example, necessitates a united effort of Mexican, US, and Canadian workers and their organizations. A transnational labor movement needs to be elaborating an approach
reflecting the standpoint of workers rather than the standpoint of capital.

Opposition to right-wing populism is directly linked to a revitalization of organized labor, and the revitalization of organized labor necessitates a political Left.
A great portion of the weakness of the union reform efforts in the 1990s was the
attempt to resolve the contradictions labor was facing within a failed paradigm.
This means that revitalization must tackle the specific realities of neoliberal globalization, growing authoritarianism, and the convergence of crises related to the
economy, the environment, and the state. In that sense, organized labor must begin to advance not only a critique of contemporary capitalism but also an alternative approach to the economy that bases itself on the needs of working-class
people. Indeed, such an approach must truly be internationalist in order to address the reorganization of global capitalism. As demonstrated in the rise of the
Industrial Workers of the World and, in the 1930s, the growth of the Congress of
Industrial Organizations, labor needs a dedicated and invigorated Left in order
to be reborn. Tactical innovation and provocative ideas are insufficient. The Left,
when it is at its best, challenges progressive social movements to go beyond the
"acceptable" and to confront power. This can be uncomfortable for the pragma-
tists within organized labor, but it is essential if the movement is to be emanci-
patory in its practice and objectives.

Organized labor must engage with community-based allies in progressive electoral challenges, state by state and territory by territory. Organized labor's approach to electoral politics must shift fundamentally not only toward engaging
their members democratically and pedagogically but also building alliances with
strategic allies on a state-by-state and territory-by-territory basis in an effort to
build progressive electoral blocs that are prepared to operate both inside and outside the Democratic Party and, in some cases, within the Republican Party. This
is beginning to happen, as in the work of the Washington State Labor Council,
but it has not been advanced as a comprehensive strategy by the movement. Independent working-class politics begins with an independent working-class analysis and program.

History demonstrates that timing is everything. History is very unforgiving,
and it reminds us that once an opportunity is lost, it may be lost for decades, if

not longer. Organized labor is in a race against time with right-wing populism. The inability of organized labor to respond to the reconfiguration of capitalism and its skittishness in addressing race and gender have placed it in a decidedly weakened position and made it more difficult to capture the imagination of the working class.

Addressing what amounts to a strategic defeat of the working class in no way means that the war is over, however. Consider those in France who in early summer 1940 could only look in despair at a country that had collapsed in weeks under the treads of the German invasion and the gutlessness of its own generals. It took time, but the battle cry of resistance was heard and a spirit emerged: a spirit of resistance, represented by the outgunned but never dispirited Maquis resistance fighters, who had to employ strategies, tactics, and organization in circumstances that only a few short months earlier could never have been conceived of—an asymmetric situation, to borrow a term from the current era. In our opinion, *this is the hour of the Maquis!*

References

Berlet, Chip, and Matthew N. Lyons. 2000. *Right-Wing Populism in America: Too Close for Comfort.* New York: Guilford Press.

Fletcher, Bill, Jr. 2015. "Stars and Bars: Understanding Right-Wing Populism in the US." In *Socialist Register 2016: The Politics of the Right*, edited by Leo Panitch and Greg Albo, 296–311. London: Merlin Press.

Fletcher, Bill, Jr., and Fernando Gapasin. 2009. *Solidarity Divided: The Crisis in Organized Labor and a New Path Toward Social Justice.* Berkeley: University of California Press.

Garin, Geoff, and Guy Molyneux. 1995. "Executive Summary of Focus Group Findings on Union Members' Political Attitudes in July and August 1995." Memo to AFL-CIO membership, September 19. PDF of memo in our possession.

Hiatt, Jon. 2016. "Guest Post: The AFL-CIO's Response to Trump's Presidency." *OnLabor* blog, November 29. https://onlabor.org/guest-post-the-afl-cios-response-to-trumps-presidency/.

MacLean, Nancy. 2008. *Freedom Is Not Enough: The Opening of the American Workplace.* Cambridge, MA: Harvard University Press.

Poulantzas, Nicos. 2014. *State, Power, Socialism.* Brooklyn, New York: Verso.

Spero, Sterling D., and Abram L. Harris. 1968. *The Black Worker: The Negro and the Labor Movement.* New York: Atheneum.

Trumka, Richard. 2016. "Statement by AFL-CIO President Richard Trumka on the 2016 Presidential Election." Press release. https://aflcio.org/press/releases/statement-afl-cio-president-richard-trumka-2016-presidential-election.

United Nations. 2016. *Sustainable Development Goals: 17 Goals to Transform Our World.* http://www.un.org/sustainabledevelopment/blog/2016/01/244-million-international-migrants-living-abroad-worldwide-new-un-statistics-reveal/.

Part II

HOW THE RIGHT WING ADVANCES ITS AGENDA

4

WALKER'S WISCONSIN AND THE FUTURE OF THE UNITED STATES

Jon Shelton

On November 8, 2016, the United States elected its first billionaire president, a man who had bragged about sexual assault and had run on explicit appeals to racial chauvinism. There has been much debate about what, aside from his own self-aggrandizement, Donald Trump stands for, but there is indeed a distinct politics of "Trumpism" for which he served as conduit in winning the presidency. Trumpism consists of exploiting the economic anxieties of non–college-educated Americans who have been left behind by the neoliberal agenda of the Democratic Party, scapegoating the vulnerable, and selling fictions that corporate giveaways will bring back well-paying jobs to "Make America Great Again." In 2016, this message helped catapult Trump to Electoral College victory through upsets in the Rust Belt states of Ohio, Pennsylvania, Michigan, and Wisconsin. With the exception of Ohio in 2000 and 2004, Democratic nominees had won each of these states in every presidential election since 1988.

For close observers of Wisconsin, however, the election results were, if still surprising, at least understandable. In many ways, Scott Walker's strategy in 2010 provided a working model for the politics of Trumpism six years later. Wisconsin—with its history of progressive public policy, strong industrial unions, pioneering support for public-employee labor rights, and a broadly accessible public university system—had been an exemplar of American social democracy, so Walker's approach represented a radical departure from the state's past (Kaufman 2018). At the same time, a conservative undercurrent in Wisconsin provided a well-worn path that Walker, supported by class-conscious corporate elites, rode to absolute victory. In November 2018, Walker was defeated by state superintendent of education, Tony Evers. While Walker's reign has now concluded, the tiny margin of victory for Evers (less than 30,000 votes out of about 2.6 million cast) did not represent a resounding repudiation of Walkerism. The heavily gerrymandered legislature continued to be controlled by Republicans, and a dramatic turn from Walker's policies seems unlikely. Indeed, the damage to working people in the state—as is likely to be the case in the United States under Trump—will take a long time to undo.

This chapter outlines Walker's strategy over the past decade and explains how it helps us understand Trump's success both in Wisconsin and in similar states such as Michigan, Ohio, and Pennsylvania. Walker, even before Trump, exploited the Democratic Party's failure to address corporations' class warfare from above and disinvestment in good jobs in Wisconsin. Many white, non–college-educated workers had seen downward pressure on job security, wages, and social insurance, and Walker crafted a narrative that blamed what he argued were unproductive sectors of the population (such as public employees) for these conditions. Like Trump's, Walker's political interventions resembled a funhouse mirror: instead of improving the economic reality for most Wisconsinites, he used this narrative to further disinvest in public institutions and slash taxes for the wealthy while stripping union rights from both the public and the private sectors. The consequence has been that economic security for working Wisconsinites—already under pressure before Walker took office—was further eroded from 2011 to 2018. In fact, one study (Meyers 2015) has asserted that Wisconsin has seen "the largest middle-class decline of any state" since 2000.

What can we do in these times to counteract the discord sown first by Walker and now by Trump? The only solution, as I argue in this chapter's conclusion, is to forge a long-range progressive coalition that can turn working Wisconsinites (and all working Americans) toward the possibility of enhanced social democracy and away from the empty promises of Walkerism and Trumpism.

The Rise of Walker

Scott Walker won a state assembly seat representing the Milwaukee suburb of Wauwatosa in 1993, serving until he was elected Milwaukee County executive in 2002. The Republican's political heroes were two other party standard-bearers, Ronald Reagan and Tommy Thompson, the latter the longest-serving governor (from 1987 to 2001) in the state's history (Kersten 2011). The imprint of both these figures was evident in Walker's gubernatorial campaign in November 2010, when he took on Democratic Milwaukee mayor Tom Barrett.

In 2009–2010, unemployment was at its highest level since the Reagan recession of the early 1980s. In Wisconsin, public employees faced furloughs to pay for budget deficits, and private-sector employers like Mercury Marine, a manufacturer of outboard motors in Fond de Lac, sought deep concessions from their workers to lower labor costs. Thus, like Reagan, Walker sought executive office at a time of economic catastrophe, and, like the Gipper, he argued that he could unleash broad economic prosperity by reducing the "burdens" of excessive taxation and government regulation. Central to his pitch was the audacious claim that his administration would create 250,000 new jobs in its first four years.

Like Reagan, Walker also squarely connected taxes and government intervention to the wages and benefits of public employees (Marley 2009). Here Walker drew on a growing reservoir of resentment toward public-sector workers. As I document in my book *Teacher Strike!* (Shelton 2017), during the 1970s, the uniquely toxic combination of corporate disinvestment, inflation, and fiscal crisis in many of America's cities allowed revanchist politicians to mobilize a growing "producerist" constituency, soldering together a political coalition of corporate elites and (mostly white) private-sector workers. Many of these workers, hit hard by the failure of the Democratic Party to arrest these trends, grew increasingly skeptical of the "unproductive" public employees and racialized welfare recipients they blamed for American economic decline. Reagan, noting this insurgent trend, spectacularly mobilized it when he weighed in on the New York City fiscal crisis from the presidential campaign trail in November 1975. "There is no question," he argued, "that the victims in New York are the three million taxpaying citizens working in the private sector who must put up all the money that pays for everything else, who for some twenty-five-odd years had their political leaders deceive them" (Shelton 2017, 142).

Work on the late twentieth century by historian Adam Mertz (2017) indicates that Tommy Thompson forged a winning coalition by employing a similar wedge. Mertz argues that Thompson stoked the fears of rural and suburban white Wisconsinites around the cost of public-employee contracts and the "special" privileges of minorities, such as black welfare recipients and Native Americans who enjoyed treaty rights to hunt and fish that white sportsmen did not. Campaigning in 1986, Thompson connected the notion of lowering property taxes to the state's binding-arbitration law for public employees, passed a decade earlier in the wake of the infamous Hortonville teacher strike in 1974.

Walker employed the playbook of both Reagan and Thompson in 2010, pointedly asserting that private-sector workers suffered at the hands of their counterparts in the public sector. In the general election's final debate, Walker linked excessive government regulation and taxation to the pampered position of public employees: "You can no longer have public employees who are the haves and tax-payers who foot the bill being the have-nots" (Marley and Berquist 2010). In retrospect, the rhetoric was brilliant. As important work by Thomas Frank (2016) has pointed out, the Democratic Party has offered little economic opportunity for working people who have not graduated from college. As Frank reminds us, since the 1980s, many Democrats have increasingly catered to a professional-class constituency, touting education as a panacea for the downward pressure on blue-collar wages from capital movement abroad and the Right's war on unions.

Blue-collar workers in Wisconsin indeed faced pressures exacerbated by the economic crisis of 2008. As in many other Rust Belt states, some of the state's larg-est manufacturers began to shift production elsewhere in the 1960s and 1970s, and some, such as Milwaukee's Allis-Chalmers, ceased production altogether in the 1980s (Gurda 1999, 415–420). In fact, one of the key arenas of debate in the 2008 presidential election centered on Wisconsin's history of corporate disinvest-ment. By that point, General Motors planned to close its plant in Janesville. In response, future president Barack Obama gave a major campaign address, casti-gating "a Washington where decades of trade deals like NAFTA and China have been signed with plenty of protections for corporations and their profits, but none for our environment or our workers who've seen factories shut their doors and millions of jobs disappear; workers whose right to organize and unionize has been under assault for the last eight years"(2008). When in 2009 the plant ultimately ceased production, 9,000 people in and around Janesville were out of work. As journalist Sarah Jones (2017) sums it up, "a little over 14 percent of the city's pop-ulation (at that point, around 63,540 people) were unemployed by 2010. And these were not just individual tragedies: Most workers had families to support, and the plant's closure stranded them in a flailing job market with skills that didn't necessarily transfer to other industries."

In fact, in 2010, Walker used fears of further capital flight to propel his guber-natorial campaign. For instance, Walker highlighted Mercury Marine, which had sought—in addition to concessions from workers—huge tax subsidies from state and local government by threatening to move all of its production to Oklahoma. Though his predecessor, Democrat Jim Doyle, had secured a $65 million pack-age of tax credits to keep the company in Wisconsin, Walker used the case to ar-gue that a good business climate in the state necessitated reducing both taxes and expenditures on public employees. "If I'm governor," he asserted in a pri-mary debate in 2010, "Mercury Marine doesn't even think about leaving" (2010). It might have seemed particularly galling to many private-sector workers in Wis-consin that while unions like the machinists local at Mercury Marine were un-able to prevent cuts to pay and hard-won benefits and the implementation of a two-tiered employment structure, university faculty and academic staff, after decades of effort, had finally won collective-bargaining rights in 2009, during the heart of the economic crisis (Kniffin 2011).

Furthermore, as Katherine Cramer's ethnography (Cramer 2016) has shown, rural Wisconsinites had begun to seriously resent public employees by 2010, associating them with the concerns of "urban" Wisconsinites and promulgating the narrative that urban areas received resources at the expense of rural people. Though Cramer shows this narrative was mostly untrue, it likely derived from the fact that for those Wisconsinites who failed to sufficiently invest in their own "human capital" to make it in a globalizing economy, no politician of either party had been doing very much to offer economic prosperity. For rural people, this resentment particularly revolved around the security of benefits, such as health insurance and pensions enjoyed by many college-educated public employees.

A study conducted by Jeffrey Keefe of the Economic Policy Institute (EPI) in early 2011 aptly parried Walker's claims. In fact, Keefe found, after accounting for level of education, that public employees in Wisconsin were actually underpaid relative to their counterparts in the private sector. But the very premise of the comparison—factoring in the level of education—points to the relevant wedge to help understand why Walker had been elected. As Keefe points out, "When comparing public and private-sector pay it is essential to consider the much higher levels of education required by occupations in the public sector. As a consequence of these requirements, 59% of Wisconsin public-sector workers hold at least a four-year college degree, compared with 30% of full-time private-sector workers" (Keefe 2011, 2). While Keefe concluded that public employees made about 25 percent less than their counterparts in the private sector, they still had what many private-sector workers did not: "State and local government employees also receive a higher portion of their compensation in the form of employer-provided nonwage benefits. . . . Public employers devote a larger share of their compensation packages to health insurance and pension benefits than do private employers" (Keefe 2011, 1). With the downward pressure on job security and benefits for workers in the private sector, it seems clear why some would find Walker's narrative convincing.

Though the vast majority of Wisconsin's African American working class—centered in Milwaukee, and the source of a significant number of votes—opposed Walker, it is important to point out that enthusiasm for a Democratic Party that has done very little to reduce poverty and facilitate good jobs for African Americans in Wisconsin had waned, and this likely was a factor in Walker's election in 2010 (and his subsequent reelections). As Marc Levine has shown, for African Americans in Milwaukee, corporate disinvestment has been particularly drastic: "No metro area has witnessed more precipitous erosion in the labor market for black males over the past 40 years than has Milwaukee" (Levine 2012). Furthermore, given that many blacks in the city interact with the state through a police department that has had a contentious relationship with African Americans—represented most recently by the killing of Sylville Smith in summer 2016 (Nolan and Bosman 2017)—there may very well be diminished confidence in the Democratic argument about the role government can play in improving lives.

I should also mention here that Walker also benefited from a 2010 Tea Party wave in which Republicans took sixty-three seats in the US House of Representatives (flipping it), five seats in the Senate, and six net gubernatorial spots, including Walker's. No doubt, historians will debate this phenomenon for years. Racial backlash likely played a part, but possibly so did the Obama administration's failure to hold financial capital responsible for its role in causing working Americans so much pain in 2008. In any event, it is also clear that the 2010 electoral wave, including Walker's election, was aided by a coordinated right-wing assault to undermine Obama and American liberalism through the network created by the various arms of the Charles and David Koch entities. The Supreme Court's *Citizens United v Federal Election Commission* decision in 2010 facilitated the flow of torrents of dark money (including from Wisconsin building-supply magnate Diane Hendricks and home-supply chain store owner John Menard Jr.) into politics and would amplify this money in Walker's recall election in 2012 and reelection in 2014 (Mayer 2016).

On November 2, 2010, Walker won election to his first term as Wisconsin's governor, beating Milwaukee mayor Tom Barrett by almost six points. Buoyed by a coalition of some of the state's wealthiest citizens and the resentment of many private-sector workers, Walker was ready to mount the most dramatic assault on social democracy in recent American memory.

Walkerism in Action

When Walker took office in 2010, both houses of the state legislature had flipped from Democratic to Republican majorities (and, in the lower house, Republicans held over 60 percent of the total seats). Walker thus had effective carte blanche to enact his plans, but his signature move—Act 10—put into motion almost immediately after he took office, was nonetheless shocking in its audacity.

Like many states in the years immediately after the Great Recession, Wisconsin faced a budget shortfall when Walker took office. The new governor, however, overstated the extent of the deficit, creating what one study has called a "political spectacle" (Pernsteiner et al. 2016, 507). In the process, Walker then convinced "state legislators that the only reasonable solution to the problem was to eliminate public-employee unions" (510).

Indeed, Act 10, which Walker ultimately signed into law in March 2011, was sweeping. It forced public employees to contribute significantly more to their pensions and health care premiums in order to reduce state expenditures. More devastating, however, was the almost complete elimination of meaningful collective-bargaining rights. All Wisconsin public-employee unions, with the exception of police and firefighters, now must be recertified as a bargaining agent every year and can only be recertified if they receive 51 percent of the vote of an entire bargaining unit, not simply those who cast a ballot. If that threshold seems difficult (in addition to resource intensive), recertifying under the proposal has also lost its purpose for many unions, since Act 10 bars them from bargaining over anything but salary increases capped at the rate of inflation. Fair share or agency fee arrangements, of course, are also illegal, and unions cannot even work out arrangements whereby employees can voluntarily have dues deducted from their paychecks.

Readers of this chapter will likely remember the "Wisconsin uprising" that captured national and global attention in February 2011, so I will not recount it in detail here. In short, grassroots activism facilitated an ongoing occupation of the state capitol and a series of protests unprecedented in Wisconsin's history. Wisconsinites who put their lives on pause to protest that winter were disappointed by the legislature's successful effort to ram Act 10 through, even though fourteen Democratic state legislators were still absent from the state, preventing the quorum needed for the initial version of the bill to move through the state senate. Still, in the same way that Trump has galvanized a resistance, the Act 10 protests served to create a base of collective memory, as John Nichols (2012) and other observers (Kersten 2011; Buhle and Buhle 2012; Yates 2012) have shown, for those who participated. In 2018 as in 2011, protests at the capitol tried to stop the legislature from ramming through unprecedented legislation. In 2018, as in 2011, the protests could not overcome the Republican legislature, and in Walker's last month in office, the lame-duck legislature passed a battery of laws limiting the power of Evers and incoming attorney general Josh Kaul (Elbow 2018).

Though many remember it fondly, we must recall that the resistance to Act 10 (as well as the resistance to the lame-duck laws in 2018) was ultimately futile. Following the legislature's gambit in 2011, some labor activists—such as the South Central Federation of Labor (SCFL), located in Madison, which passed a resolution supporting a general strike—pushed for radical action. Many of the state's labor leaders, however, were lukewarm about the idea, and it never gained significant traction (Sustar 2012). Given the GOP's unwillingness to compromise on Act 10, such an action would likely have required a shutdown of government services in the state for some time before it would have forced Walker and the legislature to repeal the law.

Public employees in Wisconsin in 2011 (like many workers in the United States these days) probably did not have the kind of infrastructure to build and sustain such a strike, however. Since the Wisconsin legislature passed the Mediation Arbitration Law of 1977, public-employee strikes have been virtually nonexistent, meaning that such an action would have little precedent—even on a local basis—for most of the public employees in the state. Instead, grassroots activists put their energy into recalling Walker from office, garnering 900,000 petition signatures in just sixty days, a more than sufficient number to force a new election in June 2012 (Davey and Zeleny 2012). Unfortunately, however, the election was a rematch between Walker and Barrett, which hamstrung the effort from the start. Though turnout was higher than in 2010, Walker actually won by a slightly higher margin (almost 7 percent). Had the question of public-employee rights been framed as it was in Ohio, where in November 2011 voters repealed Senate Bill 5, Governor John Kasich's similar attack on public-employee rights (Fields 2011), the effort in Wisconsin might have borne more fruit. In any event, the failure to recall Walker seemed to ratify his moves, and it has left many of the activists who immersed themselves in the recall effort devastated to this day.

Walker's signature move has left public employees with diminished agency since 2011. Total union membership in the state has declined by 40 percent, and most public-employee unions have seen membership plummet even more precipitously (Beck 2017). The Wisconsin Education Association Council (WEAC), for instance, has seen membership fall from about 90,000 to under 40,000 (Marianno and Strunk 2018).

Furthermore, Act 10 was accompanied by massive cuts in state appropriations, and education bore the brunt of the shortfall. In fact, Walker's 2011–2013 budget deprived the state education system of over $1 billion: $792 million in aid to school districts, $250 million to the twenty-six campuses in the University of Wisconsin (UW) system, and another $70 million to the state's technical colleges (Umhoefer 2012). Cuts to education are unsurprising for two reasons. First, education was the largest government expenditure in Wisconsin when Walker took office, and any significant state budget cutting would require cuts to it. Second, and more importantly, education has for some time been at the forefront of claims, especially by Democrats, about the need to provide economic opportunity in a global "knowledge" economy. Weakening the power of educators while taking aim at the cost of education helped Walker harness the growing resentment of those left behind by this narrative.

Budget cuts and the elimination of collective-bargaining rights allowed many school districts to cut costs, at least in the first couple of years after Act 10. The consequence, however, has been education on the cheap, with diminished working conditions for teachers and diminished quality for many students. As David

Madland and Alex Rowell of the Center for American Progress have pointed out (Madland and Rowell 2017), teacher turnover has increased substantially, undermining the long-term relationships between schools, families, and teachers. Some teachers near Illinois or Minnesota have moved across these borders for better pay and more stability, while others simply left the profession or retired. University schools of education now produce far fewer teachers than they used to. According to Madland and Rowell, there is now a significant teacher shortage. Those who do teach in Wisconsin now have less experience than the average teacher did a decade ago.

Walker's attack on public employees in the state continued unabated after Act 10. Following his reelection in 2014 (when he defeated Mary Burke, a former Trek Bicycle executive who garnered little enthusiasm), Walker focused his next assault on the university system. Using the budget process again, in late January 2015, Walker pushed the legislature to pass what he called "the Act 10 for higher education" (Herzog and Marley 2015). The 2015–2017 budget bill cut $250 million from a UW system that, already subject to a freeze on tuition that began in 2013 and continues to this day, could scarcely afford another drastic reduction. Signed into law in July 2015, Act 55 also eliminated the rights of faculty, staff, and students to meaningful shared governance and formally empowered campus chancellors to act as chief executive officers. Furthermore, it eliminated faculty statutory rights to tenure and mandated new possibilities to facilitate chancellors' removal of tenured faculty (Shelton 2015). Wisconsin was once a national model for tenure and shared governance; now it is the subject of condemnations from the American Association of University Professors, such as that of October 23, 2017 (see its website: https://www.aaup.org/file/2017-Wisc_AFT.pdf). Academic freedom on the campus—for students, staff, and faculty—is indeed under threat. In the first draft of his 2015–2017 budget, Walker even proposed altering the mission of the UW system in proto-Trumpian ways, eliminating the "search for truth" in order to prioritize "workforce needs." A vehement public response caused Walker to assert lamely that the change to the mission had been a "drafting error" (Strauss 2015).

At the same time, Walker also finally made good on his promise to billionaire Diane Hendricks to turn Wisconsin into a "right-to-work" state. (Infamously, filmmaker Brad Lichtenstein, in his 2012 documentary *As Goes Janesville*, recorded Walker in January 2011 telling Hendricks that the "first step" in a "divide-and-conquer" strategy was to critically weaken public-employee unions.) This move upended a promise Walker had made to unions endorsing him in both 2010 and 2014 that "right to work" would be off the table (Kaufman 2015). Nevertheless, the legislature passed—and Walker signed—a bill making Wisconsin the twenty-fifth right-to-work state in March 2015. By this point, Walker seemed to be on the short list, with other anti-union ideologues such as Chris Christie and John Kasich, of viable 2016 presidential contenders.

Anticipating Trump's corporate tax cut, passed in December 2017, Walker and state legislators also moved to expend a massive amount of tax dollars on the state's wealthiest citizens. Like Trump's class warfare, Walker's also included some minimal tax cuts for working Wisconsinites, but the wealthy benefited much more. While Walker cut aggregate taxes by several billion dollars, there has been little relief for working people: since 2013, about $117 a year in income-tax reduction and, since 2014, about $94 in property-tax cuts for the average Wisconsinite (Sullivan 2015). On the other hand, one of Walker's major initiatives slashed tax rates on profits in manufacturing and agriculture from 7.9 percent to virtually zero. According to the state's nonpartisan Legislative Fiscal Bureau, in 2016 alone, over 75 percent of these credits went to millionaires, and the LFB estimated that eleven tax filers (each worth at least $30 million) received about $22 million each (Kertscher 2017).

If the average Wisconsinite did not benefit very much from Walker's tax cuts, did their overall economic outlook improve? Certainly, the security and well-being of public employees in the state have suffered, and Walkerism has undermined public institutions such as the UW system, which once had a national reputation as one of the best state university systems in the nation. Indeed, public K-12 schools in Wisconsin lost over $1 billion in funding, and the UW system was deprived of $795 million in total from 2011 to 2017.

But Walker did not do much for those Wisconsinites who resented public employees either, except paying them in Schadenfreude. Walker's policies came nowhere close to providing 250,000 new jobs in his first term (and still had not done so by summer 2018), nor did they significantly raise wages, beyond the dead-cat bounce all working Americans have received since the Great Recession. An EPI study (Cooper 2018) has shown the widely divergent paths between Walkerism in Wisconsin and the "progressive priorities" sought by Democratic governor Mark Dayton in Minnesota. By virtually every metric, Wisconsin's recovery from the crisis of 2008 lagged behind that of its similarly situated neighbor. From 2010 to 2017, Wisconsin added about 225,000 jobs (9.7 percent growth), while Minnesota added 280,000 (12.5 percent growth) over the same period. From 2010 to 2016, median household income in Minnesota grew by 7.2 percent, while in Wisconsin it grew by just 5.1 percent.

By 2017, Walker realized that he had failed to deliver on his promise of widespread prosperity, and Republicans only maintained their continuous grip on state politics through extreme partisan gerrymandering and a series of discriminatory voter identification laws that Ari Berman (2017) has asserted provided the margin of victory for Trump in Wisconsin in 2016. Furthermore, Wisconsinites were

starting to feel the long-term effects of Trump's public policy, especially in education, and because of the efforts of organized educators, connecting it to Walkerism. Preparing for reelection, Walker proposed in his last budget to restore a
pittance of what had been lost since 2011.

In a desperate gambit, in summer 2017, Walker brokered a deal to bring
Foxconn—a company chaired by Terry Gou, whose manufacturing facilities
in China installed nets to prevent suicides of workers toiling in deplorable
conditions—to Wisconsin at a cost of around $4 billion over the next fifteen
years. For two reasons, this deal threatened to bring the demise of Walkerism if a
Democratic candidate could attack it appropriately. For one thing, because the
tax rate on manufacturers in Wisconsin was already practically zero when the
deal was brokered, the vast majority of state expenditures will be direct payments.
Thus, the average Wisconsinite, from factory worker to small-business owner,
will be paying taxes to enrich a Taiwanese billionaire who is already one of the
wealthiest people in the world. Second, the factory will be nestled in the southern
part of the state, near the Illinois border. The expenditure on Foxconn will hardly
have a lasting positive impact on other areas of a vast and diverse state. Still, as I
argued elsewhere, Democrats could only use Foxconn to transform Wisconsin
politics in a more social democratic direction by laying out an alternative plan to
create good jobs (Shelton 2018). Though Evers roundly criticized the Foxconn
deal on the campaign trail, to date neither his administration nor other prominent Democrats in the state have offered a compelling argument for how to create
sustainable jobs that would reach Trump and Walker voters.

What Is to Be Done?

In 2018, Republican incumbents across the country contended with angry and
motivated Democratic voters. Evers needed just about every bit of this enhanced
turnout—about 140,000 more votes than Walker's 2014 challenger won—to win
Wisconsin's citizens a reprieve from Walkerism. Indeed, it is important to remember that Walker also won about 40,000 more votes in 2018 than he did in 2014.

Though Evers was clearly a more progressive candidate than Burke had been
in 2014—he supports a $15 minimum wage, for instance, as well as restoring bar-
gaining rights to public employees—his basic strategy was to run as an alternative to the dismal politics of Walkerism and count on turning out voters. As we
learned in the presidential election of 2016, however, simply running as the alternative to bad politics is not always a winning strategy, and though Evers won
by a razor-thin margin, Democrats in Wisconsin must still contend with both intentional voter suppression and the continued consequences of gerrymandered

legislative districts. Though Democrats won 53 percent of the total votes in state assembly races, for instance, they captured only thirty-six out of ninety-nine seats (Gilbert 2018). The governor in Wisconsin has a line-item veto, and this power will give Evers some leverage in negotiating with Republicans, particularly with regard to the budget process. Even so, repealing Act 10 or the state's right-to-work law seems highly unlikely, at least in 2019 or 2020.

The bigger challenge after upending Wisconsin's forty-fifth governor—just as it is for terminating the disastrous policies of the forty-fifth US president—is more than winning one election. It is building a new majority capable of winning many future elections, one that includes a Democratic Party capable of furthering an agenda that excites working people. Charting a course away from the politics of Trump nationally is going to mean charting a clear course away from the politics of Walker in Wisconsin. Indeed, as in the Badger State, perhaps the single characteristic that best captures the political divide in the United States today is that, in 2016, college graduates voted for Hillary Clinton by a margin of eleven points, while those who did not graduate from college voted for Trump by a margin of eight points. Whites who were not college graduates voted for Trump 67 percent to 28 percent (Tyson and Maniam 2016). There are a number of reasons why this split occurred, but the Democratic argument that college education is essential for economic opportunity seems likely to have played a significant role. Any movement capable of shifting American political economy left must find a way to connect public employees and private-sector workers, blue collar and white collar, manufacturing and service sector.

So the challenge is: how do we, as unionists, help facilitate such a movement? First, just as the ascendance of Walkerism and Trumpism has been decades in the making, we have to acknowledge that our project is a long-term one, and we must constantly consider three dimensions in its pursuit. Of course, we have to organize our own workplaces, but we also must ensure that this work extends both horizontally (into our communities) and vertically (into political and electoral structures). The latter entails not only educating Democratic candidates but also encouraging and facilitating activists running for office.

In Wisconsin, union activists, by necessity, have recommitted to both organizing and building alternative ways to exercise collective power in the workplace. I am not Pollyannaish about the effort—more consistent and sustained work is needed—but there are important developments at the grassroots level that deserve our attention. For example, the Milwaukee Teachers Education Association (MTEA, affiliated with WEAC)—constrained by Act 10 from negotiating anything but salaries and not allowed to strike—in May 2018 threatened "bold action" (if not an outright call to walk out, the implication was obvious) if the school district went through with a 5 percent-per-pupil budget reduction proposed by the school board. At the same time, MTEA substitute Alex Brower went on a twenty-one-day hunger strike to win health insurance for substitute teachers. Faced with substantial pressure from city teachers and the public, the school district cut administrative costs rather than teacher and student services and funded health insurance for a majority of substitute teachers (Dombrowski 2018).

AFT-Wisconsin has also seen locals commit to engaging members in collective actions outside the bargaining framework. For instance, the Hortonville Federation of Teachers (HFT), a union no longer certified to represent the teachers of this small-town district, responded to an abusive administrator in 2016–2017 through a collective on-site protest and by recruiting and electing school board candidates responsive to teachers and parents. Our higher-education locals, barred from collective bargaining of any kind, coordinated a historic wave of faculty senate no-confidence votes in UW system president Ray Cross and the Walker-appointed board of regents in May 2016. In spring 2017, AFT-W higher-education activists intervened in the budget process through a campaign called #FundtheFreeze. Faculty and staff across the UW system insisted that a continuation of the tuition freeze necessitated a greater investment in public higher education. Thousands of Wisconsinites signed letters of support either through old-fashioned petitions or through social media, and campuses held various events across the UW system. At UW-Green Bay, for instance, we organized a panel discussion with two state legislators, followed by a march and a rally. It is not a coincidence that the state's 2018 budget provided the UW system with its first funding increase since Walker took office. Nor was it surprising that Evers, while running for governor in August 2018, used the very language of "fund the freeze" to criticize the UW system regents' 2019–2021 biennial budget request (Meyerhoffer 2018).

What is the common denominator between the actions of teachers in Milwaukee and Hortonville and those of higher-education activists? Member-driven organizing and mobilizing of the community. With Wisconsin's labor laws not favorable to workers in either the public or the private sector, it is imperative to build organizing capacity both at our workplaces and within the communities that anchor them. The latter is much easier to do in the public sector, where "consumers" of public services, such as students and parents, are natural allies, but since the Wisconsin Uprising, the most important labor victory in the private sector was achieved through mobilization in the community.

In the wake of the economic crisis in 2008, some companies forced workers to accept two-tiered wage structures in which new hires would make significantly less money and have fewer benefits than top-tier workers. At the Kohler Company plant in Sheboygan, however, workers ultimately refused to accept the two-tiered system, and it took a strike to roll it back. In newly "right-to-work" Wisconsin, United Auto Workers Local 833 at Kohler went on strike in November 2015, and the company relented, agreeing to bring some lower-paid workers to parity with those in Tier A and the rest to near parity. What was so important about the strike is that the Tier A workers—about 80 percent of Kohler's workforce in the Wisconsin plant—could have easily ignored the plight of their Tier B brothers and sisters, but, with 94 percent voting to strike, they risked their own livelihoods in the name of solidarity. A vast outpouring of support from community members in the Sheboygan area gave the strikers the fortitude to maintain their stand at Kohler for over a month (Wilkes 2016).

Efforts to empower private-sector workers in Wisconsin have also come from outside the union framework. The immigrant rights organization Voces de la Frontera, for example, which has worker centers in Milwaukee, Madison, Racine, and elsewhere in the state, has helped to give a voice to Latino workers in Wisconsin who face both hostility in their workplace and the fear of deportation. In 2016, Voces mobilized 15,000 Latino workers and their allies to march on Madison to stop a bill (similar to Arizona's infamous Senate Bill 1070, passed into law in 2010) that would have made it illegal for local governments to prevent police from asking about immigration status (Krieg 2016). Since Trump's election, Voces has emerged as a prominent voice in Wisconsin advocating sanctuary for the undocumented and the abolition of Immigration and Customs Enforcement (ICE).

We know what works to build power in the workplace and in the community. There is simply no substitute for the painstaking effort of building collective courage over time for high-stakes actions like strikes that force employers to do better by their workers. While local action may be necessary, however, it is not sufficient when the trajectory of the global economy so disadvantages just about everyone who works for a living. In Wisconsin, as in the nation, working people must solve the problem of what Mike Davis (1986) has called the "barren marriage" between labor unions and the Democratic Party.

There is a long-standing debate in left circles, of course, about whether most Democrats are capable of truly acting in the interests of working people. I do not have the space here to fully address this question. Given the iron constraints of the American political system, however, in which a lasting third-party alternative is highly unlikely, it seems that we are stuck with changing the Democratic Party from below. We should hold no illusions about the difficulty of this endeavor. In Wisconsin, as in the United States, most Democrats have offered little systematic resistance to the class war from above that has been waged for the past fifty years. In large part, this weakness stems from the necessity of seeking campaign donations from those who have benefited from the status quo, but it also stems from a path dependency in which the party's primary narrative about economic opportunity is that working people must educate themselves better in order to compete in a global economy.

This narrative will only change if there is confrontation. As working people organize their communities, they must also confront local Democratic politicians, only offering support when candidates pursue a distinct vision capable of bringing working people together: the right to a job with a living wage; universal health care; high-quality public education and transportation; immigrant rights; an end to police murders; and higher taxes on millionaires and billionaires. Democrats must offer this vision as a clear contrast to the notion that heavily subsidizing the profits of corporations like Foxconn is the only way to bring decent economic opportunity to workers. The $4 billion price tag for taxpayers in Wisconsin represents a unique opportunity on the left since it gives the lie to the claim that there are not enough public resources to fund our priorities, but Democrats will not offer such a vision unless we show them how—and pressure them—to do it. Using workplace fights—from wage increases for low-paid workers to education budgets—as the avenue to engage and educate candidates and officeholders is vital. Making the provision of votes and of volunteers to knock on doors and make phone calls in elections contingent on support for the required policies is crucial, too. Equally important in ensuring that candidates support a social democratic vision is recruiting people with lived experience as workers to run for office themselves.

In short, we need a government that facilitates not private capital accumulation for the wealthy but opportunity and security for all. The party that can make that aim central to its politics can permanently transform American politics. Labor must be foundational to that vision, and only by organizing our workplaces and communities can we build the solidarity that is necessary for us to make our government into a force for good again. Doing so, in turn, will relegate the reactionary policies of Scott Walker and Donald Trump to the dustbin of history.

References

Beck, Molly. 2015. "WEAC Turns to Local Focus after Massive Membership Loss." *Wisconsin State Journal*, February 22. http://host.madison.com/wsj/news/local /education/local_schools/weac-turns-to-local-focus-after-massive-membership -loss/article_4e31a55e-575b-598f-bb40-6b8ab1e440c5.html.

Berman, Ari. 2017. "Rigged: How Voter Suppression Threw Wisconsin to Trump." *Mother Jones*, November-December. https://www.motherjones.com/politics/2017 /10/voter-suppression-wisconsin-election-2016/.

Buhle, Mary Jo, and Paul Buhle. 2012. *It Started in Wisconsin: Dispatches from the Front Line of the New Labor Protest.* London: Verso.

Cooper, David. 2018. *As Wisconsin's and Minnesota's Lawmakers Took Divergent Paths, so Did Their Economies.* Economic Policy Institute. https://www.epi.org/publication /as-wisconsins-and-minnesotas-lawmakers-took-divergent-paths-so-did-their

-economies-since-2010-minnesotas-economy-has-performed-far-better-for
-working-families-than-wisconsin/.

Cramer, Katherine. 2016. *The Politics of Resentment: Rural Consciousness in Wisconsin
and the Rise of Scott Walker*. Chicago: University of Chicago Press.

Davey, Monica, and Jeff Zeleny. 2012. "Walker Survives Wisconsin Recall Vote." *New
York Times*, June 5. https://www.nytimes.com/2012/06/06/us/politics/walker
-survives-wisconsin-recall-effort.html.

Davis, Mike. 1986. *Prisoners of the American Dream: Politics and Economy in the History
of the American Working Class*. New York: Verso.

Dombrowski, Diana. 2018. "MPS Interim Superintendent Posley Finds $11.6 Million to
Return to Schools." *Milwaukee Journal-Sentinel*, May 25. https://www.jsonline
.com/story/news/education/2018/05/25/mps-interim-superintendent-finds-11-6
-million-return-schools/638142002/.

Elbow, Steven. 2018. "Protesters Descend on Wisconsin Capitol to Demonstrate against
Republican Lame-Duck Agenda." *Capital Times*, December 3.

Fields, Reginald. 2011. "Ohio Voters Overwhelmingly Reject Issue 2, Dealing a Blow to
Gov. John Kasich." *The Plain Dealer*, November 10. https://www.cleveland.com
/politics/index.ssf/2011/11/ohio_voters_overwhelmingly_rej.html.

Frank, Thomas. 2016. *Listen, Liberal: What Ever Happened to the Party of the People?*
New York: Henry Holt.

Gilbert, Craig. 2018. "New Election Data Highlights the Ongoing Impact of 2011 GOP
Redistricting in Wisconsin." *Milwaukee Journal-Sentinel*, December 6. https://
www.jsonline.com/story/news/blogs/wisconsin-voter/2018/12/06/wisconsin
-gerrymandering-data-shows-stark-impact-redistricting/2219092002/.

Gurda, John. 1999. *The Making of Milwaukee*. Milwaukee: Milwaukee County Historical
Society Press.

Herzog, Karen, and Patrick Marley. 2015. "Scott Walker Budget Cut Sparks Sharp
Debate on UW System." *Milwaukee Journal-Sentinel*, January 28. http://archive
.jsonline.com/news/education/scott-walker-says-uw-faculty-should-teach-more
-classes-do-more-work-b99434737z1-290087401.html/.

Jones, Sarah. 2017. "In La Follette Territory." *The Nation*, July 25. https://www.thenation
.com/article/the-lefts-opportunity-in-wisconsin/.

Kaufman, Dan. 2015. "Scott Walker and the State of the Union." *New York Times
Magazine*, June 12. https://nyti.ms/2kpcF2j.

Kaufman, Dan. 2018. *The Fall of Wisconsin: The Conservative Conquest of a Progressive
Bastion and the Future of American Politics*. New York: W. W. Norton.

Keefe, Jeffrey. 2011. "Are Wisconsin Public Employees Over-compensated?" Economic
Policy Institute, February 10. https://www.epi.org/publication/are_wisconsin
_public_employees_over-compensated/.

Kersten, Andrew. 2011. *The Battle for Wisconsin: Scott Walker and the Attack on the
Progressive Tradition*. New York: Hill and Wang. Kindle edition.

Kertscher, Tom. 2017. "Did 11 People Get $22 Million from Wisconsin's GOP-Backed
Manufacturing and Agriculture Tax Credit?" *Politifact*, February 17. http://www
.politifact.com/wisconsin/statements/2017/feb/17/gordon-hintz/11-people-get-22
-million-wisconsins-gop-backed-man/.

Kniffin, Kevin. 2011. "Organizing to Organize: The Case of a Successful Long-Haul
Campaign for Collective Bargaining Rights." *Labor Studies Journal* 36(3):
333–362.

Krieg, Gregory. 2016. "Thousands Protest 'Anti-Immigrant' Legislation in Wisconsin."
CNN.com, February 18. https://www.cnn.com/2016/02/18/politics/wisconsin
-immigration-day-without-latinos-protest/index.html.

Levine, Marc V. 2012. "Race and Male Employment in the Wake of the Great Recession: Black Male Employment Rates in Milwaukee and the Nation's Largest Metro Areas 2010." UW-Milwaukee Center for Economic Development Working Paper. http://www4.uwm.edu/ced/publications/black-employment_2012.pdf.

Madland, David, and Alex Rowell. 2017. *Attacks on Public-Sector Unions Harm States: How Act 10 Has Affected Education in Wisconsin.* Center for American Progress, November 15. https://www.americanprogressaction.org/issues/economy/reports /2017/11/15/169146/attacks-public-sector-unions-harm-states-act-10-affected -education-wisconsin/.

Marianno, Bradley, and Katharine Strunk. 2018. "After Janus." *Education Next* 18(4).

Marley, Patrick. 2009. "Walker Says He Would Cut Taxes in First Budget." *Milwaukee Journal-Sentinel*, November 2. http://archive.jsonline.com/blogs/news/68643847 .html.

Marley, Patrick, and Lee Berquist. 2010. "Barrett, Walker Stick to Game Plans in Final Debate." *Milwaukee Journal-Sentinel*, October 29. http://archive.jsonline.com /news/wisconsin/106353728.html.

Mayer, Jane. 2016. *Dark Money: The Hidden History of the Billionaires behind the Rise of the Radical Right.* New York: Doubleday.

Mertz, Adam. 2018. "Lessons in Insurgency: Teacher Unions and Populist Politics in Wisconsin." Unpublished PhD diss., University of Illinois, Chicago. In possession of author and cited with permission.

Meyerhoffer, Kelly. 2018. "Tony Evers: UW System's Budget Proposal 'Sends Wrong Message' to Lawmakers." *Wisconsin State Journal*, August 23. https://madison .com/wsj/tony-evers-uw-system-s-budget-proposal-sends-wrong-message/article _e0f28caa-fe12-5ea0-9be0-2e1a711b6802.html.

Meyers, Scottie Lee. 2015. "Wisconsin Has Seen Largest Middle-Class Decline of Any State, Study Finds." Wisconsin Public Radio, April 2. https://www.wpr.org /wisconsin-has-seen-largest-middle-class-decline-any-state-study-finds.

Nichols, John. 2012. *Uprising: How Wisconsin Renewed the Politics of Protest, from Madison to Wall Street.* New York: Nation Books.

Nolan, Kay, and Julie Bosman. 2017. "Milwaukee Officer Is Acquitted in Killing of Sylville Smith." *New York Times*, June 21. https://nyti.ms/2sRvVcc.

Obama, Barack. 2008. "Obama's Speech in Janesville, Wisconsin." February 13. https:// factreal.files.wordpress.com/2012/08/obamaspeechgmplantjanesville2008.pdf.

Pernsteiner, Aimee, D'Arcy Becker, Matthew Fish, William Miller, and Dawna Drum. 2016. "Budget Repair or Budget Spectacle? The Passage of Wisconsin's Act 10." *Public Money and Management* 36(3): 507–514.

Shelton, Jon. 2015. "The State of Wisconsin: Neoliberalism's Ground Zero." LABORonline, April 7. https://www.lawcha.org/2015/04/07/the-state-of-wisconsin -neoliberalisms-ground-zero/.

Shelton, Jon. 2017. *Teacher Strike! Public Education and the Making of a New American Political Order.* Urbana: University of Illinois Press.

Shelton, Jon. 2018. "The Factory That Ate Wisconsin." *Dissent* 65(4): 99–103.

Strauss, Valerie. 2015. "How Gov. Walker Tried to Quietly Change the Mission of the University of Wisconsin." *Washington Post*, February 5. https://www .washingtonpost.com/news/answer-sheet/wp/2015/02/05/how-gov-walker-tried -to-quietly-change-the-mission-of-the-university-of-wisconsin/?utm_term= .f0bac5eabc86.

Sullivan, Martin. 2015. "Walker in Wisconsin: A $1 Sweater and $2 Billion in Tax Cuts." *Forbes*, May 6. https://www.forbes.com/sites/taxanalysts/2015/05/06/walker-in -wisconsin-a-1-sweater-and-2-billion-in-tax-cuts/#52e6e85d31cc.

Sustar, Lee. 2012. "Who Were the Leaders of the Wisconsin Uprising?" In *Wisconsin Uprising: Labor Fights Back*, edited by Michael Yates. New York: Monthly Review Press.

Tyson, Alec, and Shiva Maniam. 2016. *Behind Trump's Victory: Divisions by Race, Gender, Education*. Pew Research Center, November 9. http://pewrsr.ch/2ffF1bU.

Umhoefer, Dave. 2012. "Recall Candidate Kathleen Falk Says Governor Scott Walker Enacted 'the Biggest Cuts to Education in Our State's History.'" *Politifact*, February 19. http://www.politifact.com/wisconsin/statements/2012/feb/19/kathleen-falk/recall-candidate-kathleen-falk-says-governor-scott/.

Walker, Scott. 2010. "Wisconsin Governor Republican Primary Debate" August 25. https://www.c-span.org/video/?295182-1/wisconsin-governor-republican-primary-debate.

Wilkes, Kathy. 2016. "How UAW Won the Wisconsin Kohler Strike." *In These Times*, March 10. http://inthesetimes.com/working/entry/18955/how_uaw_won_the_wisconsin_kohler_strike.

Yates, Michael, ed. 2012. *Wisconsin Uprising: Labor Fights Back*. New York: Monthly Review Press.

5

WHOSE CLASS IS IT ANYWAY? THE "WHITE WORKING CLASS" AND THE MYTH OF TRUMP

Sarah Jaffe

Since the early days of the 2016 presidential race, there has been no stickier narrative than the one that tells us that Donald Trump's base is the "white working class." It began sometime early in the primary process, and it lingered well into his presidency. Pundits attempt to explain Trump's latest move, and the papers of record go on exotic safaris to the parts of "real America" where the "white working class" lives to hear about its sadness, illness, joblessness, addiction, and unflagging love for The Donald.

The persistence of this narrative in the face of all sorts of contradictory evidence tells us more about the power of stereotypes than it does about the Trump election, but to get out from under it we have to do two things: look at the reasons why Trump actually won—or, perhaps more importantly, the reasons why Hillary Clinton lost—and then ask ourselves what work this narrative is doing, which realities about power and politics in the United States today it is concealing. The second part is, inevitably, harder than the first.

The widespread acceptance of the idea that the white working class is Trump's base has led to an ongoing debate about "racism" versus "economic anxiety" as motivating factors for those voters, as if the two were subjects that could ever be disentangled in a country like the United States. This has done more to obfuscate the realities than to clarify them. "The economy" does not exist outside of the social relationships among humans, and those relationships are always structured by race and gender, and by this widely misunderstood thing called class. We cannot understand what happened in 2016—and certainly not what needs to happen now—without understanding this basic fact.

It is important to understand why Clinton's vote collapsed in certain places, places that have become the poster locales for American industrial decline, and why Donald Trump, of all Republican candidates, was poised to sweep up just enough of those voters to swing key counties and eke out a victory without a majority of the popular vote. But it is perhaps even more important to shatter the story of Trumpism as workers' revolt.

The Trump Coalition

In the months leading up to the presidential election, one strange story briefly grabbed headlines—the candidacy of Deez Nuts. Deez Nuts, for those who do not remember that brief blip in the 2016 election season, was fifteen-year-old Brady Olson's idea of a joke. He filed with the Federal Election Commission to run for president under the joke name and then e-mailed Public Policy Polling, asking the pollster to include his name. In summer 2015, when Deez Nuts polled at 9 percent in a potential three-way race with Hillary Clinton and Donald Trump, his "candidacy" went viral, made MSNBC, and became the top trending topic on Twitter. In retrospect, Deez Nuts was a harbinger for the 2016 election: the options so widely disliked that voters suggested they might vote for an obvious joke just to avoid the two major-party candidates (Collins and Shire 2015).

When Election Day came, it seemed that the Deez Nuts vote broke Trump's way. There was a spike in the vote for actual third-party candidates Gary Johnson and Jill Stein, potentially enough in key states to swing the race to Trump, but the bigger story was voters' disenchantment with the status quo. Voters did not buy the "America is Already Great" narrative that the Clinton campaign had dredged up in response to Trump's barnstorming promises to "Make America Great Again." Deez Nuts was the Rexnord plant worker from Indiana, a lifelong Democrat, who told me "I can do four years standing on my head, let's give this man a shot and see what happens." Chuck Jones, the former president of the union that represented workers at Rexnord and Carrier, said, "People wanted a change. If it wasn't Trump, it could've been Captain Kangaroo" (Jaffe 2017).

Many of these voters were from the mythical white working class, but before we delve too deeply into that, we should look at the other parts of the coalition. And to do that is to realize that Donald Trump won mostly because the same people who usually vote Republican voted Republican. As Mike Davis noted, "The 'miracle' of the mogul's campaign, apart from his cunning success in manipulating negative media coverage to his advantage, was capturing the entirety of the Romney vote, without any of the major defections (college-educated Republican women, conservative Latinos, Catholics) that the polls had predicted and Clinton had counted upon" (Davis 2017). Clinton, in contrast, did not manage to hold the Obama coalition together in key locations—had she done so, she would have won the Electoral College as well as the popular vote.

The wealthy voted for their tax cuts and for continued attacks on organized labor; the religious voted for vice presidential candidate Mike Pence and for Trump's repeated jeremiads against abortion; the "deplorables," as Hillary Clinton so unfortunately called them, voted for a border wall, mass deportations of immigrants, and imprisonment of black activists (CBS News 2016). Pollsters, unfailingly polite, rarely asked the people they polled, "So, was it the moment he called all Mexicans rapists that swung your vote?," and so we are left to guess at the exact splits. But despite the refrain of a certain type of liberalism, the "deplorables" probably were not even close to the half of Trump's base that Clinton claimed. Still, the toxic atmosphere of white supremacy, misogyny, nationalism, and xenophobia that Trumpism released, that Trump himself seemed to revel in bringing everywhere with him like *Peanuts*' PigPen with his cloud of dust, was certainly, as Lauren Berlant said, a source of "enormous pleasure" for some part of his base (Malsky 2017).

The Trump movement (as much as it can be differentiated as a movement within the Republican Party) is similar to the Tea Party movement—older, whiter, and more affluent than the average. It is suburban and middle class to its core, and motivated by the same right-wing populism as the Tea Party, a fear of falling out of the middle to the bottom combined with a feeling of being squeezed by elites at the top and the undeserving poor below. The squeezing from the top was accurate, the scapegoating of those on the bottom less so. Those undeserving poor are inevitably pictured as black or brown people, scary immigrants who are both mooching off the government and also stealing American jobs. Barack Obama was the perfect foil for this kind of thinking, a representative of both parts of the fantasy at once: the Columbia-and-Harvard-educated lawyer and the black community organizer giving handouts to the poor, rolled into one bogeyman. This is where the seeds of Trumpism began, with Trump one of the loudest voices baying for Obama's birth certificate, his presidential ambitions stoked with every headline.

The Tea Party, as former partisan operative Paul H. Jossey explained in *Politico*, was always at least half grift, turning money from true believers into profits for Tea Party salesmen. There were always two Tea Parties, Jossey argued: the grassroots conservatives and "lawyers and consultants who read 2009's political winds and saw a chance to get rich" (Jossey 2016). If you believe Michael Wolff, the Trump campaign and now the Trump presidency are nearly all grift. Wolff, arguing that Trump was in the game to build his brand for more television projects, quoted Trump telling Roger Ailes, formerly of Fox News, the week before the election, "I don't think about losing, because it isn't losing. We've totally won" (Wolff 2018). To the Tea Party profiteers and the Trump family, these campaigns were ways to fleece the angry, the unsettled, to mobilize the fear of falling to collect windfall donations for campaigns that barely existed. That Trump managed, despite all this, to actually win tells you something about the desperation—or the exhaustion—of America circa 2016 (Jossey 2016).

That the story of the Tea Party has mostly been absent from the attempts to explain 2016's results is a reminder that Americans seem to have a particular capacity for political forgetting. We treat each election cycle as though it sprang fully grown from the forehead of Zeus rather than understanding that it was shaped by decades, even centuries, of history. For the last two election cycles, this has meant that results that one side saw as inevitable progressions were treated by the other side as utterly impossible, as bolts from the blue. The Tea Party treated Barack Obama as a literal foreigner and implied that ACORN stole the election for him, unwilling to understand an America that could elect a black president. When Trump came along, liberals found their own version of this in the Russia question. Whatever role Russian hackers or anyone else had in twisting the narrative and driving votes to Trump, it is indisputable that millions of people did vote for Trump, and the groundwork was laid for his victory by the right-wing populist outburst that was the Tea Party in the wake of the 2008 economic crisis. Trump was not an anomaly but rather a symptom of a particular kind of rage, and the right kind of hustler to take advantage of the anger that had faded from the front pages but still sought a political outlet. Even if the Electoral College's vicissitudes had gone the other way and Hillary Clinton's three-million-vote majority had propelled her to the Oval Office, we would still have to deal with Trumpism.

Enter the Worker

Americans are prone to rediscovering the working class, or at least our pundits are. To the millions of actual working-class people, this constant uncovering verges on ludicrous. Working-class people were rediscovered in 2012, when the first Walmart workers and then the first fast-food workers went out on strike, demanding $15 an hour. In 2015, the pundit class realized that the working class still existed just in time to make proclamations about its loyalty to the real estate mogul and reality TV star most famous for firing people.

It is hard to figure out who first declared that Trump's base was going to be the white working class. Matthew Cooper at *Newsweek* wrote a piece titled "Donald Trump: The Billionaire for Blue-Collars" in late June 2015 (Cooper 2015), a week after Trump's campaign launch; soon after, the *Washington Post* and the *New York Times* were echoing this language. Michael Barbaro, Maggie Haberman, and Jonathan Martin at the *Times* wrote of Republican leaders in July 2015, "They fear insulting the white working-class voters who admire [Trump]" (Barbaro, Haberman, and Martin 2015). The *Post* explained Trump's popularity with less-educated voters in terms of Rust Belt job decline. The shorthand was complete—Trump's base was white workers (Ross 2015a).

As Nicholas Carnes and Noam Lupu (2017) noted, most of the stories that relied on any evidence for this assertion used polls that did not gather enough detail about how people earned their living to give a coherent picture of their social class. Instead, they relied on educational attainment—specifically, whether they had a college degree. Though this is a common metric, it is deeply flawed. "When journalists wrote that Trump was appealing to working-class voters, they didn't really know whether Trump voters were construction workers or CEOs," Carnes and Lupu point out—and the difference certainly matters when we are talking about one's class position. Plenty of small-businesspeople lack college degrees, and these days one can find plenty of baristas with them. Yet polling people to ask their occupation alongside their political opinions is rare. As for income, around two-thirds of Trump supporters made more than the household median income. Carnes and Lupu reported that during the Republican primaries Trump's percentage of the non–college-educated vote was the same as the percentage of all Republicans without college degrees and about the same as the national average. In the general election, "among white people without college degrees who voted for Trump, nearly 60 percent were in the top half of the income distribution" (Carnes and Lupu 2017).

Anecdotal evidence from pundits at Trump rallies who assumed someone's class background from their clothing choices, combined with those flawed polls, led to flawed assumptions about what the working class is, but those same assumptions—that class is a baseball cap, a way of talking, even a part of the country—have been animating our politics for quite a while. Remember Joe the Plumber in 2008, the man who was neither a plumber nor named Joe but very concerned that Barack Obama was going to raise his taxes? Joe—a small- businessman who rode his brief moment in the spotlight for all it was worth—was concerned about Obama's pledged tax hike for those who made over $250,000 a year, yet became the tribune of the working man, taking the stage with Sarah Palin to denounce Obama as a socialist. (Joe, reached for comment in 2016, was a Trump fan.) Or recall Hillary Clinton herself, taking shots of whiskey in Indiana and talking about the "pattern" that Obama's "support among working, hard-working Americans, white Americans, is weakening again, and how whites in both states who had not completed college were supporting me" (Reid 2016; Brusk et al. 2008; Simon 2008; Phillips 2008).

What was Trump's real working-class support? While it was not central to his vote total, neither was it wholly mythical. As Mike Davis noted, "The phenomenon is real but largely limited to a score or so of troubled Rust Belt counties from Iowa to New York where a new wave of plant closure or relocation has coincided with growing immigrant and refugee populations. Election punditry has consistently conflated blue-collar votes long captured by Republican presidential candidates with the more modest and localized defection of working-class Democrats to Trump. Several hundred thousand white, blue-collar Obama voters, at most, voted for Trump's vision of fair trade and reindustrialization, not the millions usually invoked" (Davis 2017).

These were the workers I spoke to from Carrier and Rexnord, working at factories scheduled for closure during the presidential campaign and finding themselves showered with attention from Bernie Sanders and Trump. The union local that had endorsed Sanders in the Democratic primary was formally neutral in the general election, since so many of its members were determined to give Trump a chance. They were people like Richard Robinson, a sixty-year-old retired activist in his Utah mobile home community, who told me, "I voted for Donald Trump, on the assumption that he was going to keep a promise and drain the swamp, not fill it deeper with the people that's already in bed there. My hope was that he was not a career politician, that maybe things would be run differently in Washington." Another was Brittany Bucholtz, who told *Time* of her disappointment with Obama. "There's no more middle class. There's poor or there's rich and there's nothing in between," she said. "He's the one who's speaking to us. He would come and do these rallies or you'd hear him on TV and he'd just say all the things we wanted to say." (The same article featuring Bucholtz, a certified nursing assistant, also featured a woman identified as a "real estate investor," posed glamorously in a fur coat next to her bright yellow sports car, once again showing how class lines get blurred in these stories; see Dias, Edward, and Vick 2016).

They voted for Trump to drain the swamp or because he promised to save their jobs—their personal, specific jobs in some cases—or because the signs of decline were visible around them and Clinton did not have any solutions. They voted for Trump because, unlike the rest of the Republican primary crowd, he indicated that he did not want to cut social security and that his replacement for "Obamacare" would improve health-care options for people stuck in the limbo between the Medicaid expansion and undercoverage on the stingier Affordable Care Act plans. On a panel shortly after the inauguration, I listened as Pratik Chougule, then editor of *The American Conservative* magazine, lamented that this election

had taught him that "there is no constituency anymore for small-government conservatism." Trump voters wanted government action, he said. They wanted social security and health care and they wanted the government to save their jobs
(Lopez 2016).

One blogger wrote:

> Here's the thing: from where I live, the world has drifted away. We aren't
> precarious, we're unnecessary. The money has gone to the top. The wages
> have gone to the top. The recovery has gone to the top. And what's worst
> of all, everybody who matters seems basically pretty okay with that. . . .
> If there's no economic plan for the Unnecessariat, there's certainly an
> abundance for plans to extract value from them. No one has the option
> to just make their own way and be left alone at it. It used to be that people
> were uninsured and if they got seriously sick they'd declare bankruptcy
> and lose the farm, but now they have a (mandatory) $1k/month plan
> with a $5k deductible: they'll still declare bankruptcy and lose the farm
> if they get sick, but in the meantime they pay a shit-ton to the sharehold-
> ers of United Healthcare, or Aetna, or whoever. (Amnesia 2016)

They voted for Trump as a last-ditch effort; they voted for him as a fuck-you
to the system that failed them; they voted for him holding their nose. Exit polls
showed that, of the nearly 18 million voters who thought both candidates were
unfit, 69 percent went for Trump. This is the "Deez Nuts" vote, or the "screw it"
vote. These are the people dismissed as "voting against their own interests" over
and over again, but the interest they are mostly aware of is that their life is getting
worse when they hoped it would be getting better, and all politicians seem equally
untrustworthy (Heath and Agiesta 2016).

These people are real, and their problems matter—and Trump is unlikely to
solve them, considering his signature accomplishment thus far is a tax "reform"
law that slashes taxes on the rich and pays for them with tax hikes on working
people, and has opened the way for what Republicans are calling "welfare reform"
but actually means even bigger cuts to what is left of the social safety net, including the social security that Richard Robinson lives on (Grim 2017; Stein 2017).

But these people are only one chunk of the working class, though the one most
often used as a metonym for the entire class. Even when talking purely about the
working-class vote in the 2016 presidential election, the biggest story is not how
many workers voted for Trump. It is how many workers did not vote at all.
Whether that is because of the gutting of the Voting Rights Act and the rapid
spread of voter ID laws, curtailment of early voting, and other voter-suppression
measures passed since 2008 or frustration with all their options, it is a story that
has not received nearly as much attention as that lavished on "Trump Country."

One study found that in Wisconsin—a pivotal state in Clinton's loss—a new voter ID law reduced turnout by 200,000 votes. As Ari Berman at *The Nation* noted, Clinton lost there by 22,748 votes. Those voters who were turned away skewed Democratic and, more importantly, skewed black and lower income. In counties formerly covered by the VRA, there were 868 fewer polling places in 2016 than in the previous elections, and that is just where such data were available. Yet, when election stealing is discussed in the media, it is mostly Russian hacking, not good old-fashioned American racist voter suppression (Berman 2017, 2016).

Then there are those who did not vote by choice. They often share a lot of characteristics with those who held their nose and voted—frustration, anger, disappointment, a grinding kind of acceptance. In Milwaukee—again, Wisconsin—the *New York Times* visited a black barbershop and spoke to four men, all of whom had voted for Obama. "But only two could muster the enthusiasm to vote this time," the *Times* wrote. "And even then, it was a sort of protest. One wrote in Mrs. Clinton's Democratic opponent, Senator Bernie Sanders of Vermont. The other wrote in himself." They expressed frustration with liberal racism as much as the more overt kind expressed by Trump. "He was real, unlike a lot of liberal Democrats who are just as racist" but keep it hidden, one customer said. "You can reason with them all day long, but they think they know it all. They want to have control. That they know what's best for 'those people'" (Tavernise 2016).

In obsessing over the members of the (white) working class who did vote for Trump, the media has obfuscated the millions who did not. Moreover, it has reified a picture of the working class that was never complete and by 2016 was totally unreflective of the working class in the United States. In 2016, the fastest job growth was in home health care, a field dominated by women of color, many of them immigrants. The most visible labor movement was the Fight for $15, led by minimum-wage workers in fast food who had organically connected their movement to the movement for black lives, understanding that the cheapening of their lives at work helped to justify the cheapening of their lives at the hands of police. Teachers' unions were organizing in the community, bringing restorative practices into their schools and demanding more control over the workplace. Young people with college degrees, left out of surveys that assume a college degree means middle class, were struggling with underemployment and flocked to Bernie Sanders and then to the Democratic Socialists of America. Immigrant workers on farms and in food-processing plants made up a significant swath of the rural population in places known popularly these days as "Trump Country," where the *New Yorker* and the *New York Times*, as well as less-prestigious publications, sent reporters to uncover the secrets of Trump's success (Kaplan 2016; MacFarquhar 2016; Debenedetti 2018).

Trump Country is populated by Iraqi, Somali, and Syrian refugees pushed into chicken plants, as Patrick Dixon of the Kalmanovitz Initiative for Labor and the Working Poor at Georgetown University wrote: "Displaced foreign workers don't disembark at a New York City harbor as they did one hundred years ago; they arrive in rural resettlement centers in places like north Georgia and central Virginia. In some cases, these workers are highly educated" (Dixon 2017). Yet they are doing the most thankless grunt work our economy has to dish out. They cannot vote, so they do not count in the glowing or faintly mocking Trump Country profiles, but they nevertheless are part of the working class in America. And no one is talking about making their lives great again (Dixon 2017).

Whitewashing

The problem with discussing the "white working class" is that every time we give in to this formulation, we reify the whiteness of the working class. We allow those two words, "white" and "working," to be glued together even more firmly—so firmly that even when one of them is left out of the frame, assumptions plug it back in anyway.

It was not Karl Marx who told us that discussing class means wiping all other struggles—against racism, sexism, and homophobia—off the table. Instead, it was a slew of pundits right and left who blame "identity politics"—itself a term coined by the black queer women socialists of the Combahee River Collective—for the decline of the presumably white working class (Taylor 2017). They implicitly inject the word "white" into any mention of class, turning class into an identity category for those who do not fit into any of the others, not realizing that in doing so they are actually upholding the very "identity politics" they decry.

If "white" and "working" go together, the corollary is that nonwhite people are not working. In making the working class white, writers too often counterpose it to the "black poor" or to "people of color" who have no class descriptor at all. These narrative conventions have political consequences—to intimate that black people are not "working" is to imply, as politicians from Ronald Reagan, to Bill Clinton, to Paul Ryan have, that black people simply live off "handouts" and that the solution—backed cheerily by Trump and his administration—is to cut off those handouts. To obsess over the "white working class" is to lay the narrative foundations for Trumpism.

Class in this formulation is not a relationship of power, one's relationship to the workplace and the means of production, but simply an identity category to be lined up next to (and inevitably in competition with) others. In this essentialized notion of the white working class, class is just something you are, as immutable as the color of your skin. It is in fact intertwined with that skin color in people's minds, to the point where the whiteness of the white working class is actually its primary characteristic. This reached peak absurdity in a *New York Post* article in which a "highly regarded chief of surgery at a suburban Pittsburgh hospital" is included among those described in this jumble of contradictory words: "They are the upper-middle-class suburban voters who live in a blue-collar, upper-middle-class exurb whose vote most pollsters missed in their calculations on who would support Trump in 2016" (Zito 2018).

This slippage between "working class" and "white" happens constantly. People who are white and do not live in New York City or California or perhaps have blue-collar ancestry are thus considered working class forever, no matter how their situation might change—becoming chief of surgery or a real estate investor or just, like my own mother, a successful small-business owner. This slippage in turn leads to an assumption that all white working-class people share similar cultural traits—conservatism on issues of gender and sexuality, a deep-seated antipathy toward all nonwhite people, and a distaste for environmentalism, the arts, and anything else popular with latte-sipping coastal liberals.

These formulations shape how we react to people, and they are based on a fundamental misunderstanding of what class is. On some level, it is understandable for the Clintons to do it—they built a career turning the Democratic Party from workers to Wall Street. If workers can be boiled down to one special identity that carries with it all these undesirable beliefs and characteristics, then they are a constituency that can be safely dismissed. They are "deplorables," in Clinton's terms, or they "cling to their guns and religion," in Obama's slightly kinder earlier description (Pilkington 2008). They voted for Trump and they should get him. Markos Moulitsas of the liberal blog *Daily Kos* expressed this framework perfectly, writing, "Don't weep for these coal miners, now abandoned by their GOP patrons. They are getting exactly the government that they voted for. Democrats can no longer offer unrequited love and cover for them. And isn't this what democracy is all about? They won the election! This is what they wanted!" (Fang 2017; Ross 2015b; Johnson 2016).

And yet at the same time as class is boiled down to something deep seated and immutable, it is also perceived—often by the same writers, in the same publications—as something that can be put on like drag, like Trump's Make America Great Again baseball cap. The second-generation real estate profiteer whose claim to fame was a TV show about firing people somehow looked less like "the guy who just fired you" than the Republican Party's previous presidential nominee, Mitt Romney, or the rogue's gallery of Republican also-rans that Trump defeated in the primary. And in eight years the Clinton campaign shifted from assuming that "hard-working voters, white voters" were her natural constituency when in 2008 her opponent was the suave African American senator from Illinois to writing them off in 2016, her campaign surrogates Ed Rendell and Chuck Schumer telling the press repeatedly—in a way that made clear that it was campaign strategy—that for every blue-collar voter Clinton lost, she would pick up two middle-class suburbanites. Those middle-class suburbanites, the implication went, would be turned off by Trump's racism, while the working class gleefully embraced it (Glueck 2016; Chozick and Healy 2016; Balz and Rucker 2016).

In this case, it is not just the whiteness of the working class that has been reified; it is its essential racism. It is an opposition between white and nonwhite workers that has been assumed in this country since the days of Andrew Johnson. In this line of thinking, bigotry is the only reason that one might have voted for Trump—or, as some polls showed, against Clinton. The most interesting part of this whole narrative is that somehow a vote for Hillary Clinton, whose own track record cheering on welfare reform and referring to black youths as "superpredators" came back to haunt her in 2016, was seen as sufficient proof that one was not racist. Though Clinton made plenty of her cracks in the glass ceiling and assumed—wrongly—that Trump's *Access Hollywood* tape, in which he talked gleefully about committing sexual assault, would be the end of him, it was racism that stuck in the narrative. Racism had to be the reason people liked Trump.

Passive Racism

It is surely true, as noted, that for some percentage of Trump voters, the gleeful nastiness of the man was a draw. There have been enough white supremacist marches, attacks, and speeches at universities in the past year to make sure we are constantly reminded of this fact. One should not downplay the degree to which overt white supremacy has been let out of the bag, given a hasty face wash, and legitimated by the president and his Confederate hangover of an attorney general, Jeff Sessions, whose latest outrage at press time was touting the "Anglo-American" history of law enforcement, in case listeners were not clear that the administration's border control and policing policies were about whiteness (Vazquez 2018).

But Clinton's math notwithstanding, a far larger number of Trump voters may not have enjoyed Trump's racism and sexism. They may even have been embarrassed by it, but it was not a deal breaker for them. The ability of millions of people to bracket his racism, overlook it, or laugh it off is actually the more concerning fact in this election cycle, and this is the issue that requires much more attention.

"Many people are uncomfortable with a lot of the stuff they've heard about him but accept it as a necessary evil: the main thing is to tell Washington elites that they're not safe in their sinecures any more, that the common man is about to have his day," wrote Linda Tirado in *The Guardian*, adding, "Trump can behave as badly as he wants. It's no worse than people expect from the power elite. America, as seen from Meigs County [Ohio], is a place where bankers can unfairly foreclose on your house and then get paid by Washington for doing it—and then Washington will demand you sign the bill" (Tirado 2016). For these voters, this is the tension between a sense of embarrassment at Trump's vulgarities, the ones you are not supposed to say out loud, and the understanding and acceptance that the world is different for rich people. As more than one woman who voted for Trump shrugged, all men talk like that. And if there is anything we can learn from the #MeToo moment, it is that they are not far off in their assessment (Tirado 2016; Jaffe 2018).

But for so many people—even for the Clintons, frankly, and many of their supporters—calling Mexicans rapists and other such Trumpisms were far from anything that might happen to any real people they knew (or even real people they did not know). Evangelical Christians, another constituency wrongly assumed to be conflicted over Trump, looked past the reality star's long history of infidelity and crassness and voted for him in lockstep. The other Trump tension was that voters liked that "he says what he thinks" but also assumed he did not mean what he said. Voters always pick and choose what they like about a politician, but Trump seemed to benefit from this phenomenon more than most others, perhaps because his bluster was so overwhelming. Meanwhile, to liberal critics like Moulitsas, each Trump voter is wholly responsible for endorsing everything the president ever said or did—a rule they would hardly apply to their own votes for Obama and his less savory accomplishments.

As Kurt Newman wrote shortly after the election, "Trumpism triumphs because nice people can be won—to a minimal degree, to the degree that they pull the lever for Trump, decline to vote for the Democrats, or stay home—to white racism. . . . Our question, rather, is: under what conditions can the 'possessive investment in whiteness' take hold of white Americans who would, under other circumstances, want not to be racist (or, at [the] very least, not to be seen as racist)?" (Newman 2016). In other words, Trumpism wins when people who do not want to be racist or seen as racist put that desire below some others—to stick it to the liberals and/or the Clintons, to save the Carrier plant, or to feel they are striking a blow against an encroaching Other.

We can see this operating in precisely those moments where Clinton voters assume that their own vote has left them with clean hands, unstained by the history of American white supremacy, and that if only Trump can be removed—

perhaps if Russian election tampering and Trump's complicity with it can wipe him away—we can wash our hands as a country as well. The truth—that racism is complicated, structural, and not something we can wake up in the morning and decide to be free of—is hard and ugly, and it implicates all of us. There was no better example of this than the postelection battle for the leadership of the Democratic National Committee, where the same Democrats who were shocked by Trump's Islamophobia marshaled arguments that Keith Ellison, the black representative from Minnesota who is the country's first Muslim member of Congress, was just too extreme a choice. "We like Keith," an anonymous source described only as a "longtime Obama political ally" told *Politico*'s Glenn Thrush, "But is he really the guy we need right now when we are trying to get all of those disaffected white working-class people to rally around our message of economic equality?" (Thrush 2016).

The work of getting rid of white supremacy for good certainly cannot be done by brushing the Keith Ellisons and the millions they represent to the side, hoping they will just disappear from public view long enough to win back the racists. Congress has no stronger champion of the real working class than Keith Ellison, who has spent more time on a picket line than the entire Clinton family and is the constant sponsor of bills that would actually improve the lives of working people. There are also few who know more about battling a renascent white supremacist movement. But Ellison himself is mostly beside the point; the point is that confronting Trumpism requires confronting the complications of racism.

The workers at Rexnord were members of a union that now has a black man as its president; several of them explained to me that they did not blame the Mexican workers who would be working at the plant in Monterrey that was replacing the one in Indianapolis. Yet those same men—fans of Bernie Sanders—shrugged and gave Trump a chance. To them, there was not enough difference between the two.

This is not to say that "Bernie Bros" are the same as Trumpists. Yet we cannot simply hold our breath and hope that a tenuous coalition comes together; nor can we pander to the fears of racists and expect black and brown workers to hold their noses and vote anyway. The assumption that certain categories of voters were in the bag shaped the 2016 election, and we can see what the results of that kind of thinking are.

About the Suburbs

The assumption that the white working class was going to vote for Trump actually affected Clinton's campaign strategy and which voters she chose to compete for. That is the reality behind the Rendell and Schumer sound bites. As Mike

Davis noted, the Clinton campaign abdicated any real effort in the industrial Midwest, focusing on major metropolitan counties and media markets. Donald Trump, meanwhile, took nothing for granted. Two days before the election, he was in Minneapolis—Keith Ellison's hometown—holding a rally at the airport (Davis 2017).

The story of the Clinton loss—which, when all is said and done, is really what the 2016 election was, rather than a Trump win, and the difference matters—is best summed up in Wisconsin and Michigan. Both states went to Bernie Sanders in the Democratic primaries, yet the Clinton campaign assumed they were safe.

The Service Employees International Union, doing campaign work on the ground in Iowa, felt before the election that Clinton would certainly lose the state. They wanted to go to Michigan, where distress signals were coming loud and fast a week and a half before the election, but according to *Politico*, the union was told to turn their bus around and go back to Iowa. Michigan, the campaign's polls said, was Clinton's by five points. She lost the state by just over 10,000 votes—despite Trump drawing fewer votes there than George W. Bush had when he lost it in 2004 (Dovere 2016).

Clinton's lack of campaigning in Wisconsin became something of a joke. Wisconsin reporters even poked at Clinton for her treatment of the state when she arrived in Milwaukee for her book tour, ribbing her about showing up to sell books but not to court crucial voters. In the book, Clinton dismissed the concern that she had neglected the state, but she did admit, "Enough voters switched, stayed home, or went for third parties in the final days to cost me the state" (Stein 2016; Glauber 2017).

Though organized labor leaders were almost entirely on Clinton's side, the combination of a sanguine attitude toward losing blue-collar votes to Trump and the assumption that union members needed no prodding to vote Democrat was deadly. Clinton got 51 percent of the union household vote, a record low for a Democrat and much lower than Barack Obama had received in 2012 (a reminder of the fact that "union households" these days are likely not to be white). In Ohio, another state presumed to be safely Clinton's, Trump actually won union households 49 percent to 44 percent (Greenhouse 2016).

One study looked into the effects of so-called right-to-work laws on voter turnout and found that such laws decreased Democrats' share of the presidential vote by 3.5 percent, finding that "The effect of right-to-work laws, according to this research, [is] large enough that it could have easily cost Hillary Clinton Wisconsin and Michigan—two states that went right-to-work before the 2016 election"(McElwee 2018). Such laws, however, are not designed to decrease Democratic voter turnout—they are designed to weaken the working class as a whole, to ensure that it has less political power to see its goals pursued by politicians of either party. That is why states like North Carolina, which until 2010 were dominated by Democrats, nonetheless remained right-to-work. Political scientists note that it is union power, not Democrats' power, that determines whether public policy will favor working people or the elites. Framing right-to-work laws as an attack on Democrats treats unions—and union membership—as though they have a one-to-one correlation with membership in the Democratic Party. Looking at Clinton's abysmal record with union households, we should be reminded that this is not the case. It is safe to assume that at least some work to turn out union voters in 2016 turned out votes for Trump.

Whose Class Is It?

There are differing opinions about what working class is because at bottom we do not understand class in this country. Yet, since the 2008 financial crisis at least, we have seen a resurgence of what these days could be called "class consciousness." Socialism is back on the menu, thanks in no small part to Bernie Sanders's presidential campaign. That campaign was possible thanks to a series of social movements of various parts of the working class: the "graduates with no future" of Occupy, the low-wage workers of the Fight for $15, the movement for black lives, and now the new Poor People's Campaign.

In this space, there is tremendous cause for hope, even as Trump and the Republican Party—which has found, after all, that it can live with the blustering billionaire as long as he focuses in on longtime party priorities like the upward redistribution of wealth—dismantle safety net programs and deport and incarcerate immigrants at record speeds. There is hope because, despite the pundits, the working class recognizes itself as more complicated than the picture of it that Donald Trump paints.

An exit poll on Election Day found that 72 percent of voters—all voters, not Democratic or Republican voters—agree that "the American economy is rigged to advantage the rich and powerful" (Kahn 2016). Many of those who stayed home would likely also agree with this statement; indeed, it is a major reason why people do not bother to vote. In the same poll, a slightly higher number, 75 percent, agreed that "America needs a strong leader to take the country back from the rich and powerful."

Since Trump's election, politicians and pundits of both parties have argued against his Muslim ban, his deportations, and his gleeful grift as being opposed to "what America represents." Yet, for many working people, America represents a rigged game that they cannot win, and this feeling is becoming increasingly common. Two days after the election, an editor commented to me that Trump's victory had this much in common with that of Barack Obama: it proved that anything could happen (Dixon 2017).

Trumpism promised much, but it will not deliver for most people who voted for the president. Some may be content with the emotional representation Trump offers, the gleeful middle finger that he continues to present to the world. For many others, he will be yet another elite who has failed them. They will be looking around for new answers or joining the numbers already given over to despair. The man Mike Davis called "the Great God Trump" (Davis 2017) has no answers for the working class, white or otherwise, but the working class is beginning to offer some of those answers on its own.

References

Amnesia, Anne. 2016. "Unnecessariat." *More Crows than Eagles* (blog), May 10. https://morecrows.wordpress.com/2016/05/10/unnecessariat/.

Balz, Dan, and Philip Rucker. 2016. "In Final 100 Days, Clinton and Trump to Chart Different Paths to White House." *Washington Post*, July 30. https://www.washingtonpost.com/politics/in-final-100-days-clinton-and-trump-to-chart-different-paths-to-white-house/2016/07/30/ac58a59e-55c4-11e6-b7de-dfe509430c39_story.html?utm_term=.75b7fc19d7f5.

Barbaro, Michael, Maggie Haberman, and Jonathan Martin. 2015. "Can't Fire Him: Republican Party Frets over What to Do with Donald Trump." *New York Times*, July 9. https://nyti.ms/1IM0Yrh.

Berman, Ari. 2016. "There Are 868 Fewer Places to Vote in 2016 Because the Supreme Court Gutted the Voting Rights Act." *The Nation*, November 4. https://www.thenation.com/article/there-are-868-fewer-places-to-vote-in-2016-because-the-supreme-court-gutted-the-voting-rights-act/.

Berman, Ari. 2017. "Wisconsin's Voter-ID Law Suppressed 200,000 Votes in 2016 (Trump Won by 22,748)." *The Nation*, May 9. https://www.thenation.com/article/wisconsins-voter-id-law-suppressed-200000-votes-trump-won-by-23000/.

Brusk, Steve, Tasha Diakides, Peter Hamby, Ed Hornick, Sasha Johnson, and Alexander Marquardt. 2008. "McCain, Palin Hint That Obama's Policies Are 'Socialist.'" CNN, October 18. http://www.cnn.com/2008/POLITICS/10/18/campaign.wrap/.

Carnes, Nicholas, and Noam Lupu. 2017. "It's Time to Bust the Myth: Most Trump Voters Were Not Working Class." *Washington Post*, June 5. https://www.washingtonpost.com/news/monkey-cage/wp/2017/06/05/its-time-to-bust-the-myth-most-trump-voters-were-not-working-class/?utm_term=.840b5dccc5fc.

CBS News, "Hillary Clinton says half of Trump's supporters are in a 'basket of deplorables.'" September 10, 2016, accessed April 9, 2019, available on Youtube. https://www.youtube.com/watch?v=PCHJVE9trSM.

Chozick, Amy, and Patrick Healy. 2016. "Inside the Clinton Team's Plan to Defeat Donald Trump." *New York Times*, February 29. https://nyti.ms/1LRmxEX.

Collins, Ben, and Emily Shire. 2015. "Presidential Sensation Deez Nuts Is a 15-Year-Old Iowa Farm Boy." *The Daily Beast*, August 19. https://www.thedailybeast.com/presidential-sensation-deez-nuts-is-a-15-year-old-iowa-farm-boy.

Cooper, Matthew. 2015. "Donald Trump: The Billionaire for Blue-Collars." *Newsweek*, June 23. http://www.newsweek.com/2015/07/03/donald-trump-billionaire-blue -collars-345677.html.

Davis, Mike. 2017. "The Great God Trump and the White Working Class." *Jacobin*, February 7. https://www.jacobinmag.com/2017/02/the-great-god-trump-and-the -white-working-class/.

Debenedetti, Gabriel. 2018. "Is Pennsylvania Still Trump Country?" *New York Magazine*, May 18. http://nymag.com/daily/intelligencer/2018/05/is-pennsylvania-still -trump-country.html.

Dias, Elizabeth, Haley Sweetland Edward, and Karl Vick. 2016. "Voices from Democratic Counties Where Trump Won Big." *Time*, December 7. http://time.com/voices -from-democratic-counties-where-trump-won-big/.

Dixon, Patrick. 2017. "Playing Chicken: Discovering a Diverse Working Class in Trump Country." *Working-Class Perspectives* (blog), March 21. https:// workingclassstudies.wordpress.com/2017/03/21/playing-chicken-discovering-a -diverse-working-class-in-trump-country/.

Dovere, Edward-Isaac. 2016. "How Clinton Lost Michigan—and Blew the Election." *Politico*, December 14. https://www.politico.com/story/2016/12/michigan-hillary -clinton-trump-232547.

Fang, Marina. 2017. "Hillary Clinton: Calling Trump Supporters 'Deplorables' Handed Him 'a Political Gift.'" *Huffington Post*, September 10. https://www .huffingtonpost.com/entry/clinton-trump-deplorables-2016-election_us _59b53bc2e4b0354e44126979.

Glauber, Bill. 2017. "Hillary Clinton Was Caught by Surprise by Wisconsin Loss, She Says in Her Book, 'What Happened.'" *Milwaukee Journal-Sentinel*, September 12. https://www.jsonline.com/story/news/2017/09/12/hillary-clinton-discusses -wisconsin-loss-herds-book-lands-wisconsin-filled-explanations-her-loss-her /657485001/.

Glueck, Katie. 2016. "How Pennsylvania Will Be Won." *Politico*, July 30. https://www .politico.com/story/2016/07/pennsylvania-general-election-battleground-226461.

Greenhouse, Steven. 2016."What Unions Got Wrong about Trump." *New York Times*, November 26. https://nyti.ms/2g3T5p1.

Grim, Ryan. 2017. "The GOP Plan Is the Biggest Tax Increase in American History, by Far." *The Intercept*, December 1. https://theintercept.com/2017/12/01/the-gop -plan-is-the-biggest-tax-increase-in-american-history-by-far/.

Heath, David, and Jennifer Agiesta. 2016. "How Voters Who Found Both Candidates Unfit Broke." CNN, November 11. https://www.cnn.com/2016/11/11/politics /hillary-clinton-donald-trump-voters-dislike/index.html.

Jaffe, Sarah. 2017. "Back at the Carrier Plant, Workers Are Still Fighting on Their Own." *The Nation*, April 20. https://www.thenation.com/article/back-at-the-carrier -plant-workers-are-still-fighting-on-their-own/.

Jaffe, Sarah. 2018. "Why Did a Majority of White Women Vote for Trump?" *New Labor Forum*, January. http://newlaborforum.cuny.edu/2018/01/18/why-did-a-majority -of-white-women-vote-for-trump/.

Johnson, Adam. 2016. "Daily Kos Founder Gleefully Celebrates Coal Miners Losing Health Insurance." FAIR.org, December 14. https://fair.org/home/daily-kos -founder-gleefully-celebrates-coal-miners-losing-health-insurance/.

Jossey, Paul H. 2016. "How We Killed the Tea Party." *Politico*, August 14. https://www .politico.com/magazine/story/2016/08/tea-party-pacs-ideas-death-214164.

Kahn, Chris. 2016. "U.S. Voters Want Leader to End Advantage of Rich and Powerful: Reuters/Ipsos Poll." Reuters, November 8. https://www.reuters.com/article/us-usa

-election-poll-mood/u-s-voters-want-leader-to-end-advantage-of-rich-and
-powerful-reuters-ipsos-poll-idUSKBN1332NC.

Kaplan, Thomas. 2016. "This Is Trump Country." *New York Times*, March 4. https://nyti
.ms/2lt9IPa.

Lopez, German. 2016. "Most Ohio and Pennsylvania Counties That Flipped from
Obama to Trump Are Wracked by Heroin." *Vox*, November 22. https://www.vox
.com/policy-and-politics/2016/11/22/13698476/trump-opioid-heroin-epidemic.

MacFarquhar, Larissa. 2016. "In the Heart of Trump Country." *New Yorker*, October 10.
https://www.newyorker.com/magazine/2016/10/10/in-the-heart-of-trump
-country.

Malsky, Bea. 2017. "Pleasure Won: A Conversation with Lauren Berlant." *The Point*.
https://thepointmag.com/2017/politics/pleasure-won-conversation-lauren
-berlant.

McElwee, Sean. 2018. "How the Right's War on Unions Is Killing the Democratic Party."
The Nation, January 22. https://www.thenation.com/article/right-to-work-laws
-are-killing-democrats-at-the-ballot-box/.

Newman, Kurt. 2016. "On White Racism and the Trump Vote: A Marxist Perspective."
Sad Billionaire (blog), November 12. https://sadbillionaire.wordpress.com/2016
/11/12/on-white-racism-and-the-trump-vote-a-marxist-perspective/.

Phillips, Kate. "Clinton Touts White Support." *New York Times*, May 8. https://thecaucus
.blogs.nytimes.com/2008/05/08/clinton-touts-white-support/.

Pilkington, Ed. 2008. "Obama angers Midwest voters with guns and religion re-
mark." *Guardian*, April 14. https://www.theguardian.com/world/2008/apr/14
/barackobama.uselections2008.

Reid, Tim. 2016. "'Joe the Plumber' Praises Trump, Cites His 'Beautiful Women.'"
Reuters, March 4. https://www.reuters.com/article/us-usa-election-plumber/joe
-the-plumber-praises-trump-cites-his-beautiful-women
-idUSMTZSAPEC34J3246U.

Ross, Janell. 2015a. "Donald Trump's Surge Is All about Less-Educated Americans."
Washington Post, July 27. https://www.washingtonpost.com/news/the-fix/wp/2015
/07/27/donald-trumps-surge-is-heavily-reliant-on-less-educated-americans-heres
-why/.

Ross, Janell. 2015b. "Obama Revives His 'Cling to Guns or Religion' Analysis—for
Donald Trump Supporters." *Washington Post*, December 21. https://www
.washingtonpost.com/news/the-fix/wp/2015/12/21/obama-dusts-off-his-cling-to
-guns-or-religion-idea-for-donald-trump/?utm_term=.4dac90c2422b.

Simon, Roger. 2008. "Hillary Clinton the Straight Shooter." *Politico*, April 14. https://
www.politico.com/story/2008/04/hillary-clinton-the-straight-shooter-009596.

Stein, Jeff. 2017. "Ryan Says Republicans to Target Welfare, Medicare, Medicaid
Spending in 2018." *Washington Post*, December 6. https://www.washingtonpost
.com/news/wonk/wp/2017/12/01/gop-eyes-post-tax-cut-changes-to-welfare
-medicare-and-social-security/.

Stein, Sam. 2016. "The Clinton Campaign Was Undone by Its Own Neglect and a Touch
of Arrogance, Staffers Say." *Huffington Post*, November 16. https://www
.huffingtonpost.com/entry/clinton-campaign-neglect_us
_582cacb0e4b058ce7aa8b861.

Tavernise, Sabrina. 2016. "Many in Milwaukee Neighborhood Didn't Vote—and Do Not
Regret It." *New York Times*, November 20. https://nyti.ms/2feAFhh.

Taylor, Keeanga-Yamahtta, ed. 2017. *How We Get Free: Black Feminism and the Combahee River Collective*. New York: Haymarket Books.

Thrush, Glenn. 2016. "Keith Ellison's One-Man March." *Politico*, December 20. https://www.politico.com/story/2016/12/keith-ellison-democrats-dnc-232838.

Tirado, Linda. 2016. "This Is the Hollowed-Out Heart of America: Pain, Rage and Donald Trump." *The Guardian*, October 30. https://www.theguardian.com /commentisfree/2016/oct/30/heart-america-pain-fear-vote-donald-trump-ohio.

Vazquez, Maegan. 2018. "Sessions Invokes 'Anglo-American' Heritage of Sheriff's Office." CNN.com, February 12. https://www.cnn.com/2018/02/12/politics/jeff -sessions-anglo-american-law-enforcement/index.html.

Wolff, Michael. 2018. "Donald Trump Didn't Want to Be President." *New York Magazine*, January 3. http://nymag.com/daily/intelligencer/2018/01/michael -wolff-fire-and-fury-book-donald-trump.html.

Zito, Salena. 2018. "Donald Trump Is Still the Man to This Pennsylvania Home." *New York Post*, January 31. https://nypost.com/2018/01/31/donald-trump-is-still-the -man-to-these-blue-collar-voters/.

6

PRIVATIZATION—CHIPPING AWAY AT GOVERNMENT

Donald Cohen

Ronald Reagan ushered in a full-throated assault on American government when he declared in his 1981 inaugural address, "In this present crisis, government is not the solution to our problem; government is the problem" (1981). His vision and agenda were clear: reduce the size and power of the federal government. Handing over services and assets to the private sector one by one was at the center of that vision. Donald Trump, nearly forty years later, riding a wave of right-wing populism and hatred for nearly everything government, came to office with a privatization movement already making major gains.

Trump has surrounded himself with free-market ideologues, crony capitalists, and conservative operatives bent on downsizing and outsourcing government and dismantling public-sector unions. The former president of the Heritage Foundation, Edwin Feulner, who was head of domestic policy for the Trump transition, argued, "Any government function that can be found in the yellow pages should be a candidate for privatization" (Tracy and Feulner 2012, 80). The administration is filled with former Heritage employees and Heritage-recommended conservatives such as billionaire education secretary Betsy DeVos, a staunch advocate for charter schools and voucher programs (Mahler 2018). Trump's appointee to run the Centers for Medicare and Medicaid Services, Seema Verma, helped Iowa privatize its Medicaid system, which sputtered into crisis within months. The administration has its sights set on privatizing the US Postal Service, the Tennessee Valley Authority, the air traffic control system, and much more.

Trump and those he appoints are eager to boost the privatization process, but they are part of a much larger wave, and most of the action is likely to be at the state and local levels, especially in the numerous states with a trifecta of Republican control—the governorship and both houses of the legislature. But the trend is popular not only with Republicans—many Democratic mayors and governors continue to be attracted to privatization schemes in infrastructure, education, and more.

There is an even larger, and more important, frame through which to view privatization of public goods: as a major threat to both labor and democracy. First, there is a lot of money to be made—about $7 trillion is spent each year by federal, state, and local governments. Second, it is a chance to severely weaken public-sector unions, which are a powerful pro-government force and a formidable political opponent in elections. Third, free-market ideologues see an opening to fundamentally redefine the role of government. In a democratic society, citizens have rights and responsibilities to each other. In a market society, people are individual consumers of a limited set of public services.

At its core, privatization is at the center of a critical battle over the fundamental role of government, the relationship between public and private institutions, the appropriate and inappropriate roles of markets in the provision of public goods and services, and the core public values that define a democratic society. It is about how we as a nation define the common good, and whether our democratic institutions are able to pursue it. A fully realized privatization agenda would have each of us pay for the specific services we can afford rather than establishing a baseline of democratic rights that are available to all regardless of their ability to pay. The battle is well under way, embedded deeply in current American politics and governance.

Today, after fifty years of attack on government (Cokorinos 2007), privatization has become a standard response to tight public budgets, a key pillar of attacks on government, and a lucrative market opportunity for domestic and global corporations. Large corporations now operate virtually every type of public service, including prisons, welfare systems, infrastructure, water and sewer services, trash, and schools. For example:

- Private prisons did not exist forty years ago. Today, publicly traded, billion-dollar corporations are key players in prisons and immigrant detention (Pauly 2016). In 2016, privatized immigration facilities housed 65 percent of all detained immigrants (Homeland Security Advisory Council 2016). That number is likely higher today in the wake of Trump's immigrant sweeps.
- In 1988, American Federation of Teachers (AFT) president Al Shanker proposed a new idea: to create charter schools where teachers could experiment and innovate and bring new ideas to the nation's public

schools (Kahlenberg and Potter 2014). Today, nearly three million children attend charters. Large corporate chains and billionaires are funding the rapid growth of privatized, publicly funded charter schools (National Alliance for Public Charter Schools 2015).

- Former defense contractors, IT corporations, and publicly traded corporations are running welfare, food assistance, and other safety net systems in many states across the country.

- Today, the federal government employs more than three times as many contract workers as government workers, and state and local governments spend a combined $1.5 trillion on goods, services, and capital contracting (Conway 2012).

- Across the country, a well-established network of conservative think tanks, industry associations, investors, and corporate lobbyists—including the State Policy Network, a member of the American Legislative Exchange Council (ALEC), and others—are on the front lines, developing privatization legislation and proposing privatization projects.

A History of Privatization

The year Trump was born, 1946, was also the year that kicked off the career of the best American promoter of free-market ideas. That year, Milton Friedman joined the faculty at the University of Chicago, where he would eventually become the foremost economist in the so-called Chicago school of economics. Friedman was an effective promoter of two critical ideas: governments were just like markets (and should function like them), and government was a public monopoly that should be broken up. Both ideas became central arguments for privatization advocates in the 1970s and 1980s.

Privatization advocates chipped away at government through the 1970s, but it was not until the 1980s, with the election of Ronald Reagan as president, that privatization went mainstream. By 1987, Reagan's budget plan included more privatization proposals than any president had ever recommended, including the sale of two federally owned airports, a railroad, four regional power agencies and their electricity-generating dams, and weather satellites. Stymied by a Democratic Congress, Reagan only succeeded in privatizing Conrail, the northeastern freight railroad taken over by the federal government from the bankrupt Penn Central. In 1988, the Presidential Commission on Privitization developed a road map of federal functions to privatize, including low-income housing, federal loan programs, air traffic control, education, the Postal Service, prisons, Amtrak, Medicare, and urban mass transit, but congressional Democrats stood up again, thwarting the commission's recommendations (Cohen 2017a).

In the face of Reagan-era failures, pro-privatization forces realized that they needed a new approach. Fred Smith of the Competitive Enterprise Institute charged that privatization "had quickly been captured by the forces of the status quo in and out of government." In a somewhat bitter article analyzing the reasons for this failure, Smith tore into Reagan for failing to develop an effective strategy to take the offensive against core Democratic constituencies. Smith argued that in order for a privatization proposal to "make it through the political process," it is necessary to "create a viable privatization coalition" in favor of it (Smith 1987). "Thus a top priority," Smith wrote, "should be to identify Democratic senators and representatives who might be persuaded to support privatization and convince them to take the lead on the issue" (Smith 1987).

The liberal think tanks were also targeted. In 1988, the conservative Olin Foundation provided funding to the Brookings Institution for a book on education vouchers and, throughout the 1990s, to the program on education policy at Harvard's Kennedy School of Government. In the words of Olin's executive director, James Piereson, "We were interested in getting these ideas ensconced at liberal places" (Cokorinos 2007).

Smith based his argument on the writings of Stuart Butler, an analyst at the Heritage Foundation (especially his 1985 book *Privatizing Federal Spending: A Strategy to Reduce the Deficit*), and Madson Pirie, the architect of Margaret Thatcher's privatization efforts and the founder and current president of the London-based Adam Smith Institute (who had just published *Dismantling the State: The Theory and Practice of Privatization*, a handbook for his American audience), considered to be the two most important strategists of the privatization movement in the United States and the United Kingdom. The problem in the Reagan years, as Butler saw it, was not a lack of determination but rather that the administration had failed to change the "underlying political dynamics that favor increased Federal spending," specifically the influence of pro-spending constituencies (1985, 326). Butler wrote several influential strategy papers, including "Privatization: A Strategy to Cut the Budget" (1985) and "Changing the Political Dynamics of Government" (1987). They gave conservatives a fresh approach by showing that government responsibility could be separated from government provision of services. This meant that privatization did not necessarily require cutting popular public services—instead they could be handed to private contractors. Privatization of public services and assets could be used to "reverse the momentum towards ever-larger government in the United States"(Butler 1987, 4). Butler argued that privatization could alter the fundamental political dynamics that favored increased federal spending:

> As long as constituencies see it in their interest to demand government spending, and as long as politicians risk electoral damage when they vote against those demands, it is going to be very difficult to restrain spending. Thus a strategy to control the size of government needs a powerful "demand-side" element if it is to be successful. . . . Conditions must be created in which the demand for government spending is diverted into the private sector. This is the beauty of privatization. Instead of having to say "no" to constituencies, politicians can adopt a more palatable approach to cutting spending. They can reduce outlays by fostering private alternatives that are more attractive to voters, thereby reducing the clamor for government spending. Changing the political dynamics of government spending in this way is the secret of privatization.

Butler argued for using privatization "to reshape the interest group environment," for detaching key elements of the coalition supporting federal, state, and local government programs. Butler's insight led to a focused effort to recruit and engage corporate America as a new and focused political force for privatization (Henig 1989).

In fact, local and state governments had been contracting with private companies for many years. For example, Waste Management, Inc.—today a $6 billion company—formed in 1968 and grew rapidly in the wake of federal policy that increased waste disposal requirements. American Water Works Company, later renamed American Water, the largest water and wastewater company (now worth $19 billion), has had municipal contracts for over a century (American Water 2018).

Stuart Butler's strategy called for organizing these types of companies that would benefit from privatization, the companies that could get lucrative government contracts. In 1985, a group of large firms created the Privatization Council (Donahue 1989). The driving forces were David Seader and Stephen M. Sorett, the latter was the privatization coordinator for Touche Ross & Co., a top-tier consulting firm that became Deloitte and Touche in 1989. Touche was involved because it wanted to change the tax codes standing in the way of private municipal sewerage work. Seader went on to lead the privatization and infrastructure group of Price Waterhouse, the global consulting and accounting firm. (In the early 1990s, the council was renamed the National Council for Public-Private Partnerships.)

By 1990, the Privatization Council boasted 150 members, a who's who of consulting firms, corporations, and industry associations that had their sights on contracting opportunities in water treatment, transit, prisons, trash pickup, airports, and finance. The council's 1987 conference brought together strategists

Emanuel Savas and Stuart Butler and companies that coveted public contracts in these areas as well as in health care and infrastructure. Lockheed and Bechtel Corporation were attempting to capture a market to build and privatize airports. Construction giant Parsons wanted to build, own, and operate municipal water and wastewater plants. ATE Management and Service Company, owned by Ryder, had its eyes on transit systems (Cohen 2017a).

Taking It to Cities and States

Despite Reagan's failure to privatize significant sectors, early in his administration he had planted the seeds (Ayres 1981) that would create favorable conditions for ALEC and its corporate partners to ultimately force local and state governments toward privatization as a means of shedding responsibility and cutting costs.

Conservative direct-mail guru Richard Viguerie wrote in 1981 that conservatives had only recently determined that the state and local level "is the missing piece of the puzzle for us." ALEC stepped in to fill that role and increased and operationalized corporate involvement in moving state-level privatization policy. In the 1980s, ALEC played a pivotal role for the privatization movement in the states, and it continues to do so. ALEC's executive director in the mid-1980s, Kathleen Teague, told the *National Journal* in 1984 that the interest of mainline business corporations in state legislative affairs was rising so fast that "I have more big corporations who want to see me, get involved and become members than we can practically cope with" (Pierce and Guskind 1984).

ALEC put together working groups of corporations, think tanks, and legislators, such as one that brought together the Reason Foundation's director Robert Poole of its Local Government Center, Heritage's Stuart Butler, Seader from the Privatization Council, a private prison company (Corrections Associates, Inc.), and the National Solid Wastes Management Association (NSWMA) to set priorities and draft legislation to make it easier to outsource public services. The NSWMA was an early supporter of ALEC and conservative efforts to fight increased environmental regulation (Cohen 2017a). ALEC, too, has been funded by right-wing foundations such as Scaife and Coors, as well as by major American corporations, many of which had an eye on public contracts (Pierce and Guskind 1984).

Reagan spent much of his first term pushing what he called the "New Federalism" (CQ Researcher 1981), which others described as the "devolution revolution" (Kousser 2014), shifting federal responsibilities to state and local governments. Despite pushback from governors, he was ultimately successful in reducing the amount of federal aid going to states and cities, giving an added push toward outsourcing. Local and state governments were already dealing with the fiscal straitjacket created by the property tax revolt launched by California's Proposition 13 in 1978, which helped make taxes the new third rail of state and local politics. Governors and mayors were faced with a painful dilemma: raise taxes or cut services. Outsourcing promised cost savings—primarily by cutting labor costs.

Cuts in federal funding of programs and revenue sharing with local governments was the push the privatizers needed. "Revenue sharing is dead and other programs have been cut significantly," the Privatization Council's David Seader told the *Milwaukee Journal-Sentinel* in 1986 (Masterson 1986). Seader described it as an opportunity to shift public services to private operations, saying, "Cities have been discovering that public services do not necessarily have to be reduced by government or paid for by taxes" (Masterson 1986). Individuals could pay for what they use, and private companies were ready to take their money.

Reason Foundation founder Robert Poole saw cutting costs as a means to fundamentally redefine the role of government, writing that, "Most local services have few attributes of true public goods. Most of them—garbage collection, park and recreation services, libraries, airports, transit, and aspects of police and fire protection—have specific, identifiable users, who are the services' beneficiaries" (Heritage Foundation 1983).

In the context of the growing acceptance of a neoliberal worldview, the impacts of Reagan's devolution gave proprivatization strategists like Butler and Poole the opportunity to reframe existing government contracting practices (long common in municipal governments) as a larger theory of practical governance. Thus, standard practice became ideological mission.

For the Reason Foundation's Poole, it became the perfect incremental strategy. "I figured that if you could gradually build up to socialism, you could probably undo it, dismantling it step by step," he said. Government could be dismantled "by privatizing one function after the other, selling each move as justified for its own sake rather than waiting until the majority of the population is convinced of the case for a libertarian utopia" (Minto and Minto 1999, cited in MacLean 2017, 144n64). These ideological, political, and fiscal changes laid the groundwork to turn privatization into a bipartisan effort.

Clinton Makes It Happen

President George H. W. Bush, a president more focused on foreign policy, did not maintain Reagan's drive for privatization. Vice President Dan Quayle led the administration's Council on Competitiveness but did not make much progress. Bush's one significant privatization-related action in the final year of his presidency was to sign an executive order that would make it easier for states and cities to sell or lease public facilities such as housing projects, roads, or sewage treatment plants built with federal money (Yang 1992). The order did not launch a selloff of public assets, however.

President Clinton, the business-friendly New Democrat, got the job done. Clinton had warmer attitudes toward the role of government, but Reagan's attack on government had shifted the political terrain. While Reagan famously proclaimed that "the nine most terrifying words in the English language are, 'I'm from the government and I'm here to help'" (1986), Clinton took it further and in 1996 declared, "The era of big government is over" (Nunberg 2005).

In fact, Clinton succeeded where Reagan and Bush had failed. Writing in 1997, the Heritage Foundation's Ron Utt (who had been Reagan's "privatization czar") praised Clinton for pursuing "the boldest privatization agenda put forth by any American president to date" and noted that his proposals were "virtually all drawn from recommendations made in 1988 by President Reagan's Commission on Privatization" (Cohen 2017a). In 2006, the Reason Foundation's Robert Poole declared that "the Clinton administration's privatization successes exceeded those of Reagan" (Reason Foundation 2006, 23).

In the first year of his administration, Clinton assigned Vice President Al Gore to oversee a major initiative to "reinvent" government under the auspices of an intergovernmental task force, the National Performance Review (NPR) (see Gore 1995). Clinton's 1992 campaign promises included a commitment to cut 100,000 federal jobs (Clinton for President 1992). The NPR took it further and recommended downsizing the bureaucracy by 272,900 civilian positions (Jones 1998). These commitments created the illusion of reducing the size of government while merely increasing pressure to contract out public services and functions that still needed to be performed.

Perhaps Clinton's most significant contribution to privatization was ideological. The NPR reports redefined government services in market terms: "citizens" became "customers" of public services, competition became a guiding management principle, and "privatization" became "public-private partnerships"—a far less politically charged term (LawTeacher 2013). Conservative arguments to privatize Social Security were beginning to get traction in policy circles, including both the Brookings Institution and Cato Foundation, but there was broad public opposition to the idea. Privatization supporters who understood the nexus of policy and politics saw that the word "privatization" was in danger of damaging the prospects for other privatization efforts.

The 1996 welfare reform law supercharged privatization. The law removed restrictions that prohibited states from contracting out welfare intake and eligibility in what the *Washington Post* described as potentially "the largest transfers of public sector operations into private hands" (Havemann 1997).

The law represented a significant shift in the history of privatization. The contractors were not simply managing public services. They would make important public decisions—helping to determine which Americans received welfare and under what circumstances.

The 1996 law gave the states the green light to privatize. Texas and Wisconsin moved quickly to privatize their welfare intake programs. Texas governor George W. Bush wanted to go further than the law permitted and extend outsourcing of eligibility screenings beyond welfare to other programs such as food stamps and Medicaid—a lucrative $2.8 billion, seven-year contract.

The 1996 law opened the door for national and global corporations to make millions as providers of human services and to become powerful advocates for privatization. Large corporations, including EDS, IBM, Lockheed, and a subsidiary of Arthur Andersen and Co., saw welfare reform as a lucrative new market that promised to become a multibillion-dollar industry (Bernstein 1996).

For example, in 1996, Maximus, Inc. (founded in 1975) was a relatively small company, with only $100 million in government contracts. Today, Maximus, with over $2 billion in annual revenue (Maximus 2017), is one of the largest for-profit managers of health and human services in the United States and across the globe.

Assault on Democracy

Privatization's consequences are widespread and well documented. In neoclassical economic theory, public savings result from superior efficiencies driven by "market discipline." For-profit corporations, conservative think tanks, and ideologically driven policymakers claim that outsourcing offers cheaper, better, and faster services. The track record shows a different reality. Taxpayers see a consistent pattern of cost overruns, greater economic inequality, and service failures. Where there are "savings," they come from lower pay to workers, fewer benefits, and, in the pursuit of profits, contractors cutting corners, lowering the quality of public services.

But privatization also cuts deeper, to the foundation of American democracy. It is an assault on public control of public goods. In fact, the details of contracts, leases, and public-private agreements codify private interests into public goods in ways that distort and threaten the public interest in profound ways. Many of these legal agreements weaken democracy and the role of all Americans in participating equally in determining our common goals and finding solutions to our social, economic, and environmental problems, and as public services are increasingly outsourced, government loses the capacity to supervise the contractors, opening the door to corruption and contractor lock-in. These contracts, leases, and agreements limit democratic policy making in many areas of government responsibility, including fiscal policy, safety net services, economic development, environmental protection and public lands, criminal justice, urban planning, transportation, public education, and immigration. In effect, private companies gain power over vital public decisions in all of these arenas under contracts that can last for decades.

Corporations certainly have legitimate private interests focused on generating revenue and return on investment for owners and shareholders. The success of profitable and productive private businesses that create good middle-class jobs and a good quality of life is also important to the nation, but democracy encompasses a set of civic motives and public interests far broader than the fortunes of individual businesses. An educated and healthy public, clean air and water, economic security, and a decent standard of living for everyone are some of our most important public goals and are thwarted when private interests insert the profit motive into their pursuit.

There are six specific ways that short- and long-term agreements have weakened and continue to weaken the core elements of American democracy— transparency, participation, accountability, shared prosperity, and democratic control.

1. Fine-print contract clauses make it difficult, if not impossible, to make decisions to improve our cities, our transportation systems, and many other public services.

For example, Chicago leased 36,000 city parking meters for $1.2 billion to Morgan Stanley and private investors for a period of seventy-five years in exchange for the meters' revenues. The contract commits the city to pay the private vendor if the city makes any decision that impacts the company's revenues during the seventy-five-year term of the contract—whether it decides to hold street fairs, add bicycle lanes, eliminate rush-hour parking, make other land-use changes to make cities more livable, or allow the construction of other public parking facilities that compete with the privately controlled parking meters and lots (Farmer and Cohen 2014). Mayor Richard Daley executed a similar deal in 2006 to lease city parking lots for ninety-nine years in exchange for a $563 million upfront payment. In November 2014, a judge ruled that Chicago must compensate the private operators of four downtown parking garages owned by the city and park district for $62 million in lost revenue and interest stemming from the city's approval of a competing parking facility (Mihalopoulous 2015).

Similarly, the city of Denver gave up control of the Northwest Parkway toll road to a consortium led by Brisa Auto-Estradas de Portugal. The ninety-nine-year contract forbids local governments from upgrading surrounding free public roads because they would compete with the toll road for commuters (Lewis and Dow Jones Newswires 2007).

CoreCivic (formerly Corrections Corporation of America, or CCA), the nation's largest private prison company, often stipulates in their contracts that prisons must be filled to 90 percent or even 100 percent capacity, or else municipalities (i.e., taxpayers) are slapped with penalties for empty beds. In 2012, CCA even sent a letter to forty-eight governors offering to buy prisons from cash-strapped states in exchange for the governors' promise to "maintain a minimum 90 percent [inmate] occupancy rate during the course of the contract" (Lappin 2012).

2. We lose the right to know important details about how public services are delivered.

When services are outsourced, public information goes behind a private wall. Advocates lose access to critical information essential in many policy arenas, and even policymakers lack information to hold contractors accountable. We simply do not have the information we need to evaluate whether we are getting what we pay for. Access to information is a critical component of contractor accountability, as most public agencies lack adequate capacity for contract oversight.

Basic financial information such as CEO salaries, profits, employee wage rates, and even the work produced become "proprietary information" exempt from disclosure. Performance data, such as audits and records that describe how a program or service is performing, are often confidential. This includes information about the type of care a child is receiving in a state's foster care system.

For example, despite public records and open meetings laws, private organizations that receive public money have been allowed to keep their operations shrouded in secrecy. The governing board of a publicly funded Ohio charter school had to file suit to force White Hat LLC, the for-profit education management operator the board hired to run the school, to provide basic financial, curriculum, and other information about the operation of the school (Marshall 2010). For-profit charters often refuse to share curricula they develop while operating a tax-funded charter school, claiming that it is proprietary information.

In Texas, State Highway 130, a privatized road between San Antonio and Austin, filed for bankruptcy in March 2016 when expected traffic projections failed to materialize. A Texas news outlet's information requests for the original projections were rejected by the company, the Texas attorney general, and the US Department of Transportation. The road concessionaire claimed the projections contained proprietary information or included "trade secrets" that might help competitors (Blunt 2016).

3. Private contractors get "skin in the game" and have the right to weigh in on any policy debate that could impact their revenues, profit margins, and market share.

As the market share of contractors grows, so does their lobbying and campaign spending—in other words, their political power—and their interests can directly conflict with the public interest. For example, in their annual 10-K filing to the SEC, publicly traded companies list the "risk factors" that could negatively impact company health and growth. The following are excerpts from some SEC filings from 2017:

- CoreCivic (2017 revenue $1.77 billion) (Market Watch 2017a): "The demand for our facilities and services could be adversely affected by the relaxation of enforcement efforts, the expansion of alternatives to incarceration and detention, leniency in conviction or parole standards and sentencing practices or through the decriminalization of certain activities that are currently proscribed by criminal laws. For instance, any changes with respect to drugs and controlled substances or illegal immigration could affect the number of persons arrested, convicted, and sentenced, thereby potentially reducing demand for correctional or detention facilities to house them. Immigration reform laws are currently a focus for legislators and politicians at the federal, state, and local level."
- American Water Works (2017 revenue $3.4 billion) (Business Wire 2017): "Our water and wastewater operations and the operations of our Market-Based Businesses are subject to extensive federal, state and local laws and regulations and, in the case of our Canadian operations, Canadian laws and regulations that govern the protection of the environment, health and safety, the quality of the water we deliver to our customers, water allocation rights, and the manner in which we collect, treat, discharge and dispose of wastewater."
- Waste Management, Inc. (2017 revenue $14.5 billion) (MarketWatch 2017c): "The adoption of climate change legislation or regulations restricting emissions of 'greenhouse gases' could increase our costs to operate. Our landfill operations emit methane, identified as a GHG. There are a number of legislative and regulatory efforts at the state, regional and federal levels to curtail the emission of GHGs to ameliorate the effect of climate change. Should comprehensive federal climate change legislation be enacted, we expect it could impose costs on our operations that might not be offset by the revenue increases associated with our lower-carbon service options."

While these statements may accurately describe risks that each company may face, it is also true that they spend millions lobbying and contributing to candidate campaigns and PACs as an important way to mitigate those risks. Their obligation to shareholders to increase returns guarantees that they make these expenditures. For example, prison companies lobbied for tougher mandatory sentencing and immigrant detention laws to increase the need for prison beds. Private prison companies that stand to gain billions in revenue are already benefiting as detention centers fill up as a result of the Trump administration's "crackdown" on "illegal immigration." Similarly, for-profit education companies lobby for mandatory online classes and online-only charters.

4. Bad deals and poorly negotiated agreements rob taxpayers of funds that we should be spending on important public services.

According to the Chicago inspector general, the city's parking meter agreement could have generated $1 billion more for the city. In the Public Interest found that two-thirds of state private prison contracts contain "occupancy guarantees" of between 80 percent and 100 percent (In the Public Interest 2013). In one instance, an investigative reporter found that Tennessee taxpayers paid $487,917.27 for empty beds in one CCA-operated prison in 2012 (Watson 2015). After it came to light publicly, the guarantee was removed from the contract upon its renewal in 2015.

Cost overruns and change orders are typical. Governments are faced with a choice when contractors declare they need more funds to complete the job: pay more to finish the job or stop halfway. The Florida Department of Law Enforcement contracted with Motorola in 2007 to build a $7.4 million fingerprint identification system. By October 2013, they had spent an additional $11.3 million (Korten 2014). Florida's $92 million contract with Accenture to automate the state's procurement process was revised upward to $114 million. Florida's $68 million contract to upgrade its twenty-five-year-old accounting and cash management system rose to $100 million (Chicago Tribune 2017). In 2007, then chief financial officer Alex Sink stopped the project, declaring the privatization effort an expensive failure. By that time, $89 million had been spent (Dockery 2013). New York City's CityTime payroll processing contract ballooned to more than $700 million from an initial price of $73 million (Grynbaum 2012).

Legal fees on outsourcing deals that happen, that do not happen, and/or are litigated after the deal is done have cost state governments millions. The state of Pennsylvania spent $3 million on lottery privatization that did not happen (Sweeney 2014), and a lawsuit over Indiana's public benefits contract with IBM cost taxpayers about $78 million, counting the judgments and outside legal fees.

Finally, the government (that is, us) shells out billions of dollars that are not spent for on-the-ground service delivery but rather become company profits and business expenses such as executive compensation and debt service. For example, the following companies receive virtually all their revenue from taxpayers. The net incomes (2017 figures are shown here) of each are resources that would be far better spent on direct provision of public services, whether it be higher worker pay, increased productivity, or increasing the amount of services provided.

- Geo Group: $146 million (Market Watch 2017b)
- CoreCivic: $177 million (Market Watch 2017a)
- Maximus: $209 million (Amigo Bulls 2017)
- Waste Management: $1.95 billion (Market Watch 2017c)
- American Water: $552 million (Business Wire 2017)

5. We lose the ability to make services affordable to poor, working-class people, seniors, and small businesses.

Many contracts give private operators authority to set user fees to guarantee their return on investment. We must pay for things, but there are lots of things that should be available to everyone regardless of their ability to pay, such as parks, health care, and getting to work and school. For example, parking costs are now $6.50 per hour in the Chicago Loop, and, typical of many water privatizations across the country, the North Texas town of Blue Mound's privatized system saw their water rates increase, hurting poor seniors (Permenter 2013). Intuit, the maker of TurboTax, consistently wages legislative battles to limit or eliminate publicly provided free online tax services that compete with their product (Day 2013).

6. Incentive structures written into contracts and agreements can distort and work against public policy goals and quality of services.

Some contracts base their size and schedule of payments on process and volume over product and quality service. For example, volume-based contracts at Colorado Foster Care paid contractors for each "match" they completed, so the contract provided an incentive for companies to approve people who were unqualified to be foster parents. The private foster care contractors in Colorado are responsible for monitoring and self-reporting their own cases of abuse or negligence. The companies have a clear financial incentive to underreport cases to ensure steady income, and, sure enough, incidents of abuse in the system went up (Callahan and Mitchell 2000).

In Texas, a contract with Accenture (formerly Andersen Consulting) to administer the children's health insurance and other state benefit programs was canceled after a report by the state comptroller found a pattern of lost applications, wrongly denied coverage, and poorly trained staff (Batheja 2015). The contract performance metrics were process based rather than outcome based, such that the contractor was paid for each time that employees "touched" an application. The state thought they were incentivizing the contractor to work quickly to get families approved, but, according to the comptroller, it actually had the effect of encouraging the contractor to process applications "slowly, inefficiently and incorrectly" by having employees touch an application more times than necessary in order to maximize the payments it received from the state (Strayhorne 2006). (Note that Texas has taken the original comptroller report that had this finding about the contract's perverse incentives off the web. The original link, http://www.window .state.tx.us/comptrol/letters/accenture/accenture_letter.pdf, no longer works).

Many private prison contractors are paid by the number of "heads in beds." That creates incentives to maintain and increase prisoner populations, incentives that may be counter to public goals of reducing the number of people in prison.

Public investment and policy decisions are increasingly driven by the potential for revenue and the need to protect revenue streams of private investors. For example, if infrastructure agreements are based on long-term traffic projections that create pressures to maintain high traffic levels, that works against clean-air, climate-change, and smart-growth initiatives to reduce the number of autos on the road or reduce speed limits. In this vein, Texas increased the speed limit of a privatized highway—a major truck route between Austin and San Antonio—to 85 miles per hour to generate more revenue.

The Attack on Unions and Workers

In the age of Trump, the attack on workers and unions, long under way, is now in full swing—in the courts, in the states, and in the boardrooms.

The impacts on wages and benefits are clear, with over twenty million public-sector workers in local, state, and federal government agencies across the country. At that scale, any outsourcing that reduces wages becomes a significant factor in increasing inequality. In fact, that number hides the true size of the government and its impact on wages and benefits. The federal government spends $500 billion on private contractors, and some departments have as many contract employees as regular full-time civilian workers (DiIulio 2014).

In addition to lowering costs from reduced contractor wages and health care benefits, mayors, county administrators, and governors of both parties see outsourcing as a way to reduce the number of people covered by their defined-benefit pension systems, which they see as a constant drag on their budgets. For conservatives, though, the attack on defined-benefit pensions is an example of the synergy between their political and their economic agendas. Reducing public-sector pensions advances several goals at the same time: reducing government spending; weakening workers' commitment to public-sector unions as benefits are reduced; and eliminating workers' power to enforce corporate standards through their pension investments, while boosting the finance industry by increasing workers' investments in 401(k) programs it controls.

Eliminating public-sector unions is a central and strategic objective for the corporate and ideological Right. Unions, quite simply, are in the way of their political and policy agendas, as well as, of course, their ability to secure maximum profit. For example, according to historian Nancy MacLean, "Breaking the spine of the labor movement would hobble any future defense of Social Security" (MacLean 2017, 181).

Reducing the number and political clout of union members is central to the conservative program for permanent political control of the nation. Grover Norquist, head of Americans for Tax Reform and one of the most influential Republican strategists in Washington, has long recognized the partisan value of vouchers, sometimes euphemistically referred to as "choice." "School choice reaches right into the heart of the Democratic coalition and takes people out of it," he said in a 1998 interview with *Insight*, the magazine of the conservative *Washington Times* (Miner 2004).

The issue comes down to "a matter of power," said Terry Moe, a senior fellow at the conservative Hoover Institution and coauthor of the book *Politics, Markets, and America's Schools*, in a summer 2017 interview with the Heartland Institute in Chicago. "School choice allows children and money to leave the system, and that means there will be fewer public teacher jobs, lower union membership, and lower dues" (Miner 2004).

The State Policy Network (SPN), the alliance of conservative policy centers across the country, is clear about the central purpose of weakening public-sector unions. A 2016 SPN fundraising appeal focused on "a once-in-a-lifetime chance to reverse the policies of the American left. . . . I'm talking about government employee unions," declared SPN president Tracie Sharp. "Today," she continued, "coercive Big Government unions are the biggest source of funding and political muscle for the Left—and a major obstacle to the ability of voters to reclaim control of American government. Which is why, to win the battle for freedom, we must take the fight to the unions, state by state, with key reforms" (Sharp 2016).

Nowhere is the importance of reducing the labor movement's political power clearer than in the court case *Janus v. AFSCME*, over the union's use of dues to advocate on behalf of workers. An amicus brief filed by the Competitive Enterprise Institute (2017) in the case specifically points to AFSCME's opposition to privatization as "evidence" that the union is engaging in political activity with members' dues.

Rebuilding a Pro-public Movement for the Common Good

All is not lost. Unions, advocates, and others are defeating privatization proposals and, perhaps more importantly, are winning campaigns that are starting to turn the tide. Water systems are being remunicipalized, private prison companies are losing contracts, and a growing movement is focused on rebuilding our national commitment to public education.

They are winning by mounting comprehensive campaigns, asking the hard questions about privatization proposals that highlight the underlying myths—and facts—about cost, quality, and control of public services. They do research, build coalitions, and make the case to the public.

For example, in 2017:

- The University of Tennessee at Knoxville, responding to a community labor campaign, decided to reject Governor Bill Haslam's privatization proposal. According to the university, "The decision is due to the university's extensive financial analyses, the complexity of the work done on the research-intensive campus, and its commitment to East Tennessee's economy and its workforce" (Davenport 2017).
- Atlantic City decided to reject Governor Chris Christie's push to privatize the city's water system. Food and Water Watch led a broad-based coalition of civic associations, local groups, the NAACP, NJ Appleseed, the ACLU of New Jersey, and public-sector unions in the successful campaign (Smith 2017).
- In November 2018, by a wide margin, voters in Baltimore adopted a charter change banning privatization of their water system and declared the system to be "a permanent, inalienable asset of the city."
- In a landmark decision, the Los Angeles Superior Court ruled that information related to job promises in a Los Angeles Metro contract with Canadian multinational bus manufacturer New Flyer should be released to the public. The company had claimed that job statistics needed to perform the public contract were a trade secret (Cohen 2017b).

There is also a growing realization that it is not sufficient for cities or states to stop new efforts at privatization. Ultimately, the public needs to support—and demand—quality public services that are controlled by the public and serve the public interest. Activists, organizations, and leaders across the country are also starting to see—and say—that effective, responsive, and inclusive government is essential to protecting and promoting the common good.

It is important to note that local, state, and federal governments do, and will always, enter into contracts and agreements with private companies. The preceding discussion demonstrates the potential loss of democratic rights and goods when public responsibilities are handed over to private interests without clarity about how the public, and the public good, must always be in the driver's seat. The solution must include government agencies at all levels adopting and rigorously enforcing a robust set of public protections that fortify the basic pillars of democratic government: transparency, accountability, public voice, and democratic control of vital services and infrastructure and our collective well-being.

Conservative and corporate forces have waged a multidecade, multifaceted campaign to delegitimize government and public collective solutions to our common problems and aspirations. They have created structures, lockboxes, and rules that advance their interests and agenda, and they have effectively organized day-to-day discontent with inadequate government services into a broad rejection of government as both an idea and a set of complex institutions.

Despite the success of these forces, there is ample evidence that the American people want control of public services and want more government action, not less, but distrust of government and complaints about specific services—some valid, some exaggerated, and some fake news—urge a new approach by pro-public forces. Progressives need a long-game, multisided strategy to rebuild trust in competent public institutions that protect and advance the common good. The following are some elements of such a strategy.

1. The idea and values of "public" (and the need for public control over public goods).

A focus on specific campaigns or advocating for solutions that rely on government action is essential to winning specific things, but campaigns on their own do not advance fundamental ideas about the need for collective action to advance the common good.

We need government action because there are essential things that we have to do together. Only together can we make sure everyone has access to education and health care. These are things we all benefit from, regardless of whether we use the specific service or asset or whether it impacts us directly, and these are things that make us a better nation. We need to start articulating these ideas and saying them over and over again.

2. Expose how private interests get in the way of public interests.

We need to make crucial distinctions between the real failures of government agencies (with limits that are human, political, financial, and bureaucratic) and corporate control of government institutions. Such corporate control has implications for and impacts almost every aspect of our lives. We need a continuous effort to expose those interests but do it in a way that makes clear that the problem is not "the government" but rather the interests that control it today—interests that can be dislodged.

3. The successes of the public in our lives.

We have to talk (a lot) about the many things government action has done effectively. If we do not, the idea of public solutions and government action has no defenders. You cannot win a battle when there is only one side, especially with the constant focus on (real or supposed) public failures, corruption scandals, and the general ugliness of political campaigns.

On the other hand, we cannot simply be the defenders of a status quo that most people do not like and that falls short in significant ways. The Right has repeatedly attacked the idea and institutions of government, while the progressive movement has left the ideas and successes of government action undefended. It is possible—and essential—to be both pro-public and pro-reform.

4. Transform public institutions for the common good.

We need an agenda that creates effective, responsive, inclusive, and innovative government institutions. We also must be about accountability, efficiency, openness, cutting waste, and stopping corruption. But ultimately the question will be whether governments deliver quality services, economic prosperity, and health and safety for the American people.

Conclusion

Today, privatization is weakening democratic public control over vital public goods, expanding corporate power, and increasing economic and political inequality. Domestic and global corporations and Wall Street investors covet the $7 trillion in local, state, and federal annual public spending on schools, prisons, water systems, transit systems, roads, bridges, and much more. Over the last forty years, private interests have gained control over important public goods, and the impacts are clear. The next forty years are ripe with opportunity to put the public solidly back in control.

References

American Water. 2018. Corporate profile. http://ir.amwater.com/corporate-profile.

American Water Works Company, Inc. 2017. 10-K filing to the Securities and Exchange Commission. http://ir.amwater.com/Cache/392756756.PDF?O=PDF&T=&Y=&D=&FID=392756756&iid=4004387.

Amigo Bulls. 2017. "Maximus." https://amigobulls.com/stocks/MMS/income-statement/annual.

Ayres, B. Drummond. 1981. "Reagan's Acts Renew, with Vigor, Nation's Debate about Federalism." *New York Times*, June 1. https://nyti.ms/2KxdTBc.

Batheja, Aman. 2015. "In State Contracting, Failure Is an Option." *Texas Tribune*, February 1. https://www.texastribune.org/2015/02/01/cost-overruns-and-bungles-state-contracting/.

Bernstein, Nina. 1996. "Giant Companies Entering Race to Run State Welfare Programs." *New York Times*, September 15. https://nyti.ms/2KvOZSr.

Bill Clinton for President. 1992. Campaign brochure. http://www.4president.org/brochures/billclinton1992brochure.htm.

Blunt, Katherine. 2016. "The End of the Road." *San Antonio Express-News*, September 16. http://projects.expressnews.com/the-end-of-the-road-texas-130-toll-road.

Business Wire. 2017. "American Water." https://www.businesswire.com/news/home/20180220006588/en/American-Water-Reports-Fourth-Quarter-Year-End-Results.

Butler, Stuart M. 1985a. *Privatizing Federal Spending: A Strategy to Reduce the Deficit.* New York: Universe Books.

Butler, Stuart M. 1985b. "Privatization: A Strategy to Cut the Budget." Cato Institute. https://object.cato.org/sites/cato.org/files/serials/files/cato-journal/1985/5/cj5n1-17.pdf.

Butler, Stuart M. 1987. "Changing the Political Dynamics of Government." *Proceedings of the Academy of Political Science* 36(3): 4–13. doi:10.2307/1174092.

Butler, Stuart M., and Kim R. Holmes. 1997. *Mandate for Leadership IV: Turning Ideas into Action.* Heritage Foundation.

Callahan, Patricia, and Kirk Mitchell. 2000. "Foster Care Too Often Fails to Keep Kids Safe." *Denver Post*, May 21. http://extras.denverpost.com/news/foster0521a.htm.

Chicago Tribune. 2017. "Judge: IBM Owes Indiana $78M for Failed Welfare Automation." August 7. http://www.chicagotribune.com/business/ct-ibm-indiana-penalty-20170807-story.html.

Cohen, Donald. 2017a. "The History of Privatization: How an Ideological and Political Attack on Government Became a Corporate Grab for Gold." Talking Points Memo. http://talkingpointsmemo.com/features/privatization/one/.

Cohen, Donald. 2017b. "Huge Win in California Regarding Access to Public Information." *In the Public Interest*, October 13. https://www.inthepublicinterest.org/huge-win-in-california-regarding-access-to-public-information/.

Cokorinos, Lee. 2007. *Upsizing Democracy: Confronting the Right Wing Assault on Government.* CreateSpace Independent Publishing Platform.

Competitive Enterprise Institute. 2017. "Amicus brief in Janus v AFSCME Council 31 submitted to U.S. Supreme Court." http://www.scotusblog.com/wp-content/uploads/2017/07/16-1466-cert-tsac-CEI.pdf.

Conway, Danielle M. 2012. "Sustainable Procurement Policies and Practices at the State and Local Government Level." In *Greening Local Government*, edited by Keith Hirokawa and Patricia Salkin. American Bar Association.

CoreCivic, Inc. 2017. 10-K filing to the Securities and Exchange Commission. https://
corecivic.gcs-web.com/static-files/6e38a54c-cdea-4ff9-ba06-f24d38a6ad60.
CQ Researcher. 1981. "Reagan's 'New Federalism.'" April 3. http://library.cqpress.com
/cqresearcher/document.php?id=cqresrre1981040300.
Crane, Edward H. 1998. *America's Social Security System: The Case for Privatizing*. Cato
Institute, April 15. https://www.cato.org/publications/commentary/americas
-social-security-system-case-privatizing.
Davenport, Beverly J. 2017. "University of Tennessee, Knoxville Office of the Chancellor:
Outsourcing Update," October 31. https://chancellor.utk.edu/2017/10/31
/outsourcing-update/.
Day, Liz. 2013. "How the Maker of TurboTax Fought Free, Simple Tax Filing." Pro-
Publica, March 26. https://www.propublica.org/article/how-the-maker-of
-turbotax-fought-free-simple-tax-filing.
DiIulio, John J., Jr. 2014. "Want Better, Smaller Government? Hire another Million
Federal Bureaucrats." *Washington Post*, August 29. http://wapo.st/1vulpCG?tid=ss
_mail&utm_term=.686f7c5eedc4.
Dockery, Paula. 2013. "When Government, Outsourcing and Technology Meet, It Isn't
Always Pretty." *Tampa Bay Times*, November 1. http://www.tbo.com/list/news
-opinion-commentary/when-government-outsourcing-and-technology-meet-it
-isnt-always-pretty-20131101/.
Donahue, John D. 1989. *The Privatization Decision: Public Ends, Private Means*. New
York: Basic Books.
Farmer, Stephanie, and Donald Cohen. 2014. "Why Chicago's Botched Parking Meter
Privatization Is Also Bad for the Environment." Next City, June 4. https://nextcity
.org/daily/entry/infrastructure-projects-p3-contracts-chicago-parking.
Gore, Al. 1995. *Common Sense Government Works Better and Costs Less*. Third Report of
the National Performance Review. Washington, DC: US Government Printing
Office. ERIC Number: ED387065.
Grynbaum, Michael M. 2012. "Contractor Strikes $500 Million Deal in City Payroll
Scandal." *New York Times*, March 14. https://nyti.ms/2v5oGv4.
Havemann, Judith. 1997. "Welfare Reform Incorporated: Social Policy Going Private."
Washington Post, February 7. http://www.washingtonpost.com/wp-srv/politics
/special/welfare/stories/wf030797.htm?noredirect=on.
Henig, Jeffrey R. 1989. "Privatization in the United States: Theory and Practice." *Political
Science Quarterly* 104(4): 649–670. doi: 10.2307/2151103.
Heritage Foundation. 1983. *Municipal Services: The Privatization Option*. Report.
January 11. https://www.heritage.org/government-regulation/report/municipal
-services-the-privatization-option.
Homeland Security Advisory Council. 2016. *Report of the Subcommittee on Privatized
Immigration Facilities*. December. https://www.dhs.gov/sites/default/files
/publications/DHS%20HSAC%20PIDF%20Final%20Report.pdf.
In the Public Interest. 2013. *Criminal: How Lockup Quotas and Low-Crime Taxes
Guarantee Profits for Private Prison Companies*. September 19. https://www
.inthepublicinterest.org/wp-content/uploads/Criminal-Lockup-Quota-Report
.pdf.Jones, Vernon Dale. 1998. *Downsizing the Federal Government: The Manage-
ment of Public Sector Workforce Reductions*. Armonk, NY: M. E. Sharpe. https://
books.google.com/books?id=Jr5JuQpASJwC.
Kahlenberg, Richard D., and Halley Potter. 2014. "The Original Charter School Vision."
New York Times, August 30. https://nyti.ms/1n9L5wD.
Korten, Tristram. 2014. "Florida Spent Millions on Flawed Fingerprint System." *Miami
Herald*, March 9. http://www.miamiherald.com/news/state/article1961182.html.

Koussier, Thad. 2014. "How America's 'devolution revolution' reshaped its federalism" *Revue française de science politique* 64 (2): 265–287.

Lappin, Harley, 2012. Link published in "Private Prison Corporation Offers Cash in Exchange for State Prisons." *Huffington Post*, February 14. https://www.huffingtonpost.com /2012/02/14/private-prisons-buying-state-prisons_n_1272143.html.

LawTeacher. 2013. *Origin of Public-Private Partnerships*. https://www.lawteacher.net/free -law-essays/commercial-law/origin-of-public-private-partnerships-commercial -law-essay.php?vref=1.

Lewis, Al, and Dow Jones Newswires. 2007. "Parkway Lease Fool's Gambit." *Denver Post*, August 31. https://www.denverpost.com/2007/08/31/parkway-lease-fools-gambit/.

MacLean, Nancy. 2017. *Democracy in Chains: The Deep History of the Radical Right's Stealth Plan for America*. New York: Viking Press.

Mahler, Jonathan. 2018. "How One Conservative Think Tank Is Stocking Trump's Government." *New York Times*, June 20. https://nyti.ms/2MI4k4n.

MarketWatch. 2017a. *CoreCivic, Inc*. https://www.marketwatch.com/investing/stock/cxw /financials.

MarketWatch. 2017b. *Geo Group, Inc*. https://www.marketwatch.com/investing/stock /geo/financials.

MarketWatch. 2017c. *Waste Management, Inc*. https://www.marketwatch.com/investing /stock/wm/financials.

Marshall, Aaron. 2010. "10 Northeast Ohio Charter School Boards Sue White Hat Management Firm." *The Plain Dealer*, May 18. https://www.cleveland.com/open /index.ssf/2010/05/for-profit_management_company.html.

Masterson, Peg. 1986. "Privatization: Should the State Divest?" *Milwaukee Journal-Sentinel*, October 14. https://news.google.com/newspapers?id=zzcjAAAAIBAJ &sjid=fRIEAAAAIBAJ&pg=1856%2C5369791.

Maximus. 2017. *Annual Income Statement*. https://amigobulls.com/stocks/MMS/income -statement/annual.

Mihalopoulous, Dan. 2015. "The Watchdogs: City Hall's $62 Million Blunder." *Chicago Sun-Times*, May 23. https://chicago.suntimes.com/the-watchdogs/the-watchdogs -city-halls-62-million-blunder/.

Miner, Barbara. 2004. "Why the Right Hates Public Education." The Progressive, February 1. http://progressive.org/public-school-shakedown/right-hates-public -education/.

Minto, William, and Karen Minto. 1999. Interview with Robert Poole. *Full Context* 11 (May–June). http://www.fullcontext.info/people/poole_intx.htm. (Link no longer active.) National Alliance for Public Charter Schools. 2015. *A Growing Movement: America's Largest Charter School Communities*. November. http://www.public charters.org/sites/default/files/migrated/wp-content/uploads/2015/11/enrollment share_web.pdf.

Nunberg, Geoffrey. 2005. "Thinking about the Government." *American Prospect*, April 19. http://prospect.org/article/thinking-about-government.

Pauly, Madison. 2016. "A Brief History of America's Private Prison Industry." *Mother Jones*, July–August. https://www.motherjones.com/politics/2016/06/history-of -americas-private-prison-industry-timeline/.

Permenter, Cody. 2013. "Blue Mound Residents Boiling over Water Rate." *Texas Tribune*, March 18. https://www.texastribune.org/2013/03/18/high-water-rates -cause-angst-texas-town/.

Pierce, Neal R., and Robert Guskind. 1984. "The New Right Takes Its Political Show on the Road to Win Power in the States." *National Journal*, October 13. https://www .prwatch.org/files/New_Right_Takes_to_States.doc.

Pirie, Madson. 1985. *Dismantling the State: The Theory and Practice of Privatization*. Dallas, TX: National Center for Policy Analysis.

Reagan, Ronald. 1981. "Text of President Ronald Reagan's Inaugural Address," January 20. https://www.presidency.ucsb.edu/documents/inaugural-address-11.

Reagan, Ronald. 1986. "The President's News Conference," August 12. https://www.reaganfoundation.org/ronald-reagan/reagan-quotes-speeches/news-conference-1/.

Reason Foundation. 2006. Environmental Services and Issues. In Leonard C. Gilroy (ed.), *Transforming Government Services through Privatization*. Annual Privatization Report: 20th Anniversary Edition, August 1. https://reason.org/wp-content/uploads/files/d767317fa4806296191436e95f68082a.pdf.

Sharp, Tracie. 2016. State Policy Network (SPN) fundraising letter, April 22. http://www.documentcloud.org/documents/3984715-SPN-Letter.html#document/p1.

Smith, Fred L. 1987. "Privatization at the Federal Level." *Proceedings of the Academy of Political Science* 36(3): 179–189. doi: 10.2307/1174107.

Smith, Lena. 2017. "We Win! Atlantic City's Water Stays Public." Food and Water Watch, December 22. https://www.foodandwaterwatch.org/impact/we-win-atlantic-city%E2%80%99s-water-stays-public.

Strayhorne. Carole. 2006. "Letter from Texas Comptroller of Public Accounts on Accenture Contract to Senator Shapleigh, Chairman Uresti and Representative Casteel." October 25. http://web.pdx.edu/~pcooper/TexasComptrollerReportonAccentureContract2006.pdf.

Sweeney, Marlisse Silver. 2014. "Critics Alarmed over Pa. Legal Fees Paid to Firms." Corporate Counsel, April 1. https://www.law.com/corpcounsel/almID/1202649211704/Critics%20Alarmed%20Over%20Pa%20Legal%20Fees%20Paid%20to%20Firms/?slreturn=20180519155442. Waste Management, Inc. 2017. 10-K filing to the Securities and Exchange Commission. http://investors.wm.com/mobile.view?c=119743&v=201&d=3&id=12062694&idParam=RV^.

Tracy, Brian, and Edwin J. Feulner. 2012. *The American spirit: celebrating the virtues and values that make us great.* Nashville, Tenn: Thomas Nelson.

Watson, Joe. 2015. "Report Finds Two-Thirds of Private Prison Contracts Include 'Lockup Quotas.'" *Prison Legal News*, July 31. https://www.prisonlegalnews.org/news/2015/jul/31/report-finds-two-thirds-private-prison-contracts-include-lockup-quotas/.

Yang, John E. 1992. "Bush Moves to Ease Sale of Federally Financed Facilities." *Washington Post*, May 1. https://www.washingtonpost.com/archive/politics/1992/05/01/bush-moves-to-ease-sale-of-federally-financed-facilities/3d386795-3591-4992-8369-08c210df24a3/?utm_term=.15de5084eaf4.

Part III

CHALLENGES AND COALITION OPPORTUNITIES

7

BUILDING A PRO-WORKER, PRO-UNION CLIMATE MOVEMENT

Lara Skinner

Addressing climate change requires a major transformation of our economy. Most greenhouse gas emissions come from burning fossil fuels, and we burn fossil fuels to drive our cars, heat and power our homes, produce food, transport goods, and so much more. Every sector of our economy relies on fossil fuels to some extent, and, as a result, transitioning to a sustainable, low-carbon economy is going to require a lot of change—and the change has to happen quickly.

The climate science community agrees that, to avoid the worst impacts of climate change, we need to cut our emissions drastically. In some cases, addressing climate change means entire sectors of the economy, and their associated jobs, will go away. In 2017, several automakers, including General Motors, Volkswagen, Volvo, and Jaguar Land Rover, committed to transitioning their production completely to electric vehicles by the early 2020s. That means we will make far fewer combustion engines and all the related component parts that accompany them. This is akin to the early 1900s, when mass production of the Model T revolutionized transportation and caused the decline of the horse and buggy. Yet, just as the new automobile industry created thousands of new manufacturing jobs, so will the transition to a sustainable, low-carbon economy. The questions at hand are whether this transition will happen quickly enough to stave off the worst effects of climate change and whether the new jobs will be good jobs that will build the middle class of the future or bad jobs that will serve to increase inequality in the United States.

Responding to climate change and transitioning our economy away from high-carbon activities present a number of challenges for unions, especially those connected to the energy sector. This chapter outlines approaches to three major tensions that must be addressed to build a pro-union climate movement. First, I describe the jobs-versus-environment debate that has pitted workers against environmentalists. Second, I discuss the dynamics of ensuring that new energy jobs are good, union jobs. Third, I describe the challenges of implementing "just transition" for workers who are displaced as we move away from fossil fuels. I outline these strategies for building a pro-worker climate movement by drawing on contemporary cases of unions' climate activism, mostly using examples in New York State. In doing so, I examine the challenges that responding to the climate crisis presents for the labor movement and explore how these challenges can be overcome.

We cannot gloss over or trivialize these tensions. Acknowledging and addressing these challenges is essential to enable the labor movement to engage positively in the struggle to stop climate change and create dignity at work. In fact, the dual crises of climate change and inequality of wealth and power are two of the greatest challenges of our time, and, by creating good jobs while addressing climate change, we can address these challenges simultaneously. Put another way, climate change impacts working people first and worst, and the environmental degradation we are experiencing, including climate change, is inextricably linked to a political-economic system that degrades workers and the environment alike. The solutions are linked.

Crafting a pro-worker, pro-union climate agenda opens up important opportunities for the labor movement. With the tremendous amount of work that needs to be done to build a low-carbon economy, this could be an opportunity to expand union membership dramatically. Labor's leadership on climate change also opens up opportunities for labor to build alliances with other social movements, including the growing climate and environmental justice movements, which I argue is important to beat back attempts to weaken unions and transfer wealth and power from working people to the political-economic elite.

Political Divisions on Jobs and the Environment

Within the scientific community, there is no doubt that we have a crisis of climate change. The latest data from climate scientists are deeply disturbing. A report from the National Oceanic and Atmospheric Administration released in March 2018 projects that high-tide flooding may occur every other day or every day in US East Coast and Gulf Coast cities by late this century (National Oceanic and Atmospheric Administration 2018), and these projections assume we curb, rather than increase, our emissions in the coming decades. In February 2018, the Arctic ice was so thin that a ship passed through without the aid of an icebreaker. That is because temperatures there were forty-five degrees Fahrenheit above normal. With a fire season that is now more than a month longer than it used to be, California was ravaged by fires in the past year. Without trees to slow the fall of heavy rains, these fires were followed by unprecedented mudslides and community evacuations. In Maine, where long, cold winters typically kill off ticks, some tick-related diseases have increased thirtyfold in the past decade because ticks are surviving the winter.

One of the main impacts of rising temperatures and rising seas is more frequent and more intense storms. Indeed, the United States was hit by ten major hurricanes during the 2017 season. Hurricane Maria took an unbelievable toll on Puerto Rico. Eight months after the storm hit Puerto Rico, 10 percent of residents still did not have electricity. The economic damage from the storm is estimated at $90 billion; the island's entire GDP for 2017 was $101 billion (Pasch, Penny, and Berg 2019). Avoiding the worst impacts of climate change will require immediate and dramatic action. Scientists agree that our economy needs to be nearly 100 percent carbon-free by 2050, a goal that will require bold action and strategic leadership over the next three decades (United Nations Intergovernmental Panel on Climate Change 2014).

Under President Barack Obama, the United States was not acting at the pace and scale necessary to address the climate crisis, but there was acknowledgment that climate change exists, and Obama took a number of steps in the right direction. The United States signed the Paris Climate Accord, an agreement that took over twenty years to forge, bringing most of the world's countries to the table to pledge that they would reduce their emissions and contribute to efforts to adapt to the impacts of climate change. President Obama initiated the Clean Power Plan through executive order, proposing a path to begin to reduce emissions from power plants in the United States and protect workers and communities in the process. President Obama also increased fuel-economy standards for vehicles, and late in his second term, he denied the construction permit for the Keystone XL oil pipeline, citing the increase in greenhouse gas emissions it would facilitate as well as concerns over how pipeline spills would impact communities along the pipeline route.

President Trump has reversed almost all of the actions President Obama took to address climate change. On the campaign trail, he promised to bring back coal miners' jobs, expand oil and gas production (under Obama, gas extraction was the highest it had ever been), and approve the Keystone XL and Dakota Access pipelines. Indeed, through executive order, he has expedited the process to build the Keystone XL pipeline, initiated the repeal of the Clean Power Plan, and opened up 3.1 million acres of federal lands for drilling and mining. Trump invited leaders of the North American building trades unions to join him in the White House when he signed the executive order approving the Keystone XL pipeline, knowing that this issue has caused deep divisions within the labor movement and between the labor movement and other social movements. Unions currently representing energy-sector workers have typically been more supportive of pipeline construction and less supportive of action on climate change, while unions that do not represent members in the energy sector have often been more engaged in climate-protection efforts. Trump has effectively exploited these tensions and divisions within the labor movement through his promise to expand pipeline construction and oil and gas production. Trump has also appointed people who deny climate change is real and/or run fossil-fuel companies to a number of key positions in agencies that are responsible for protecting our environment and public health, such as Scott Pruitt and Rex Tillerson.

In explaining his actions to expand mining, drilling, and pipeline construction, President Trump points to jobs and the economy. For example, in his first days in office, Trump said, "We're ending intrusive EPA regulations that kill jobs, hurt family farmers and ranchers, and raise the price of energy so quickly and so substantially." Trump argues that he is taking these actions on behalf of working people. He has exploited the age-old narrative that you can have jobs or the environment but you cannot have both, even though a number of US states and countries, such as California, Iowa, Germany, and Denmark, have shown there are significant opportunities for job growth in clean-energy sectors. While giving lip service to the needs of working people in the United States, he has launched a flat-out attack on the environment, and there is little evidence that he will push for new jobs to be "good" jobs.

The challenging political moment at the national level has given rise to the need for positive climate-job examples at the local level. By demonstrating that we can address the climate crisis and create good, union jobs in the process at the local level, we can create scalable models that are ready for implementation when there are receptive leaders at the national level.

Are the New Jobs Good Jobs? What It Takes to Make New Clean-Energy Jobs Good Union Jobs

Hundreds of thousands of union members are currently employed in the energy and fossil-fuel sectors. The *2017 US Energy and Employment Report* estimates that 6.4 million workers are employed in the traditional energy and energy-efficiency sectors (US Department of Energy 2017). The report also estimates that 1.9 million of these workers are in electric power generation and fuel technologies; about 1.1 million in traditional oil, coal, and gas; and about 800,000 in low-carbon-emission generation technologies, including renewables, nuclear, and advanced/low-emission natural gas. Assuming a 6.7 percent unionization rate (the national private-sector unionization rate), nearly 430,000 union members could be employed in the entire energy sector.

Unions fought hard to make these energy-sector jobs good, middle-class jobs with benefits, where workers have dignity and respect on the job. The important role that unions play in improving the quality and safety of energy-sector work is clearly demonstrated in the mining sector. A study examining the relationship between unionization and coal-mine safety from 1993 to 2010 found that unionization is associated with a 14–32 percent drop in traumatic injuries and a 29–83 percent drop in fatalities (Morantz 2013).

Unions in the traditional energy sector have a real concern that the transition to renewable energy will serve to undermine decades of work, and blood, sweat, and tears, that have gone into unionizing this sector. Will there be good jobs for workers to transition to, or will the current well-paid, high-road jobs in the energy sector be replaced with low-pay, low-road jobs in solar, energy efficiency, and other clean-energy sectors? A transition from a good job to a bad job, regardless of the type of industry, is simply unacceptable for many union members and their families.

When the idea of "green jobs" entered the public discourse in the middle of the last decade, there was a lot of talk about the millions of jobs that could be created in clean-energy sectors. One of President Obama's 2008 campaign promises was to create millions of clean-energy jobs—more specifically, his administration estimated that a $150 billion investment through the American Recovery and Reinvestment Act would create five million jobs over ten years. However, green jobs, or what we now call "climate jobs," did not take off at a significant scale until the past decade, and only in certain states that have driven a local pro-climate agenda. Since 2010, the number of jobs in solar installation, for example, has grown more than 200 percent, but these jobs are concentrated in certain states. In 2010, very few workers in the United States were employed in the solar sector; now, approximately 260,000 workers spend about half their time supporting some portion of the solar industry (US Department of Energy 2017). In other words, for a long time, "climate jobs" were a promise, but now they are becoming a reality.

The pace of creation of clean-energy jobs has been increasing. As of April 2018, the fastest-growing jobs in the United States were for solar and wind installers (US Department of Labor 2018). Yet the quality of these jobs is questionable. Most of this work is done by non-union labor, and workers are not well paid, properly trained, or offered benefits for the work. California, the state with the largest number of solar jobs, is a good example of this. A 2015 study found that the majority of solar jobs in California are in the residential rooftop sector and that they are nonunion jobs with an average wage of $14.42 per hour (Jones and Zabin 2015). Conversely, a smaller number of solar jobs in California have been created in the utility-scale solar sector (about 10,000 as of 2015), and these jobs are more likely to be union construction jobs, paying an average of $39 per hour with benefits.

Even progressive states with well-established labor standards in the construction industry have skirted these standards when it comes to clean-energy work. Indeed, in California and New York, both states with powerful labor movements and strong project labor agreements (PLAs) in place for construction work, unions have had to run campaigns pressuring local and state officials to bring solar and energy-efficiency work under existing or new project labor agreements to improve the quality of these jobs. Politicians and agencies are not naturally inclined to link good, union jobs to the new clean-industry economy; creating this link has only happened through advocacy and pressure. More information about these campaigns is provided in the examples that follow.

Similarly, the mainstream environmental movement has not been naturally inclined toward ensuring that the clean-energy economy creates good, union jobs. Until just a few years ago, the mainstream environmental movement (e.g., the Sierra Club, the Natural Resources Defense Council, the National Wildlife Federation, and others) paid little attention to labor issues (Skinner 2012). Since then, however, segments of the mainstream environmental movement, in an effort to neutralize union opposition or positively engage unions in climate-protection efforts, have worked to assess and promote the job-creation benefits of clean-energy projects (see Sierra Club n.d.; Ettenson 2017).

Nevertheless, the mainstream environmental movement has paid less attention to the quality of these jobs. Even when the rhetoric of "good jobs" is used, it often is not accompanied by a deep and nuanced understanding of what it takes to ensure that these jobs are good jobs. Too often, they neglect a real accounting of the number and quality of jobs that will be lost with the transition and fail to do the more difficult work of actually figuring out how to make these new jobs good, union jobs. This neglect, coupled with the failure of some unions to prioritize climate protection, has resulted in tensions between workers' organizations and environmental groups.

Labor Activism on Climate in New York

In New York, several campaigns demonstrate how unions can lead on an agenda that is both pro-union and pro-climate. I describe several organizations that are advocating around climate and labor issues, and the lessons that we can learn from these campaigns.

Climate Jobs New York, a new union-led organization and campaign consisting of building trades, energy, transit, public-sector, and service-sector unions in New York State, provides an example of how unions in energy-related fields can turn clean-energy jobs into good jobs. Climate Jobs New York was sparked by a three-year research, education, and policy initiative led by The Worker Institute at Cornell University's ILR School that brought New York unions together to examine how ambitious climate-protection and clean-energy efforts could drive the creation of good jobs in the state. The campaign is made up of five union federations, as well as individual unions, including the International Brotherhood of Electrical Workers Local 3, Laborers Local 79, Utility Workers Union of America Local 1-2, United Association New York State Pipe Trades, Transport Workers Union, American Federation of State, County and Municipal Employees District Council 37, Service Employees International Union 32BJ, and the New York State Nurses Association. Together, the coalition's unions represent 2.6 million union members in New York State.

Since its launch in 2017, Climate Jobs New York has intervened in the state's energy policy to fight for ambitious climate action, progressive procurement policy, and strong labor standards in a host of clean-energy activities and programs. Presenting a clear, cohesive labor voice in New York's climate and energy debates, combined with lobbying and member education and organizing, has allowed Climate Jobs New York to significantly influence New York State's public debates and policy on clean energy.

In 2017, Climate Jobs New York urged Governor Andrew Cuomo to expand the scale of energy-efficiency and solar activities in New York State. The impetus for this push came from two core interests. First, the current scale and pace of work in New York has not been sufficient to address the climate crisis. Second, scaling up these programs is important for expanding the number of jobs that are created from the work. In response to Climate Jobs New York's policy proposals and numerous meetings with local and state policymakers, Governor Cuomo doubled the amount of funding available for energy-efficiency and solar work in public buildings and schools. Importantly, he also committed to undertaking this work with a project labor agreement (PLA). PLAs, among other things, ensure that workers will receive fair pay and benefits.

Climate Jobs New York also advocated that labor standards be included in all publicly funded renewable-energy projects. Since 2017 New York State has issued multiple major solicitations for the development of renewable energy, and they are important for jump-starting the renewable-energy industry in New York State. However, the solicitations have not included any labor standards. Developers applying to build new renewable-energy projects have not been required to abide by PLAs or prevailing wage or other labor standards. Climate Jobs New York worked to ensure that these solicitations required that winning bidders abide by strong labor standards, ensuring that the state's efforts to develop the renewable-energy industry would lead to the creation of good, middle-class jobs that tackle inequality.

In response to this pressure, in March 2017, Governor Cuomo announced that all renewable-energy solicitations would now require that workers be paid the prevailing wage. Moreover, the twenty-six projects that were awarded under a June 2017 solicitation will have to abide by the prevailing wage provision as well. Speaking to this shift in state policy, Mario Cilento, president of the New York State AFL-CIO, said, "We welcome this partnership with Governor Cuomo to strengthen the economy, while addressing climate change. Expanding the state's commitment to renewable-energy projects is not only an opportunity to make New York a leader in the clean-energy industry, it's an investment in long-term, sustainable middle class jobs in our state. Good paying jobs with benefits allow working men and women to provide for their families while supporting local businesses in their community" (Cuomo 2017).

Climate Jobs New York continues to push for labor standards in all climate work. Governor Cuomo announced in June 2017 that New York State would procure 800 megawatts of offshore wind power over the next two years. Other East Coast states have also made major commitments to develop offshore wind power, including Massachusetts, New Jersey, Maryland, Virginia, and Rhode Island. If all these states implement wind-energy projects, it is likely that the offshore wind power industry could become a major regional employer. In Europe, the offshore wind industry has taken off: Europe has built enough offshore wind capacity to supply 38 gigawatts of electricity (by comparison, the United States has installed only 3 gigawatts of solar and onshore wind capacity combined). Europe has 150,000 workers employed in the wind industry alone.

Unfortunately, only Maryland has included a prevailing wage requirement in its solicitation for offshore wind power. As East Coast states seek to develop a robust offshore wind industry in the United States, it is imperative that strong labor standards be included in these plans from the start. Accordingly, in New York, Climate Jobs New York has begun a push to secure a responsible contracting policy for all offshore wind and other renewable-energy solicitations. The responsible contracting policy helps ensure the state will complete its offshore wind projects on time, on budget, and safely, and will provide good jobs with fair wages and benefits to New York workers.

The success of Climate Jobs New York can in part be credited to the fact that New York has strong unions, a vibrant environmental movement, and politicians who care about workers and the environment. In addition to this, two factors were particularly important. First, unions in the building trades, energy, and transport sectors—unions that represent members in the current energy economy—spearheaded the campaign. They launched the campaign and put the concerns of their existing members in the energy sector, as well as concerns about the quality of jobs in new clean-energy sectors, at the heart of their proposal. This meant that, at its core, the work was grounded in a vision of how New York could tackle the climate crisis but also create good jobs and build more equitable communities.

In the past, union engagement in climate efforts in New York was dominated by public- and service-sector unions that typically do not represent members in the energy sector and thus are not at risk of losing their jobs in the transition to renewable power. Having unions that represent members in the existing energy sector, including constructing and operating coal, oil, and gas power plants, positions these unions as powerful and legitimate messengers for tackling climate change, and doing so in a way that protects current energy-sector workers and ensures the creation of good jobs. Speaking to this point, James Slevin, president of the Utility Workers Union of America Local 1-2, said, "As a union leader who represents thousands of workers currently employed in New York's energy system, whose livelihoods depend on those jobs, I am very concerned about protecting their jobs and addressing climate change, which affects my members, their families, and their communities. This initiative represents the best hope for protecting my members, ensuring new energy jobs are good union jobs, and addressing climate change" (Climate Jobs New York 2017).

The second reason Climate Jobs New York has been successful is that prior to launching the campaign, the unions that make up the coalition participated in a three-year research, education, and training initiative led by The Worker Institute at Cornell. Dubbed a "Climate Jobs Program for New York State," the program helped these unions identify and address challenges related to transitioning to a low-carbon economy and also helped them develop a jobs-focused agenda to drastically reduce greenhouse gas emissions, create good, union jobs, and build communities that are more resilient. The program outlined a pro-worker, pro-union infrastructure plan and allowed these unions to enter the climate-protection debate with a proactive agenda that centered on worker protections and economic justice. Most union engagement prior to Climate Jobs New York's work had been reactive, with unions often responding negatively to plans and proposals developed by the mainstream environmental movement that did not pay enough attention to the labor and employment impacts.

Climate Jobs New York is spearheaded by unions. Other climate-related work in New York has a broader umbrella that brings the power of multiple movements together. For instance, Climate Works for All is a coalition of labor, community, and environmental justice groups in New York City. It is anchored by the Alliance for a Greater New York (ALIGN), the New York City Central Labor Council, and the New York City Environmental Justice Alliance. Similar to Climate Jobs New York, it has focused on winning PLAs for renewable-energy projects. New York City mayor Bill de Blasio committed to increasing the city's solar and energy-efficiency work by including in the city's capital budget money to retrofit 1,000 public schools. Despite the Building and Construction Trades Council of Greater New York having a PLA for all public works in the city, the de Blasio administration argued that solar installations were not public works. It claimed they were separate systems, not part of the building, and thus were outside PLA requirements. The Climate Works for All campaign organized to reverse this initial decision by releasing reports to influence the public debate and through on-the-ground organizing and lobbying of relevant city officials and elected leaders. The campaign was successful in getting New York City to commit to a PLA for all energy-efficiency and solar work on public schools.

Another broad coalition of labor, community, environmental, and environmental justice groups is New York Renews. This group introduced legislation to reduce carbon emissions in New York State that would attach labor standards to clean-energy investments and provide significant funding for worker and community transition. This bill, the Climate and Community Investment Act, represents one of the most progressive carbon-tax proposals in the United States. It raises funds for clean-energy investment by taxing polluters and allocating the revenue in a way that will drive investment in high-road jobs in the renewable-energy, energy-efficiency, and public-transit sectors. In addition, it will protect workers and communities that need support in the transition to a low-carbon economy.

The groups described here organize mostly around legislation and PLAs. Another important strategy for creating good jobs in renewable energy is to unionize new shops. For instance, the Blue-Green Alliance, including the United Auto Workers, is running a campaign to organize Tesla's electric vehicle plant in Fremont, California. It is also pushing the California state government to implement a rule that Tesla must be certified as a "fair and responsible workplace" in order for its customers to qualify for publicly funded state electric-vehicle rebates. For the last several years, Tesla has expanded its electric-vehicle manufacturing facilities in California and Oregon with nonunion labor.

These examples of including a progressive procurement policy and strong labor standards in new clean-energy projects highlight two important factors in labor's engagement in climate-protection efforts. First, it is much more likely that new jobs in the clean-energy economy will be good jobs if unions are proactively involved in the development and implementation of clean-energy policy and programs. Unions are well equipped and best positioned to collaborate with local and state government, the renewable-energy industry, and other partners to identify workforce gaps and the job standards needed to help set an industry precedent for the creation of high-quality jobs.

The second lesson from these examples is that successfully linking jobs and the environment by securing PLAs for renewable-energy projects will attract broader and deeper engagement from unions in future efforts. These local examples, if scaled up, can offer important lessons for building national-level coalitions to address the dual crises of climate change and inequality, with labor unions at the helm.

For climate and environmental groups that seek to partner with the labor movement around climate change in more robust ways, learning to advocate for the specific policies that will make these jobs good jobs is important. Distrust of the environmental movement is a fairly common sentiment in the labor movement, particularly in cases where environmental organizations have called for power plants to be shut down and there has been no constructive dialogue with the union representing members at the plant. Yet building a broader movement, or a movement of movements, for climate and economic justice will be important to tackling the climate crisis at the scale and pace necessary to avoid the worst impacts of climate change. This movement-building work that combines the power of the environmental and labor movements can also help defend workers' rights and collective representation, which is an attendant benefit of this work.

The Sierra Club in New York State is a good example of how an environmental organization can become a powerful champion for both climate protection and high-quality jobs. Lisa Dix, the director of the New York State Sierra Club, has developed strong relationships with unions in the state and has worked closely with unions to secure a project labor agreement for New York's first wind farm. Not unrelated to this work, at the national level, the Sierra Club established a Labor and Environmental Justice Division to help address equity issues in the Sierra Club's climate work.

Developing a More Sophisticated Approach to Just Transition

A major aspect of developing and advancing a pro-worker, pro-union climate agenda is figuring out how to implement successful "just transition" programs. Workers and communities are negatively impacted by plant closures and other changes that come about because of the shift from high-carbon to low-carbon economic activities, and real solutions must be developed to protect them.

The concept of "just transition" was developed by Tony Mazzocchi, leader of the Oil, Chemical and Atomic Workers Union, and is a useful ideological tool for supporting and protecting workers in times of transition. Mazzocchi came up with this idea to protect his members in the nuclear sector while also advocating for the phaseout of nuclear power in support of nuclear disarmament and the health of his members. Just transition plans typically include wage and benefit replacement, retraining or education funds, retention bonuses, and financial support for the relocation of members impacted by plant or facility closures.

Unfortunately, in practice, the call for a just transition has been a way for advocates of climate action to pay lip service to protecting and supporting workers in this transition without having a plan to actually secure and implement a just transition. Understanding the tensions around just transition is an important step in more positively engaging unions in the fight against climate change. Several just transition plans have been successfully implemented in the last few years. I discuss these cases later in this section to highlight what we can learn from these efforts to inform future just transition efforts.

Just transition is complicated for several reasons. One of the most challenging parts of providing a just transition for workers and communities impacted, for example, by a plant closing is that the plant is often the main economic actor for a region. It is often the largest employer in the region and provides significant indirect economic benefits for the community. This means that the whole economy, including seemingly unrelated jobs, may be negatively impacted by the loss of the plant. In short, it is very unlikely that there will be other jobs for impacted workers to transition to unless they are willing to move. To create new economic activity that can support workers who have lost their jobs takes a tremendous amount of time and a concerted and strategic planning effort.

Instead, what usually happens is that the private company that owns or operates the plant decides to shut down the plant with very little notice for the workers or the community. This has been especially common in the last few years, with coal plants shutting down because they cannot compete with cheap natural gas and/or because of pressure to phase out fossil fuels in favor of renewable power generation. In New York, for example, large businesses are required to provide employees and the Department of Labor with early warning of a facility closure and layoffs (New York State Department of Labor n.d.). However, the law only requires businesses to provide ninety days' notice prior to closing, which is not nearly enough time to craft a successful just transition plan.

For unions in particular, successful just transition requires having the bargaining and/or political power to secure adequate resources for impacted members—wages, benefits, retraining funds, transfers to other plants, retention bonuses, and more—from the employer or government. Ideally, the union would also work alongside the local community that will be impacted, using the combined strength of the union and community to secure adequate support for their transition.

But union campaigns alone are rarely enough. Just transition is challenging in a deregulated, market-based economy. Given the scale and pace of the transition that climate change requires, from fossil fuels to renewable energy, a proactive, rational, well-funded, and well-coordinated approach to closing existing fossil-fuel plants and building new renewable-energy capacity is what is really needed. Direct, coordinated, and multilevel government intervention is required to determine which plants should close first, based on clear community- and worker-oriented criteria; to identify a source of funding for implementing just transition programs; and to involve all relevant stakeholders in crafting these plans.

Canada provides an example of what this approach could look like. The Canadian Labour Congress (the equivalent of the AFL-CIO in Canada) proposed a just transition task force and achieved this in 2018. The task force is composed of representatives from unions, industry, government, and community groups and is charged with making recommendations for how to approach Canada's just transition efforts, including developing the principles that should guide their just transition efforts.

At the provincial level, the Alberta Federation of Labour convened a multiyear process to create and implement a just transition for their coal workers in the province. At the culmination of the process, it produced a report called "Getting It Right," and it has been able to work with the Alberta government to establish a just transition task force to discuss and begin the implementation of this transition (Alberta Federation of Labour 2017). The Canadian examples of just transition are unique because they involve designing and implementing transition for whole sectors, with government intervention and involvement. The effectiveness of these task force efforts is still to be determined; clearly, continued pressure from the labor movement and other allies will be necessary to actually realize their just transition plans.

Proposals for these sorts of task forces are also emerging in the United States. Climate Jobs New York, for example, has proposed that New York State establish a just transition task force to proactively plan a transition for energy-sector workers. This proposed task force would bring together representatives from labor, industry, and government. It would examine what it will take for New York State to transition to a nearly decarbonized economy—how much generation needs to be retired and replaced, how many workers will be impacted, the quality of their jobs, the impact on the community, and other related issues.

In the United States, there are also a few examples of plant- or facility-level "just transitions." In California, the International Brotherhood of Electrical Workers (IBEW) Local 1245, Friends of the Earth, and the Pacific Gas and Electric Company came together to develop a transition plan for workers at the Diablo Canyon nuclear plant. This plant's nuclear reactors will be closed in 2024 and 2025, and it currently employs 1,500 workers. The negotiated just transition program provides $211.3 million for employee retention, $11.3 million for employee retraining, and an employee severance program. Retention bonuses of 15–25 percent will be provided, on top of annual salary, for every year workers stay until 2023.

The Utility Workers Union of America (UWUA) Local 1-2 in New York is in the process of securing a similar deal for its members at the Indian Point nuclear facility, owned by Entergy. The facility employs 450 UWUA members out of a total workforce of about 700. In their latest round of negotiations, UWUA Local 1-2 was able to secure retention bonuses for its members, retraining funds, and reassignments to other Entergy plants for those who want them. Complicating the process, Entergy pays about $30 million per year in property taxes. Some conversations have begun in the community surrounding Indian Point about how to replace the $30 million in taxes per year that it will lose.

To further complicate matters, according to federal law, Entergy has fifty years to decommission the plant (remove the nuclear reactive materials on-site) and can sell the decommission funds (about $100 million) to another company. It is possible that Entergy, or the company that it sells the plant and decommission funds to, will choose to invest those funds, in the hope of increasing their value, before applying the funds to the actual decommissioning of the plant. Delaying the decommissioning of the plant puts both the current workers at the facility and the community in limbo. The union would like its current members at the plant to be able to prolong their employment there by performing the decommissioning work, but the company might delay the decommissioning, while the funds are gaining interest through investments, for up to fifty years. The decommissioning work will likely take five to seven years, but the workers cannot wait decades for this work to begin. Of course, having the existing workers at the plant do this work seems beneficial to the company and local community, given the workers' intimate knowledge of the plant's operation, but this may not be the company's primary interest. On the community side, not knowing exactly when the plant will be decommissioned and whether the land it is on will be available for other activities makes it challenging to plan how else they might use this land and how to replace the tax revenue lost after Indian Point's closure.

Concerned with these sorts of issues, the Western New York Area Labor Federation and the Clean Air Coalition worked on legislation in New York State that allows communities to apply for tax-replacement funds. After NRG Energy decided to close the Huntley coal-fired power plant in western New York in 2015, these groups pushed for and won passage of the Fossil Fuel Plant Closure Act. Under this legislation, communities that will lose significant tax revenues because of the closure of a plant can apply to receive replacement tax payments.

In another example, at a plant in Tonawanda, New York, the IBEW local that represented plant workers was able to find positions for their members at other plants operated by NRG or to secure "bridge to retirement" funds for workers who were interested in transitioning to retirement.

However, it is important to note that there are key differences in the plant closures and transitions described here. In the case of Indian Point, the company that owns it, Entergy, is a multibillion-dollar company making billions of dollars in profits each year, including from Indian Point. This meant that there were resources that could be secured for just transition.

In the case of coal-plant closures, it is often no longer financially attractive for the owners to keep it open, often because of the low cost of natural gas, and it may be in bankruptcy. As a result, the plant is closed quickly, and with few resources available, it is difficult for the union or community to secure a good just transition plan. Of course, the strength and resources of a union representing workers at a plant and the presence of organized allies also determine the quality of a just transition plan or whether one is even negotiated at all.

Conclusion

Looking ahead, I believe unions' engagement in climate action is important for three main reasons. First, it is only through the combined power of the labor movement, the environmental movement, and other movements that climate change will be tackled, given the power of the fossil-fuel industry and its allies. Second, if unions are not involved in the transition to a low-carbon, sustainable economy, it is unlikely that the new economy will protect workers or ensure that new clean jobs are good jobs. Finally, this transition presents unions with a major opportunity to expand union jobs and power. Because of the efforts of Climate Jobs New York, all future renewable-energy developments in New York will have to pay the prevailing wage and, in many cases, participate in a project labor agreement. From the ground up, these new industries are now more likely to provide high-quality jobs with benefits and the opportunity for women and people of color to enter apprentice programs and pathways to lifelong construction careers.

But, as I explained, there are real tensions and obstacles to acknowledge and overcome in order for labor to positively and powerfully engage in climate-protection efforts. The "jobs versus environment" debate is still widely used to divide the labor and environmental movements and undermine climate-protection efforts, and these tensions are reinforced when new jobs in the clean-energy sector are poor-quality jobs or when the negative social and employment consequences of this transition are not properly or meaningfully addressed. Demonstrating that both good jobs and a healthy environment are achievable requires overcoming these obstacles. This means figuring out what it will take to make this an equitable transition with high-road jobs and adequately protecting and supporting workers and communities in the transition to a low-carbon economy.

The examples of labor's engagement in climate action discussed here provide us with some key lessons about what it will take to reposition unions as an engine to tackle the climate crisis rather than an obstacle to doing so, and to reframe the public debate to forge an unbreakable link between worker protections, economic justice, and climate justice. The active engagement of unions in the efforts to advance climate action is critical. Unions are best positioned and have the relevant knowledge to ensure that the interests and needs of workers are addressed during this transition. For many years, unions have either not been engaged in climate-protection efforts at all or have only engaged reactively, in response to other movements' efforts to implement climate action. In short, labor's leadership on this issue is essential to realizing a pro-worker, pro-union climate agenda.

Like most campaigns, tackling climate change and avoiding its worst impacts requires building and wielding power. It is difficult for labor to step up to lead on this issue at a time when workers' rights and collective representation are under increasing attack, but workers and the environment are often attacked by the same political-economic forces. This means that joining forces with other movements will greatly help the labor movement achieve economic and climate justice and in broader struggles for social justice. Simply put, a broad, diverse, inclusive, and powerful movement is needed.

The examples I discussed also point to the important role that government will play in ensuring an equitable transition to a low-carbon economy. Union and community coalitions and actions are not enough in most cases. Government regulation and legislation, including paying the prevailing wage, project labor agreements, the establishment of just transition task forces, and other initiatives, are necessary to address the needs of workers and communities.

Despite the challenges and obstacles that addressing climate change presents to the labor movement, this political moment demands a renewed effort to envision and realize a pro-worker, pro-union climate agenda that can overcome the traditional jobs-versus-environment divide. Tackling the climate crisis, and linking it to the struggle to reverse inequality, can help build a powerful movement for economic and climate justice that expands union jobs and power in new, clean-energy sectors and helps avoid the worst impacts of climate change. I hope the examples given here of labor's leadership on climate can help spark this kind of movement and inform other efforts to broadly and deeply engage unions in one of the most important social issues of our time—climate change.

References

Alberta Federation of Labour. 2017. *Getting It Right: A Just Transition Strategy for Alberta's Coal Workers.* https://digital.library.yorku.ca/yul-1121960/getting-it-right-just-transition-strategy-albertas-coal-workers.

Climate Jobs New York. 2017. "New Pro-Climate, Pro-Worker Coalition of New York's Energy, Transport and Building Trades and Service Unions." Press release, June 2.

Cuomo, Andrew M. 2017. Press Release: Governor Cuomo Announces Major Climate and Jobs Initiative in Partnership with Worker Institute at Cornell University's ILR School and Climate Jobs NY to Help Create 40,000 Clean Energy Jobs by 2020, June 2. https://www.governor.ny.gov/news/governor-cuomo-announces-major-climate-and-jobs-initiative-partnership-worker-institute-cornell.

Ettenson, Lara. 2017. "Pathways to Clean Energy Can Support Jobs and Communities." Natural Resources Defense Council Expertblog, September 21. https://www.nrdc.org/experts/lara-ettenson/pathways-clean-energy-can-support-jobs-and-communities.

Jones, Betony, and Carol Zabin. 2015. *Are Solar Energy Jobs Good Jobs?* University of California Berkeley Labor Center, July 2. http://laborcenter.berkeley.edu/are-solar-energy-jobs-good-jobs/.

Morantz, Alison D. 2013. "Coal Mine Safety: Do Unions Make a Difference?" *ILR Review* 66(1): 88–116.

National Oceanic and Atmospheric Administration. 2018. *Patterns and Projections of High Tide Flooding along the U.S. Coastline Using a Common Impact Threshold.* NOAA Technical Report NOS CO-OPS 086. https://tidesandcurrents.noaa.gov/publications/techrpt86_PaP_of_HTFlooding.pdf.

New York State Department of Labor. n.d. *Work Adjustment and Retraining Notification.* Accessed August 16, 2018. https://labor.ny.gov/workforcenypartners/warn/warnportal.shtm.

Pasch, Richard J., Andrew B. Penny, and Robbie Berg. 2019. National Hurricane Center Tropical Cyclone Report. National Oceanic and Atmospheric Organization, February 14. https://www.nhc.noaa.gov/data/tcr/AL152017_Maria.pdf.

Sierra Club. n.d. "Clean Energy Jobs." Accessed August 16, 2018. https://content
.sierraclub.org/coal/texas/clean-energy-jobs.

Skinner, Lara. 2012. *Recycle or Reimagine: Tracking the Direction of the U.S. Environmental Movement.* Rosa Luxemburg Stiftung New York Office, November. http://www
.rosalux-nyc.org/wp-content/files_mf/skinner_recycle_reimagine93.pdf.

United Nations Intergovernmental Panel on Climate Change. 2014. *Climate Change
2014 Synthesis Report.* http://www.ipcc.ch/pdf/assessment-report/ar5/syr/SYR
_AR5_FINAL_full_wcover.pdf.

US Department of Energy. 2017. *2017 US Energy and Employment Report.* https://www
.energy.gov/eere/solarpoweringamerica/2017-us-energy-and-employment-report.

US Department of Labor, Bureau of Labor Statistics. 2018. *Fastest Growing Occupations.*
April. https://www.bls.gov/emp/tables/fastest-growing-occupations.htm.

8

FROM CO-OPTATION TO RADICAL RESISTANCE: AN EXAMINATION OF ORGANIZED LABOR'S RESPONSE(S) TO IMMIGRANT RIGHTS IN THE ERA OF TRUMP

Shannon Gleeson

Introduction

When Donald Trump kicked off his presidential campaign, a key part of his message was a direct and unapologetic demonization of immigrants and communities of color. Since taking power, the Trump administration has made good on its promise not only to continue but to escalate the legacies of criminalization from previous administrations. The substantive changes are undeniable. They include rendering all undocumented immigrants at risk for deportation (Law 2017); disregarding previously recognized safe spaces (schools, churches, courthouses, and even labor commissioner hearings) (Kitroeff 2017); and ramping up the number of immigration enforcement personnel, workplace audits, and onsite raids (Kitroeff 2018; Thomsen 2018).

The union movement's response to these attacks on immigrant workers has varied, ranging from indignant rage that punches back to eager photo opportunities in the Oval Office (Scheiber 2017). In many ways, this variation is not surprising. On the issue of immigration, the labor movement has long been divided, both on the primary question of immigrant inclusion and later on the details of what inclusion looks like. The labor movement is by no means monolithic, and these differences appear not only between industries but also by geography and between rank-and-file members and their leadership.

This chapter uses unions' public statements in the press and on social media to analyze labor's position on the Trump immigration agenda. First, I adopt a historical perspective to document how the major institutions within the union movement have responded to the complex "immigration question" in the past and now, what distinct policy positions have emerged, and the coalitions that have been struck to achieve them. Second, I analyze the official positions of labor movement federation leadership. Finally, I demonstrate how the variation in union response emerges at the state and local level by examining union responses to three anti-immigrant policy changes: (1) increases in deportations; (2) elimination of temporary programs such as Deferred Action for Childhood Arrivals (DACA) and Temporary Protected Status (TPS); and (3) implementation of a travel ban for immigrants from seven predominantly Muslim countries. Through each of them, I also show how some advocates within the labor movement have tried simultaneously to build alliances with black, Muslim, and LGBT workers. I end by considering what the Trump administration has meant for the emerging platform and tactics of immigrant rights within organized labor less than two decades since the American Federation of Labor and Congress of Industrial Organizations (AFL-CIO) reversed its previously explicitly anti-immigrant platform.

Immigrants and the Labor Movement: A Retrospective

Any story of the role of immigrants in the labor movement must start with an obligatory retrospective on unions' dynamic position toward immigrants over time. Labor historians and social movement scholars elsewhere have documented this history far more meticulously than I can do here, but a few key points are important for understanding the range of positions the labor movement has taken over time.

From the founding of the AFL-CIO, the federation has been an inconsistent supporter of immigrant rights and, at times, a bastion of nativism. Samuel Gompers, whom the federation has enshrined as "the first and longest-serving president of the American Federation of Labor" and to whom "the American labor movement owes its structure and characteristic strategies" (AFL-CIO 2018b), was a renowned racist and xenophobe, despite his own immigrant origins. His words are emblazoned in union literature and on labor schools across the country, often unreflexively. Even civil rights leaders such as Cesar Chavez, the United Farmworkers icon who spearheaded the Delano grape boycott, have a mixed legacy on undocumented immigrants. Though he often viewed them as scab labor, Chavez "evolved" and, along with Dolores Huerta, has become an icon of immigrant rights, with significant influence from the Chicano movement of the era (Grossman 2014; Bender 2017).

In 1986, the Immigration Reform and Control Act granted amnesty to nearly three million undocumented immigrants but also created the current employer sanctions policy, which criminalizes the hiring of undocumented workers. The AFL-CIO initially championed this policy, citing fears that undocumented immigrants would drive down "fair wage levels" and "employment opportunities" for "American citizens and legal immigrants" (Tichenor 2015). With significant pressure from below, in 2000, the AFL-CIO denounced the employer sanctions policy and called for a range of other rights and benefits to lift up the lives of undocumented immigrants. As documented by Hamlin (2008), these efforts trace back to the Labor Immigrant Organizing Network, a coalition of advocates from the union (the Service Employees International Union, or SEIU, and UNITE HERE in particular) and immigrant rights communities. What began as a Northern California (and especially San Francisco Bay Area) effort, paired with steady organizing efforts targeting top leadership in Washington, D.C., eventually led the California State Federation of Labor to introduce the resolution. The eventual resolution included full-scale legalization of those "who are working hard, paying taxes and contributing to their communities . . . [f]ull protection of workplace rights, including the right to organize . . . and stiff and meaningful penalties for employers who break immigration and labor laws in order to exploit workers." The statement also called for support for the undocumented victims of the 9/11 attacks, reform of guest-worker policies, and investment in union democracy (AFL-CIO 2001).

In the last several decades, several immigrant union victories have been won, such as SEIU's Justice for Janitors, UNITE HERE's Hotel Workers Rising, and the Retail, Wholesale and Department Store Union's campaign to organize car washes, among others (Sherman and Voss 2000; Milkman 2006; Milkman and Ott 2014). However, immigrant advocates in the union movement have not always agreed on a way forward. Proposals for a guest-worker program (originally supported by some facets of SEIU and the United Food and Commercial Workers, UFCW) have been rejected by other labor leaders, calling for a path to citizenship (Williams 2007). During Barack Obama's presidency, the union movement also split on whether a carved-out solution for "DREAMers" would be an acceptable compromise on the road to comprehensive immigration reform (Nicholls 2013).

Enter Trump. In the first year of his presidency, Donald Trump initiated a dizzying list of immigration reforms, focused on "enforcement-first" policies that capitalize on the deportation machine perfected under the Obama administration. In a short time, Trump successfully implemented an effective "Muslim ban," ended new applications to the DACA program, attempted to decimate the TPS program, and created a deportation free-for-all. The administration's zero-tolerance policy also resulted in the separation of thousands of children from their detained parents and a litany of human rights abuses as a "caravan" of Central American refugees arrived at the southern border in late 2018. As the findings presented here will illustrate, labor's response to these and other attacks on immigrants varied across industries and places and included some critical blind spots and contradictions.

Official Position of Federation Leadership

The AFL-CIO has struggled to balance its formal position in support of immigrants with charges that it is not doing enough to reach out to current and potential immigrant union members, and that its top leadership does not reflect the backgrounds and concerns of the rank and file. Formally, the AFL-CIO has explicitly tied the fate of immigrants to that of all working people in its advocacy: "The entire workforce suffers when millions struggle to support their families without a way to speak up on the job, and ramping up fear in our workplaces only serves to increase exploitation. Instead of deporting immigrants, we need to ensure that all working people have rights on the job and are able to exercise them without fear of retaliation" (AFL-CIO 2018a). One of the AFL-CIO's most vocal champions of immigrant rights, its vice president, Tefere Gebre, reiterated the labor movement's support for full citizenship: "We don't believe anything less than a pathway to citizenship is really a true immigration reform. We are very proud to be fighting for pathway to citizenship, not just any kind of immigration reform, but fully incorporating everybody who works in this country to contribute, own it, and be part of this country" (Sampat 2016). Efforts spearheaded by key immigrant workers' unions such as UFCW and UNITE HERE also motivated the federation to promote contract language that protects workers from immigration-based retaliation and curtails the use of E-Verify, a largely voluntary web-based system meant to allow employers to confirm work authorization of newly hired employees.

The AFL-CIO began to invest in immigration training in 2006, following the massive and unprecedented (and some say never again replicated) protests that same year, when congressional conversations around comprehensive immigration were still going full steam (AFL-CIO 2015a). Following Obama's 2012 and 2014 actions, the federation also engaged its membership through workers' rights webinars and community workshops designed to prepare immigrants and their families to apply for the programs. Some unions even provided grants and loans to cover applications and legal fees. Conversations with union leaders reveal that much of this work (including outreach, documentation preparation, and referrals to legal counsel) came from the ground up, with minimal national coordination. The AFL-CIO also began to forge an intentional relationship with "Dreamer" groups, particularly United We Dream. When the 2014 Deferred Action for Parental Accountability (DAPA) program (which would have provided legal status to over four million parents of citizen and legal permanent resident children) stalled in the courts, local efforts shifted to comprehensive efforts for other forms of relief.

In 2015, the AFL-CIO kicked off a national campaign around naturalization and citizenship, also coordinated with its get-out-the-vote efforts. To do so, the federation worked with community-based organizations and other service-provider collaboratives, such as the National Partnership for New Americans and the AFL-CIO Lawyers Coordinating Committee. Initiatives such as ¡Adelante We Rise! (through Working America) in part came out of this era (AFL-CIO 2015a, 2015b; Los Angeles Federation of Labor 2016a). On the ground, unions such as the UFCW led these efforts through their Union Citizenship and Action Network. Similar initiatives were sponsored by other unions, including UNITE HERE, the Laborers' International Union of North America (LIUNA), and trade unions, but those with far fewer immigrant members, such as the Communications Workers of America (CWA) and the American Federation of Teachers (AFT), also engaged.

However, the AFL-CIO's position on immigration policy and its posture toward immigrant workers has not been without controversy, with some within the movement claiming that the leadership has not gone far enough. For example, when the Change to Win coalition split with the AFL-CIO a decade ago, it claimed that the federation had become overly political and unwilling to organize the largely immigrant workforce in key low-wage industries (Hamlin 2008). Since then, these concerns have broadened to claims that the federation is failing to address issues of racial justice, despite formal declarations from above (AFL-CIO 2017b). In particular, the departure of many women of color from the organization has raised questions about the work still needed to align the federation's rhetoric with its practices. Staff holding immigration-related positions have left the federation, such as the assistant to the president for immigrant and community action; the specialist on immigration community action; the national director of worker center partnerships and deputy director of community engagement; and the director and program coordinator of the civil, human, and women's rights department of the AFL-CIO.

The contradictions within the AFL-CIO are perhaps most visible within North America's Building Trades Unions (NABTU). NABTU is one of six trades departments within the AFL-CIO, representing members in fourteen building trade unions. Currently, the NABTU website advocates for solidarity and a "unified labor movement in urging Congress to pursue a solution to our broken immigration system that is comprehensive and puts workers first. Without reform, workers will continue to suffer at the hands of exploitative and unscrupulous employers." It also calls for an "informed" visa system that allows for temporary and permanent migration and "a plan for operational control of our borders." NABTU has long been a supporter of "operational control of our borders" (what some see as union-made border militarization), the E-Verify system, and the H-2B guest-worker program (NABTU 2018). In fact, NABTU never took an official position on 2012's DACA or 2014's DAPA. Its official statement makes no mention of stemming mass deportation or of refugee communities. In the weeks leading up to the 2016 presidential election, a top staff person for a building trades organization explained to me candidly that the best they could do for the cause of immigrant rights was to keep their organization away from the seemingly deadlocked deliberations in Congress—that, in practice, neutrality was as close as they were going to get to championing the rights of immigrants.

NABTU's position stems in part from construction unions' almost complete loss of the residential building sector, which is now filled by mostly low-road contracted labor. To many in the organization, "the anxiety of displacement is real," compared to other industries, where direct competition is more of an abstraction. This is in part because the construction industry faces distinct issues compared to other sectors. For example, E-Verify is a particularly salient issue for public works projects that receive federal funding. Furthermore, independent contractor misclassification, a rampant issue that drives the race to the bottom in an industry driven by bidding wars, has in fact become a vehicle for avoiding E-Verify liability.

This is not to say that the construction unions are uniform in their position. One of the clearest examples of this pushback took place at the NABTU Legislative Conference in April 2017, where Trump delivered a speech. Several members of the San Diego County Building and Construction Trades Council, including IBEW Local 569, donned Bernie (Sanders) shirts, held up #RESIST signs, and turned their back on Trump (Dimaggio 2017). Though not a formal part of NABTU (but certainly a major leader in the sector), the United Steelworkers (USW) has also been engaged in pushing back against anti-immigrant sentiment in the name of workers. The national USW organization recently tweeted at Ted Cruz to "please stop name-dropping #Steelworkers in your attempts to divide & distract. We stand w/ Dreamers & their families. We are proud to fight for a true path to citizenship. Next time you mention us, mention we ALWAYS welcomed all." The group pointed to the USW's founding principles, which start with a declaration to "unite in one organization, regardless of creed, color or nationality, all workmen and working women eligible for membership" (United Steelworkers 2018). This posture, however, stands in contradiction to both NABTU and USW's aligned support of the president's policies of economic nationalism and "America First."

From Triage to Sustained Resistance in the Trump Era

Changes in the Trump era have affected immigrant workers across the country. However, the way specific forms of advocacy are being deployed on behalf of immigrants varies substantially from place to place, depending on the local demography, labor market, and political context of the communities in which union affiliates are operating. These differences shape the political agendas that unions are engaging in on behalf of immigrants, and the community coalitions in which unions are participating (de Graauw, Gleeson, and Bada 2018). As these findings also reveal, the tactics adopted by particular pro-immigrant unions have also differed, in part as a result of the given organization's history vis-à-vis immigrant members, its leadership structure, and the dynamics of the industries it represents. In the remainder of this chapter, I examine these differences from the perspective of three main points of entry to immigrant advocacy that unions are approaching: (1) antideportation efforts; (2) the campaigns to save DACA and TPS; and (3) support of refugees and opposition to Islamophobia.

Fighting Deportation and Forging Sanctuary Unions

In the immediate aftermath of the election, several local labor federations called out the Trump administration's rhetoric and devotion to a ramped-up mass deportation effort. When the push toward local sanctuary cities prompted threats from the Trump administration to defund those cities and even arrest their mayors (Edelman 2018), and, many believe, target them for raids, labor organizations pushed back.

AFL-CIO federations in major immigrant-receiving cities have been the most vocal. For example, both the Los Angeles and the Orange County Federations of Labor vowed to stand "with immigrants and their families" and "against policies of hate and fear." Those federations also vowed to launch an effort to push back against the coming assault on sanctuary cities and vowed to "actively press for a large-scale immigration legal defense effort to ensure every immigrant is equipped to defend themselves" (Los Angeles Federation of Labor 2016b; Orange County Labor Federation 2017). Los Angeles Federation leader Rusty Hicks even went so far as to declare in the weeks following Trump's inauguration, "We'll stand in front of our Sisters & Brothers to stop Trump & ensure every immigrant has an attorney to defend their rights" (Los Angeles Federation of Labor 2017a). Similarly, the Chicago Federation of Labor, led by a longtime immigrant rights activist, harkened back to the nineteenth-century history of the iconic Haymarket affair as a direct parallel to the contemporary fight for immigrant rights and "committed to continuing to fight so that anyone who seeks refuge here receives the protection they desire" (Chicago Federation of Labor 2017). In Seattle, the Washington State Labor Council passed a resolution on immigration and the labor movement, and the importance of refugees to the state. It also lauded "Know Your Rights" workshops sponsored locally by UFCW, the Teamsters, SEIU, UNITE HERE, and the United Automobile Workers and reiterated King County's policies on providing sanctuary for undocumented immigrants and honoring only "detainer requests that are accompanied by a criminal warrant issued by a federal judge or magistrate" (Washington State Labor Council, AFL-CIO 2017).

In less immigrant-friendly places, unions had to contend with nativism from their state legislatures. When the Texas governor signed the "show me your papers" Senate Bill 4, the president of the Texas State Labor Federation marked it as one of the saddest days he had ever spent around the state legislature. He declared, "This bill will harm all working people. Immigrants do some of the hardest jobs in our state and are net contributors not just to our economy, but to our future. SB 4 will not only make it easier for unscrupulous employers to deny important workplace rights to immigrants, but will also undermine important labor standards for all workers" (Texas AFL-CIO 2017b). The organization similarly rebuked the bill for its effects on union members in law enforcement. Local and regional labor councils responded as well. The Harris County Labor Assembly (part of the newly formed Texas Gulf Coast Area Labor Federation) vowed to protect immigrant families and to carry out the Houston mayor's promise that his city would be a "welcoming city" (Texas AFL-CIO 2017a). Five hours north, in Dallas, the labor council reiterated its commitment to being a "sanctuary organization for those in the shadows" and vowed to continue working with the Texas Organizing Project and the Workers Defense Project to see this promise through (Lantz 2017a).

Despite these proclamations, unions have been limited in their practical ability to launch a resistance to deportation efforts. Efforts to leverage union contracts to protect immigrants can be traced back to the 1990s. In this regard, California unions have led the way, innovating policies that have ultimately had national reach (Bacon 2018). As a result, unions such as UNITE HERE Local 2 include language in their collective-bargaining contracts that protect a worker from losing seniority if their immigration status changes and prevent a change of ownership from triggering new verification requirements. California unions have also promoted the TRUST Act, which limits local jails from holding people for extra time to cooperate with federal immigration enforcement actions. In the wake of a ramp-up of worksite raids and audits, more recently targeting Northern California (Aleaziz 2018), unions also promoted California Assembly Bill 450 (currently facing a challenge by the US Department of Justice), which would limit employers' ability to cooperate with federal immigration officials in the absence of a signed judicial warrant.

Efforts to protect immigrants from deportation have also required that labor examine state policies that involve union members. These include, for example, the legacy of local "broken-windows" policing efforts that create a pipeline to deportation, even in sanctuary cities with all the official protections in place. Some immigrant rights activists have called on the AFL-CIO, as well as labor schools with which they do business, to look critically at the law enforcement unions they represent. Activists have called on the federation to expel the National Border Patrol Council, which represents 14,000 US Border Patrol agents (Vasquez 2016), as well as police unions, which are seen to "staunchly defend [bad cops and fight] reforms with inflammatory rhetoric" (Nolan 2016).

The Call to Save DACA and TPS

In addition to advocating defensive policies to protect immigrant workers at risk of deportation, unions have also pushed for programs that would provide affirmative relief in an era when comprehensive immigration reform is elusive. The two largest of these programs are Deferred Action for Childhood Arrivals (DACA) (2012), intended for young immigrants who arrived as children, and the long-standing Temporary Protected Status (TPS) program, which benefits nationals of designated countries that have suffered a recognized political or natural disaster. Both policies provide work authorization and deportation relief and have come under attack in the Trump era.

DACA, which has received far more national attention, has posed a logistical challenge to the union movement. Early on, and after significant disagreement about the policy agenda for immigration (Nicholls 2013), the labor movement was a key ally of affected "Dreamers" and a key partner of the advocacy group United We Dream. This support was revitalized when Attorney General Jeff Sessions rescinded the program on September 5, 2017, prompting a series of legal challenges and vocal denouncements from the AFL-CIO and the Labor Council for Latin American Advancement. Labor leaders framed this advocacy as a reaction to the administration's attack on young working people, which would make them even more vulnerable to employer abuse (Quinnell 2017b). DACA has benefited around 800,000 young immigrants yet poses a logistical challenge to the labor movement, given that few of its actual members are directly affected, though many of their children are. Union advocacy for DACA in the Trump era has largely been fueled by youth-centered labor-backed groups, such as UFCW's 21 Progress, which has provided support for applications and renewal-fee loans (21 Progress 2018, https://21progress.org/).

The fight for DACA has also forced unions to make good on their claims to address the needs of "all working people," not just their members, and to rethink the function of the union. Reluctance to become merely a "service union" has accompanied calls for unions to work more with community groups fighting on the front lines, with mostly nonunion workers. This has required collaborating with immigrant rights groups to disseminate information and with legal aid groups who could provide technical expertise. For example, the Northern Virginia Labor Council worked alongside the Virginia Coalition of Latino Organizations to promote free legal clinics for DACA renewal, which became urgent during the narrow window available while DACA languished in the courts (Northern Virginia Labor Federation 2018).

In contrast, TPS is a smaller program that has benefited over 300,000 people, largely from Central America and Haiti, for over two decades. Even before the 2016 election, TPS required constant advocacy, as the benefit must be reauthorized for each country every six to eighteen months. As of this writing, the Trump administration has attempted to end the program for seven countries, and a legal challenge is pending to at least partially restore the program. Whereas the labor movement has partnered with United We Dream on DACA advocacy, TPS advocacy has happened in large part in conjunction with the National TPS Alliance (National TPS Alliance 2018, http://www.savetps.com/). Yet the coalition has been split on competing goals: to save TPS or to call for a path to full citizenship that grants more than the precarious renewable two-year TPS status. Allies have also struggled to support a dual message of saving DACA and saving TPS, given the former's more prominent status in the immigrant rights community (National TPS Alliance 2017).

For unions and other immigrant rights groups, this ongoing threat has felt most urgent among those groups or industries that have welcomed beneficiaries of the programs, and it is in these places that a sustained call to save both DACA and TPS has resonated most consistently. Perhaps the most vocal has been SEIU, the leader of the Change to Win coalition that broke with the AFL-CIO in 2007.

Local affiliates in places where immigrants have settled have been particularly vocal. For example, SEIU 32BJ vice president Jaime Contreras criticized the decision to end TPS, pointing to the impact of TPS beneficiaries, who clean "every major landmark you can think of (in Washington, DC, home to one of the largest Central American communities)" (Miroff and Nakamura 2018). In Maryland, other trade unions have pushed for greater visibility for TPS. An organizer with the Painters (IUPAT DC51) recounted the severe impact that termination of TPS is having on their members who are affected, many of whom have "mortgages, wives, and kids" and have no connection to the country to which they are being returned (IUPAT DC51 2018). In response, the union has taken members to lobby in Congress and has supported media training.

Another hotspot for TPS advocacy has been the Boston region, which has a large Central American community. In December 2017, the Boston Teachers Union came together for a National Day of Action for TPS and DACA in Boston (Boston Teachers Union 2017; Massachusetts Jobs with Justice 2017). In January 2018, when Trump made his notorious racist comments characterizing Haiti and areas in Africa as "shithole countries," the labor council in Boston—home to a large Haitian population—condemned the "racist and ignorant remarks" (Boston Labor Council 2018). And when the Harvard University president issued a statement in May 2018 in solidarity with TPS beneficiaries (Guillaume 2018), it was the result of a joint effort by the Harvard Union of Clerical and Technical Workers, UNITE HERE Local 26, and SEIU 32BJ (Herwitz and McCafferty 2018).

Rejecting Islamophobia and Supporting Refugees

Another plank of labor's immigrant rights platform, one that has been harder to pin down, has been in reaction to President Trump's consistent and unapologetic xenophobic targeting of immigrants from Muslim-majority countries. The most prominent of Trump's attacks sought to curtail the flow of refugees as a whole and shut down most migration from a list of specific countries deemed at risk for sending likely security threats. When initially announced in January 2017, this travel ban prompted a wave of protests at airports across the country, where travelers found themselves caught in limbo as policies changed while they were literally in midflight. Labor organizations took part in these protests. In Dallas, for example, AFL-CIO political director Lorraine Montemayor issued a call to union supporters to join the actions at DFW airport (Lantz 2017b), citing national and local AFL-CIO policy, as support for the fight for immigrant and refugee rights (AFL-CIO 2017c). Next door, in Fort Worth, Tarrant County Central Labor Council president Brian Golden lambasted the "Trump 'Travel Ban' and the current climate of anti-immigrant, racist, xenophobia, blaming the 'other' ideologues and all those that follow," and noted that they were "on the wrong side of history" (Tarrant County Central Labor Council 2018).

Yet, despite these official declarations of support, strong advocacy on behalf of Muslim immigrants in the Trump era requires strong efforts at coalition building with a variety of community organizations. One common avenue for this has been via interfaith coalitions. In Dallas, the labor council has worked with an interreligious faith summit on worker and immigrant justice to help resist terror and intimidation tactics that were regularly being deployed outside area mosques (Dallas AFL-CIO 2017). Similarly, in Seattle, the state federation and local affiliates have worked with the Faith Action Network to combat attacks on Muslim immigrants. Outreach to Muslim-centered groups, such as the Council on American-Islamic Relations and local mosques, has been more elusive.

Another tactic has been to focus on Muslim workers, especially those in precarious gig economy jobs, as the Teamsters have done through their organizing with Uber drivers and port truckers (Washington AFL-CIO 2018). This work is difficult, however, and often challenged by Islamophobic rank-and-file members. The North Shore Labor Council in Massachusetts has responded to local Islamophobia by working through two mosques that are affiliates of the congregation-based Faith in Action (formerly the PICO National Network) to do outreach, attend events at houses of worship, and engage in dialogue (North Shore Labor Council 2018). Yet one council leader recounted how some of his members remain wedded to the perceived link between Islam, Sharia law, and terrorism. This "nonsense," as he characterized it adamantly, made intersectional work especially challenging, despite national declarations of solidarity from national labor federations in the United States and Canada (Quinnell 2017a).

The key factors that have galvanized concrete support for Muslim workers, even in the Trump era and in places with large Muslim communities, have been everyday incidents of Islamophobia that have caught national attention. For example, when a Muslim worker for New York's Metropolitan Transportation Authority (MTA) was called a "terrorist" and pushed down the stairs at Grand Central Station, it made national headlines, and the president of the Transport Workers Union of America Local 100 subsequently condemned the attack (NBC New York 4 2016). Yet labor unions and other advocates have had to balance the specific concerns of the Muslim community with calls for racial justice in other communities of color. When two good samaritans were murdered and one seriously injured on a light rail train in Portland, Oregon, while responding to an attacker who targeted two young girls of color while screaming anti-Muslim abuse, Amalgamated Transit Union Local 757 called for the strengthening of antifascist and antiracist organizing while also rejecting an escalation of policing as a poten-tial solution (Block, Longoria, and Hunt 2017).

Perhaps the biggest significance of unions' response to the "refugee crisis" and the increase of overt Islamophobia has been the need to think beyond narrow nar-ratives of economic utility and class-based solidarity, even when this solidarity seems to be a demographic imperative. For example, in Minnesota, home to a large Somali immigrant population, the president of the Minneapolis Regional Labor Federation Chelsie Glaubitz Gabiou (the first woman to be elected to this position) declared resistance and solidarity with immigrants under attack, includ-ing refugees (Gabiou 2017). Specifically referencing "the largest refugee crisis since World War II," her statement called for humanitarian support regardless of faith. The labor movement has been called on to broaden its concerns beyond the white working class: "The labour-minded have to be prepared to protect and support each other as workers and fighting Islamophobia should be seen as an integral part of that and the larger tussle for democracy" (Huq 2016). This has meant still tenuous efforts at building coalitions among black, Latino, and Mus-lim workers (Gleeson and Sampat 2018).

Toward an Intersectional Immigrant Advocacy Agenda for Labor

To be sure, the shifting of the landscape of immigration policy is not happening in a vacuum, and, for many locals, immigration and immigrant rights are part of a broader progressive agenda that pockets of the labor movement have been building from below for years (see, for example, Raise Up Massachusetts 2018, https://raiseupma.org/). An effective response to the Trump-era anti-immigrant agenda has also required meaningful collaboration with worker centers and other progressive immigrant advocates who are on the front lines of serving immigrant communities and lobbying of elected officials on their behalf (de Graauw 2016).

As part of this effort, labor has had to contend with its own history of racism, especially concerning black and immigrant workers. Following the attacks of white supremacists in Charlottesville, Virginia, in summer 2017, AFL-CIO president Richard Trumka stepped down from Trump's "American Manufacturing Coun-cil" in response to Trump's ambivalence toward the attack (AFL-CIO 2017a). More meaningfully, local unions are fighting to forge a pro-immigrant agenda that takes on issues of racial justice in a reflexive way. In Washington State, one leader candidly explained, dialogue with their local Black Lives Matter chapter led to the realization "that we have to look at our own house, the house of labor."

This led to an internal "deep-dive look at racism in the labor movement" (Washington AFL-CIO 2018).

Immigrant advocacy also cannot be separated from women's rights movements. In the first year of the Trump administration, UNITE HERE worked to recenter the voices of immigrant women workers who faced harassment and assault long before Hollywood co-opted the #MeToo campaign from founder Tarana Burke (Rekowski 2018). The same is true of the centrality of LGBTQ rights for immigrant rights. Though the AFL-CIO advocates for LGBTQ workers, and more recently for immigrant rights, through its Pride at Work initiative (Pride at Work 2017a, 2017b), trans rights activists such as Jennicet Gutiérrez (2017) have been leading this charge from within the labor movement. She and others have been at the forefront of the fight, calling for affirmation of the rights of sex workers and an end to the detention of all migrants, including Roxsana Hernández, an HIV-positive rape survivor and asylum seeker who died in ICE custody (National Center for Transgender Equality 2018).

In sum, it is possible that it has taken a no-holds-barred display of white supremacy, homophobia, and sexism in Washington, D.C., to force the labor movement to examine immigrant rights more intently and intersectionally. One potential impact of this new direction has been a renewed militancy among the rank and file, as one Seattle-based labor leader suggested. "We'll keep doing the work that we're doing building relationships with organizations that are on the front lines. We'll keep doing that work, but there's also clearly a need to be more militant in addressing this" (Washington AFL-CIO 2018). It remains to be seen whether this shift in strategy will continue over the long term, beyond press releases, tweets, and days of action. Perhaps through this return to direct action on behalf of immigrant rights, seen through an intersectional lens, labor's viability for the future will find its best hope for success.

Conclusion

In this chapter, I have examined the role of labor unions in responding to anti-immigrant policies under the Trump administration. I have done so by reviewing efforts to (1) stem deportations, (2) save temporary programs such as DACA and TPS, and (3) advocate for refugees while rejecting state-sponsored Islamophobia. Regarding the first, I find that, while national organizations have focused on broad policies at the border, local affiliates have focused on calls to defend local sanctuary policies. California unions in particular have been key innovators of workplace policies that help shield immigrants from the deportation dragnet, efforts that have been replicated across the country and that have served as a template for pioneering state policies. More challenging, however, has been the ability to have a candid conversation about the role of union labor in fortifying the southern border through the construction of a likely union-made border wall and an expanding unionized Border Patrol force. These are contradictions that few labor leaders have been willing to take on. However, the urgency of civil disobedience has become clearer in recent months, as unionized workers in state law enforcement agencies have been called on to share information with immigration officials, as teachers see ICE encroach onto their campuses, and as airline workers are asked to transport deportees to their likely death or to take their children without their consent.

At a time when comprehensive immigration reform has remained a far-fetched fantasy, the preservation of temporary programs that provide relief to immigrants has been an easier vehicle for union advocacy. The DACA program provided a framework of economic productivity and lost talent that has worked well in the context of labor advocacy, especially since the Trump administration rescinded the program in September 2017. However, alliances with "Dreamer" organizations such as United We Dream have also forced a broader narrative of human rights. This coalition has also required that unions rethink their advocacy beyond their core membership and include young workers in a movement where the average worker is well into their forties. DACA advocacy has also forced unions to think of their core functions in multifaceted ways, in order to facilitate outreach, education, and legal services, which most unions are unable to provide in-house. More recently, Trump's dismantling of the TPS program has drawn reactions, especially from regions where key beneficiaries (largely Central American and Haitian) are concentrated. Labor's responses have been critical in pushing other key institutions to voice their support as well.

Finally, unions have responded to attacks on refugees and Muslims in various ways. This advocacy has faced significant resistance from Islamophobic rank-and-file members who disagree with the more inclusive stance that their leaders (who are vulnerable during reelection season) have adopted, muting much of labor's response. Thus, the main impetus behind labor's statements of solidarity has been high-profile instances of discrimination and violence against Muslim members. More sustained coalition building with Muslim leaders and community groups is occurring largely through interfaith coalitions, though overall it is still a limited effort.

Moving forward, these findings suggest that unions' ability to engage meaningfully with immigrant rights also requires an intersectional approach that couches these issues within efforts to build race, gender, and LGBTQ justice, even during a dark era for workers and underrepresented minorities alike. Future research requires a deeper dive into the actions that follow unions' public pronouncements, and greater attention to how these efforts vary geographically and across industries.

References

AFL-CIO. 2001. "Resolution 5: A Nation of Immigrants." Presented at AFL-CIO 24th Biennial Convention, Las Vegas, NV, December 2–6. https://aflcio.org /resolution/nation-immigrants.

AFL-CIO. 2015a. Interview with the author, May 14.

AFL-CIO. 2015b. "AFL-CIO Launches Historic Campaign to Assist Workers with Immigration Executive Action and Citizenship Assistance." Press release, April 2. https://aflcio.org/press/releases/afl-cio-launches-historic-campaign-assist -workers-immigration-executive-action-and.

AFL-CIO. 2017a. "AFL-CIO Representatives Resign from Presidential Council on Manufacturing | AFL-CIO." Press release, August 15. https://aflcio.org/press /releases/afl-cio-representatives-resign-presidential-council-manufacturing.

AFL-CIO. 2017b. "Resolution 19: Diverse and Inclusive Leadership for a Thriving Labor Movement." October 25. https://aflcio.org/resolutions/resolution-19-diverse-and -inclusive-leadership-thriving-labor-movement.

AFL-CIO. 2017c. "Attacking Immigrants and Refugees Hurts All Working People." January 31, 2017. https://aflcio.org/press/releases/attacking-immigrants-and -refugees-hurts-all-working-people.

AFL-CIO. 2018a. "Immigration." https://aflcio.org/issues/immigration.

AFL-CIO. 2018b. "Samuel Gompers." https://aflcio.org/about/history/labor-history -people/samuel-gompers.

Aleaziz, Hamead. 2018. "Immigration Agents Raid 77 Northern California Workplaces; No Arrests Reported." *San Francisco Chronicle*, February 2. https://www.sfgate .com/bayarea/article/ICE-workplace-sweep-hits-Northern-California-12544863 .php.

Bacon, David. 2018. "How Unions Help Immigrants Resist Deportations." *American Prospect*, February 13. http://prospect.org/article/how-unions-help-immigrants -resist-deportations.

Bender, Steven W. 2017. "César Chávez Would Oppose Trump's Border Policies." *Oxford University Press* blog, March 31. https://blog.oup.com/2017/03/cesar -chavez-trump-border-policies/.

Block, Shirley, Mary Longoria, and Jonathan J. Hunt. 2017. "ATU Division 757 Letter to Union Members, Transit Riders, and the Greater Portland Community." March 31. http://www.atu757.org/wp-content/uploads/2017/05/MAXattack Letter.pdf.

Boston Labor Council. 2018. "The Greater Boston Labor Council Condemns President Trump's Racist and Ignorant Remarks about Haitians, Africans and Latin Americans. We Stand with All Our Immigrant Union Members and Their Families in the Boston Labor Community. #1u #SaveTPS." Tweet by @Bosto- nUnionCity (blog), January 12. https://twitter.com/BostonUnionCity/status /951871473974685696.

Boston Teachers Union. 2017. "Contract Updates, Fighting for TPS." eBulletin issue 16, November 28. https://btu.org/presidents-message/contract-updates-fighting-for -tps/.

Chicago Federation of Labor. 2017. "Statement from Jorge Ramirez, President of the Chicago Federation of Labor, Regarding President Trump's Executive Orders on Immigration." Press release, January 31. http://www.chicagolabor.org/news /press-releases/statement-from-jorge-ramirez-president-of-the-chicago -federation-of-labor-regarding-president-trumps-executive-orders-on -immigration.

Dallas AFL-CIO. 2017. Interview with the author, October 17.

Dimaggio, Dan. 2017. "Building Trades Activists Protest Trump to His Face." *In These Times*, April 7. http://inthesetimes.com/working/entry/20038/building_trades _activists_protest_trump_to_his_face.

Edelman, Adam. 2018. "Mayors' Group Calls Off Trump Meeting after DOJ Threatens Sanctuary Cities." *NBC News*, January 24. https://www.nbcnews.com/politics /politics-news/mayors-call-trump-meeting-after-justice-department-threatens -sanctuary-cities-n840721.

Gabiou, Chelsie Glaubitz. 2017. "Our Movement, Rooted in Immigrant Workers, Must Stand with Immigrants." *Workday Minnesota*, March 22. https://www .workdayminnesota.org/commentary/our-movement-rooted-immigrant-workers -must-stand-immigrants.

Gleeson, Shannon, and Prerna Sampat. 2018. "Immigrant Resistance in the Age of Trump." *New Labor Forum* 27(1): 86–95.

Graauw, Els de. 2016. *Making Immigrant Rights Real: Nonprofits and the Politics of Integration in San Francisco*. Ithaca, NY: Cornell University Press.

Graauw, Els de, Shannon Gleeson, and Xóchitl Bada. 2018."Unions and Immigrant Rights Advocacy: The Role of Local Context in Coalition Building and Framing Strategies." Unpublished manuscript.

Grossman, Marc. 2014. "Confronting Cesar Chavez's Stance on Illegal Immigration." *Huffington Post*, April 1. http://www.huffingtonpost.com/2014/03/31/cesar-chavez -illegal-immigration_n_5065654.html.

Guillaume, Kristine E. 2018. "Faust Pens Letter Urging Congress to Protect TPS Holders." *The Harvard Crimson*, February 7, 2018. http://www.thecrimson.com /article/2018/2/7/faust-tps-letter/.

Gutiérrez, Jennicet Eva. 2017. "Trans Women of Color Marching in Solidarity with #daca Recipients, #tps Holders, and All Undocumented Immigrants." Facebook, September 6. https://www.facebook.com/jenniceteva.gutierrez.9883/videos /2041342459419892/.

Hamlin, Rebecca. 2008. "Immigrants at Work: Labor Unions and Non-citizen Members." In *Civic Hopes and Political Realities: Immigrants, Community Organizations, and Political Engagement*, edited by S. Karthick Ramakrishnan and Irene Bloemraad, 300–322. New York: Russell Sage Foundation Press.

Herwitz, Edith M., and Molly C. McCafferty. 2018. "Workers, Activists Discuss Impact of TPS on Unions." *Harvard Crimson*, February 27. http://www.thecrimson.com /article/2018/2/27/tps-union-event/.

Huq, Chaumtoli. 2016. "Rallying the Working Class to Resist Trump's Registry." *Convivencia Magazine*, December 22. https://convivencia.co/rallying-the-working -class-to-resist-trumps-registry-a60eb0f98cab.

IUPAT DC51. 2018. Interview with the author, February 21.

Kitroeff, Natalie. 2017. "Officials Say Immigration Agents Showed Up at Labor Dispute Proceedings. California Wants Them Out." *Los Angeles Times*, August 3. http:// www.latimes.com/business/la-fi-ice-california-labor-20170802-story.html.

Kitroeff, Natalie. 2018. "Workplace Raids Signal Shifting Tactics in Immigration Fight." *New York Times*, January 15. https://nyti.ms/2FECnaj.

Lantz, Gene. 2017a. "Mark York: 'We Will Not Be Divided!'" *Dallas Labor News*, January 27. https://unionhall.aflcio.org/dallas/news/dallas-labor-news-january-27 -2017.

Lantz, Gene. 2017b. "We're Involved—Join the Fight!" *Dallas Labor News*, January 29. https://unionhall.aflcio.org/dallas/news/were-involved-join-fight.

Law, Anna O. 2017. "This Is How Trump's Deportations Differ from Obama's." *Washington Post*, May 3. https://www.washingtonpost.com/news/monkey-cage /wp/2017/05/03/this-is-how-trumps-deportations-differ-from-obamas/?utm _term=.48d0470fdd82.

Los Angeles Federation of Labor. 2016a. "Cliff Smith w/@RoofersLocal36 Stands with Immigrant Workers Because Everyone Deserves Dignity and Respect #1uWeR- isepic.Twitter.Com/CtnIJB721C." Tweet by @LALabor, May 6. https://twitter .com/LALabor/status/728700283539230720.

Los Angeles Federation of Labor. 2016b. "Statement by Los Angeles Labor Leader Rusty Hicks on President-Elect Trump's Proposed Next Steps on Immigration." Press release, November 14. http://thelafed.org/releases/statement-los-angeles-labor -leader-rusty-hicks-president-elect-trumps-proposed-next-steps-immigration/.

Los Angeles Federation of Labor. 2017a. "We'll Stand in Front of Our Sisters & Brothers to Stop Trump & Ensure Every Immigrant Has an Attorney to Defend Their Rights. @rustyhickspic.Twitter.Com/VEQQh5h3Pn." Tweet by @LALabor, January 14. https://twitter.com/LALabor/status/820334427729367040.

Massachusetts Jobs with Justice. 2017. "Boston National Day of Action for TPS & DACA!" Announcement, December 6. https://www.massjwj.net/events/2017/12/6 /boston-national-day-of-action-for-tps-daca.

Milkman, Ruth. 2006. *L.A. Story: Immigrant Workers and the Future of the U.S. Labor Movement.* New York: Russell Sage Foundation Press.

Milkman, Ruth, and Ed Ott. 2014. *New Labor in New York: Precarious Workers and the Future of the Labor Movement.* Ithaca, NY: Cornell University Press.

Miroff, Nick, and David Nakamura. 2018. "200,000 Salvadorans May Be Forced to Leave the U.S. as Trump Ends Immigration Protection." *Washington Post*, January 8. https://www.washingtonpost.com/world/national-security/trump-administration -to-end-provisional-residency-for-200000-salvadorans/2018/01/08/badfde90 -f481-11e7-beb6-c8d48830c54d_story.html.

National Center for Transgender Equality. 2018. "Roxsana Hernandez Is Sixth Person to Die in ICE Custody Since October." Press release, May 31. https://transequality .org/press/releases/roxsana-hernandez-is-sixth-person-to-die-in-ice-custody -since-october.

National TPS Alliance. 2017. "We Fight for #CleanDREAMact, All DACA Recipients AND All #TPSianos #TPS Beneficiaries. #laUnionhacelafuerza #SaveTPS #ExtendTPSpic.Twitter.Com/3HnZKGLLZH." Tweet by @TPS_Alliance, September 27. https://twitter.com/TPS_Alliance/status/913139664910815232.

NBC New York 4. 2016. "Muslim MTA Worker Called 'Terrorist,' Pushed Down Stairs." December 5. http://www.nbcnewyork.com/news/local/Muslim-MTA-Worker -Called-Terrorist-Pushed-Down-Stairs-New-York-NYC-404819216.html.

Nicholls, Walter. 2013. *The DREAMers: How the Undocumented Youth Movement Transformed the Immigrant Rights Debate.* Stanford, CA: Stanford University Press.

Nolan, Hamilton. 2016. "Can the Labor Movement Live with Police Unions?" *Gawker*, April 11. http://gawker.com/can-the-labor-movement-live-with-police-unions -1770261739.

North America's Building Trades Unions (NABTU). 2018. "Immigration." https://nabtu .org/workplace_standards/immigration/.

Northern Virginia Labor Federation. 2018. Interview with the author, February 2.

North Shore (MA) Labor Council. 2018. Interview with the author, January 25.

Orange County Labor Federation. 2017. "Immigrants Belong in Unions." September 5. http://www.oclabor.org/.

Pride at Work. 2017a. "Pride at Work Condemns New Anti-immigrant Executive Orders." *Pride at Work* blog, January 25. http://www.prideatwork.org/pride-at -work-condemns-new-anti-immigrant-executive-orders/.

Pride at Work. 2017b. "Pride at Work Response [to] the Trump Administration's DACA Announcement." *Pride at Work* blog, September 5. https://prideatwork.org/2gJu0Cj.

Quinnell, Kenneth. 2017a. "North American Unions Together against Islamophobia Stand in Solidarity with Immigrants, Refugees and Muslim Communities." AFL-CIO Blog, February 9. https://aflcio.org/2017/2/9/north-american-unions -together-against-islamophobia-stand-solidarity-immigrants-refugees.

Quinnell, Kenneth. 2017b. "DACA Announcement Will Not Deter Working People's Fight for Justice." AFL-CIO Blog, September 5. https://aflcio.org/2017/9/5/daca -announcement-will-not-deter-working-peoples-fight-justice.

Rekowski, Rachel. 2018. "Hotel Workers Say #MeToo and Fight Back." Blog, January 26. https://aflcio.org/2018/1/26/hotel-workers-say-metoo-and-fight-back.

Sampat, Prerna. 2016. "Tefere Gebre: The New Labor Movement Must Lead the Fight for Immigration Reform." *Mobilizing against Inequality*, March 17. https://www .ilr.cornell.edu/mobilizing-against-inequality/post/tefere-gebre-new-labor -movement-must-lead-fight-immigration-reform.

Scheiber, Noam. 2017. "Union Leaders Meet with Trump, Construction on Their Minds." *New York Times*, January 23. https://nyti.ms/2jSBIcQ.

Sherman, Rachel, and Kim Voss. 2000. "Organize or Die: New Organizing Tactics and Immigrant Workers." In *Organizing Immigrants: The Challenge for Unions in Contemporary California*, edited by Ruth Milkman, 81–108. Ithaca, NY: Cornell University Press.

Tarrant County Central Labor Council. 2018. *2017 TX AFL-CIO Constitutional Convention Report*. http://tcclc.org/?zone=/unionactive/view_article.cfm&Home ID=658286&page=President27s20Page.

Texas AFL-CIO. 2017a. "Resolution: Protection of Immigrant Families / Harris County Labor Assembly." January 26. https://www.texasaflcio.org/news/resolution -protection-immigrant-families-harris-county-labor-assembly.

Texas AFL-CIO. 2017b. "Immigrant Working People Will Suffer under SB 4, but So Will State as a Whole." *Texas AFL-CIO* blog, April 28. https://www.texasaflcio.org /news/texas-afl-cio-immigrant-working-people-will-suffer-under-sb-4-so-will -state-whole.

Thomsen, Jacqueline. 2018. "Montana State Employee Goes Viral for Quitting over Work on ICE Subpoena." *The Hill*, February 9. http://thehill.com/blogs/blog -briefing-room/news/373152-montana-state-employee-goes-viral-for-quitting -over-working-on.

Tichenor, Daniel. 2015. "The Political Dynamics of Unauthorized Immigration: Conflict, Change, and Agency in Time." *Polity* 47(3): 283–301. https://doi.org/10 .1057/pol.2015.11.

United Steelworkers. 2018. "Dear @tedcruz: Please Stop Name-Dropping #Steelworkers in Your Attempts to Divide & Distract. We Stand w/ Dreamers & Their Families. We Are Proud to Fight for a True Path to Citizenship. Next Time You Mention Us, Mention We ALWAYS Welcomed All: Http://Usw.to/2ig #USWUnity." Tweet by @steelworkers, February 15. https://twitter.com/steelworkers/status /964246012620615681.

Vasquez, Mario. 2016. "Immigrant Activists Call for AFL-CIO to Expel Border Patrol Union after Donald Trump Endorsement." *In These Times*, April 5. http://inthesetimes.com/working/entry/19028/donald-trump-border-patrol-union-mexico-immigrants-not1more.

Washington AFL-CIO. 2018. Interview with the author, February 8.

Washington State Labor Council, AFL-CIO. 2017. "2017 WSLC Resolutions: Resolution on Immigration and the Labor Movement (#22)." July 26. http://www.wslc.org/2017-wslc-resolutions/.

Williams, Krissah. 2007. "Unions Split on Immigrant Workers." *Washington Post*, January 27. http://www.washingtonpost.com/wp-dyn/content/article/2007/01/26/AR2007012601635.html.

9

TRUMPISM, POLICING, AND THE PROBLEM OF SURPLUS POPULATION

Cedric Johnson

Securitization and policing, racist exclusion, and repression were central features of Donald J. Trump's ascension to the presidency. During summer 2016, when his election still seemed like a long shot to many, Trump was emphatic in his support for police. He seized on the fatal assault on police in Dallas, saying, "We must stand in solidarity with law enforcement, which we must remember is the force between civilization and total chaos" (J. Johnson 2016), echoing the core logic of the "thin blue line" that has animated US law enforcement since the Cold War. Trump led a chorus of conservative voices that claimed that the Obama administration and Black Lives Matter protests have created dangerous conditions for police officers. Rudolph Giuliani, former New York City mayor and now Trump's attorney, was quick to attack activists, claiming that Black Lives Matter is "inherently racist because, number one, it divides us" (Larimer 2016; O'Connor 2016).

Contrary to the overheated rhetoric of Trump, Giuliani, and others, policing is not the most hazardous occupation in the United States. In fact, it is not even in the top ten, with on-the-job police fatalities ranking well behind those of construction workers, groundskeepers, fishermen, garbage collectors, and loggers, among others (Frase 2014). And contrary to the claim that the Obama administration enabled antipolice sentiment, violence against police officers actually decreased during Obama's tenure, especially when compared to the George W. Bush years (Frase 2014). Moreover, conservative attacks on Black Lives Matter are simply unfounded. Over 70 percent of the violence against law enforcement that occurred during the 2016 election year was carried out by white men (King 2016).

The mass shootings of police during the week of July 4, 2016, were tragic, but equally so is the fact of police suicide, the number of which in recent years has dwarfed the number of police officer fatalities by shootings and traffic accidents combined (O'Hara 2017; Nickeas 2018; Sobol and Koeske 2018; Donato 2017). Yet, improving the working conditions and mental health care of officers is not at the forefront of the "Blue Lives Matter" chest thumping of Trump, Giuliani, and their ilk.

Since taking the oath of office, Trump has continued to deride any dissent against police violence and abuse, infamously demanding that the National Football League's team owners fire any player who followed San Francisco 49ers quarterback Colin Kaepernick's national anthem protests. Trump also openly joked about police violence during a 2017 address to law enforcement officers at Suffolk County Community College on Long Island, New York, in a manner that encouraged rough treatment of suspects and minimized their right to due process (Washington Post 2017).

Following the well-worn playbook of GOP strategists, Trump's approach to campaigning and governing pits the deserving American middle class against the relative surplus population of welfare dependents, overpoliced minorities, undocumented migrant workers, and low-wage workers in China and other countries. Surplus population, or the industrial reserve army, is understood here as those persons not currently employed who might be pressed into service to the advantage of capital (Marx 1867). The presence of surplus population in any given historical context exerts downward pressure on wages. As a reservoir of low-wage, fragmented, and disempowered labor, surplus laborers are often employed as competitors or scabs against more established and secure workers, fomenting division within the working class. Trump endorses a punitive approach to managing surplus population that millions of Americans condone, and, believe it or not, such public support for policing has actually grown stronger during the era of Black Lives Matter.

For decades, in the rhetoric of the New Right and New Democrats alike, the poor and unemployed have been routinely blamed for societal decline and public financial woes. We are told in every election cycle that those whose survival depends on meager public assistance, housing vouchers, Medicaid, and the like do not pay their fair share of taxes and do not contribute much to the economic and social health of the nation. Blaming the most vulnerable segments of the working class, however, merely absolves corporate elites of their responsibility in worsening material conditions for millions of Americans through their decision making (e.g., offshoring of production, replacement of living labor with automation, and massive reductions in the taxation of corporations and the wealthiest households). Blaming minorities, the poor, and immigrants further distracts an already anxious middle class and secures their interests as consumer-citizens in the reproduction of the capitalist order. Trumpism appeals to the real economic anxieties of those Americans who can recall the last days of a vibrant manufacturing-based economy. His protectionist ideas as well as his xenophobia beckon many Americans, not just whites, back to a nostalgic ideal of unending compound growth and middle-class consumption. The current carceral order was built to secure that particular version of the American Dream.

The liberal antiracist perspective on policing and incarceration popularized through Black Lives Matter protests carries a powerful moral weight but does not help us understand the fundamental problems before us, which are rooted not in slavery and Jim Crow but in the discrete social contradictions of "postindustrial" capitalism. Moreover, without addressing the class character of policing, liberal solutions will only shore up the current order, making exploitation and dispossession more socially tolerable. This chapter situates contemporary carceral logics in Cold War transformations of American urbanism, class relations, and politics. When we look more closely at the livelihoods of those slain by police, and the thousands more who are incarcerated, what becomes clear is their common class predicament. Some worked in the low-wage service sector, such as Philando Castile, who was a school cafeteria worker and a member of Teamster Local 320. Others made their living through the informal economy. Both Eric Garner and Alton Sterling were killed as they sold items—loose cigarettes and music CDs, respectively—to passersby in front of convenience stores. Others killed by police were involved in the illicit drug trade. The problems of overpolicing and mass incarceration should be central to the labor left agenda, because the most dispossessed segments of the working class endure the violence of the carceral state.

Policing as we know it emerged out of the postwar urban transformation, the making of middle-class suburbia. The massive state investments in housing and real estate development, defense contracting, and infrastructure projects transformed American cities and in the process produced higher standards of living, popular acceptance of capitalism's virtues, and new social conflicts within the laboring classes. Just as the postwar transformation produced the middle-class consumer citizen, the same historical processes would also create the affluent society's walking contradiction, an industrial reserve of unemployed, mostly black and brown urban dwellers. The "thin blue line" took shape across this postwar landscape as a means of defending the consumer society. These underlying social contradictions were brought fully out into the open during the popular protests and mass urban riots of the 1960s.

This chapter also explores how the processes of neoliberal revitalization and gentrification since the 1980s intensified aggressive policing of black and brown communities, which occupied increasingly valuable real estate. Paradoxically, the expansion of the carceral state and fortressing of American cities was often carried out by black-led, Democratic, and liberal governing coalitions, a fact that also troubles any straightforward identity-based approach to the problems before us. While Trump is a dangerous and divisive figure, his antics should not distract us from local and state politics, which have long been the primary battleground over policing and punishment, and should continue to be the focus of those of us who want more just, egalitarian ways of maintaining public safety. Along with civil rights organizations and local campaigns against police abuse, unions can play a crucial role in deepening opposition to and advancing solutions that confront the very inequality our current carceral state was created to maintain.

The Postwar Urban Transformation and the Origins of Policing as We Know It

Modern policing and punishment have served as a means of disciplining the poor and protecting emergent property regimes, from the public hangings of eighteenth-century London to the fugitive slave laws of the American antebellum period, the policing of crowds in early industrial New York City, and the use of state militia to crush labor protests throughout the Fordist era (Linebaugh 2003; Whitehouse 2014; Palmer 2016). As Mark Neocleous argues, police, "along with equally fetishised sister concepts of 'order', 'security' and 'law', is a central category in the self-understanding of bourgeois society" (Neocleous 2000). Furthermore, Neocleous contends, "policing has been central not just to the repression of the working class and the reproduction of order, but to the fabrication of order . . . as order became increasingly based on the bourgeois mode of production, so the police mandate was to fabricate an order of wage labour and administration of the class of poverty" (Neocleous 2000).

Contemporary accounts of the birth and expansion of the prison state have typically neglected the significance of the post–World War II urban transformation and the new status distinctions and aspirational mythology it produced, sharpening conflicts within the working class along racial and urban-suburban divides while cementing the interests of the most secure segments, the middle class, to the interests of capital. Beginning with the New Deal and expanding after World War II under the leadership of President Harry Truman, the United States embarked on a housing revolution, a process that transformed millions of whites into nominal property holders and members of the new consumer middle class while relegating the majority of blacks to devalued and deteriorating central city neighborhoods (Cohen 2004). Suburban development and all manner of consumer activity transmutated class identity away from old urban ethnic and proletarian affinities and cemented the loyalty of more upwardly mobile and secure workers to the Cold War growth trajectory of defense spending, urban renewal, and suburbanization. This postwar spatial fix featured a transformed role for the federal government, and a turn to commercial Keynesianism, which marked a departure from the public works and racially progressive dimensions of the New Deal project (Adams 2014; Reed 2015; Levine 1988).

The development of a home realty market and mortgage market, as well as the rapid expansion of the consumer economy, were intended as remedies to the surplus-absorption problem that was partially responsible for the crisis of the Great Depression. The Depression devastated the real estate and housing construction industries. The construction of residential properties plummeted by 95 percent between 1928 and 1933, and home repair expenditures fell by 90 percent during the same period (Jackson 1985). In 1930 alone, 150,000 non-farm households lost property to foreclosure, and by 1932 that figure had reached 250,000. The rapid development and expansion of suburban homeownership created a means for the realization of surplus value.

As geographer David Harvey notes, capital never resolves its crises but rather moves them around geographically (Harvey 2008). The problems of overproduction and value realization were solved through public subsidization of the real estate industry and, consequentially, massive urban expansion. From its origins, the American liberal project has elided class, instead proffering the view that inherited bonds and social restrictions do not bridle the pursuit of individual economic autonomy and personal fulfillment, even though the nation was established as a slave-holding republic. In response to both the powerful working-class movements of the interwar period and the decisive role of the Soviet Union in defeating fascism during World War II, however, American popular ideology and institutions during the Cold War were reoriented forcefully against notions of class struggle and revolutionary socialism.

The birth of the postwar suburban middle class as lived social reality and an aspirational identity, the increasing availability of mass-produced goods and services, and the ways in which consumer capacity became synonymous with success and, sadly, with human worth within popular culture produced a new social terrain, marked by renewed mass commitments to liberal individualism, new anxieties about social status, seismic political realignments, and novel everyday preoccupations. This era produced two powerful myths of class: the relative middle class and the "underclass." These were myths to the extent that both obscured actual capitalist class relations at the time, treating those who occupied the same objective experience of dependency and exploitation as dissimilar classes, a cultural development that would have profound implications for American politics in the decades to come. The so-called middle class and the "underclass" would emerge as popular ways of talking about class that no longer focused on productive relations but instead focused on consumption. Both the middle class and the "underclass" were figments of Cold War ideology and mirrored narratives of American exceptionalism.

Blacks were largely excluded from the postwar prosperity, a pro-market policy context that treated private actors, developers, realtors, and homeowners as sovereign, enabling all manner of discrimination at the local level (Satter 2010; Katznelson 2005; Reed 2018). It would be an overstatement, however, to suggest that some segments of the black population did not enjoy versions of the good life during this era, albeit circumscribed by racism. Before and after World War II, black civic leaders and businessmen broke ground on their own affluent subdivisions in places like St. Albans in Queens, New York, the Chatham and Pill Hill neighborhoods in Chicago, LeDroit Park in the District of Columbia, Pontchartrain Park in New Orleans, and Southern Heights in Baton Rouge, among scores of others (Smith 2012; Wiese 2006; Landry 1987; Pattillo 1999). Often in the face of virulent backlash, many black families also attempted to purchase homes across the color line during the same period. The modern civil rights movement sought the restoration of black citizenship in the South but also access to the jobs and prosperity denied by Jim Crow strictures (Reed 2015; Jones 2013). It is not incidental that some of the most pitched battles for desegregation unfolded in consumption and leisure spaces—lunch counters, pharmacies, department stores, public pools and beaches, concert halls, and downtown commercial districts. Nor is it surprising that the black professional-managerial class and collegiate aspirants were often at the forefront of desegregation struggles. Of course, black nationalists and even some critics within the southern desegregation campaigns grew increasingly skeptical of the capacity of civil rights reforms to create meaningful progress, and by the mid-1960s, demands for black political autonomy and self-determination had literally spread like wildfire across America's cities. The most radical wing of the black power movement also articulated a nascent critique of the prison system, one that makes clear the class contradictions coursing through the black population and American society writ large. Civil rights reforms created the context for a long, uneven process of black integration into the consumer society and government, but the same capitalist dynamics that made all manner of goods and lifestyles available to millions of Americans also produced mass unemployment for the black urban poor through corporate restructuring and more capital-intensive production, strategies adopted by management in response to growing worker power.

We get a sense of the emergent nexus of unemployment and incarceration in the writings of George Jackson, the cofounder of the Black Guerilla Family, who was killed in an attempted escape from San Quentin prison in August 1971. "This

is my eleventh year of being shoveled into every major prison in the most populous state in the nation—and the largest prison system in the world," Jackson
wrote. "At each institution I've been in, 30 to sometimes 40 percent of those held
are black, and every one of the many thousands I've encountered was from the
working or lumpenproletariat class. There may be a few exceptions, but I simply
have not met any of them in my eleven years" (Jackson 1971). So, while Jackson
makes clear that blacks are overrepresented, he insists that there is an underlying
unity, that the vast majority of the prison population is drawn from the *lumpenproletariat* ("proletariat in rags"), the most dispossessed segments of the working
class. The Black Panther Party, of course, was born out of protests against overpolicing. The Panthers and related urban left organizations such as the Young
Lords and the Young Patriots, which also sprang from ghettoized conditions,
adopted various strategies for addressing police abuse, from the early armed
police-monitoring patrols first undertaken by Panthers in Oakland to the staging
of meetings between police and their communities and demands for greater public oversight and accountability in Chicago. These efforts were heroic but ultimately were inadequate to the enormity of the task at hand, which required not
merely the mobilization of the ghetto poor but also the transformation of a society where many workers had come to see the interests of capital as their own and
who accepted the role of domestic policing and imperial wars in maintaining the
prosperity they enjoyed. In this context of Cold War complicity, the Panthers and
other urban radical left organizations were isolated, infiltrated, and repressed by
state and federal police agencies. Their interpretations of the ghetto poor stood
in sharp contrast to the underclass moralizing of Daniel Patrick Moynihan and
Great Society liberals.

The "underclass," as the liberals called the ghetto poor, came to be reviled from
the 1960s onward as a social burden on the middle class. As Michael Zweig argues, we should cease treating the poor as some distinct and inferior entity. They
are merely ruined workers, and the vast majority of the American poor work multiple jobs to survive (Zweig 2000; Schor 1992). The New Right seized on Moynihan's imagery of the dysfunctional and dependent urban black poor, using such
imagery as justification for dismantling the welfare state, which was viewed as an
undue burden on the tax-paying middle class. This is the ideological context that
fostered the growth and racialization of policing and prisons as we know it.

Propelled by new popular commitments to an accumulation model rooted in
profit sharing, mass consumption, and real estate development, the affluent society gave rise to new social antagonisms, conflict between the suburban haves
and the inner-city have-nots. Rising anxieties over crime, and the existing role of
local and national police, were expanded to address real and imagined threats to
the Cold War order. In concert with the new class consciousness produced by the

postwar urban transformation, with the suburban middle class on one side and the urban underclass on the other, policing took a dual form: an emulatory strategy of promoting civic virtues of deference and middle-class aspiration, and a punitive strategy of defending the propertied and virtuous middle class from the outsiders, those segregated in inner-city ghettos and struggling to survive. William H. Parker, a World War II veteran and Los Angeles police chief throughout the 1950s and early 1960s, imagined his department as a "thin blue line," the only defense separating the virtuous middle class from the barbarism of organized crime, Godless communism, and ghetto criminality (Schmidt 2005).

As Ronald Schmidt Jr. argues in his analysis of the Los Angeles Police Department (LAPD) under Parker, the middle class was policed through this softer emulatory model. Schmidt describes Parker's approach as "a vision of an elite corps that would control crime but, more important, provide the citizens of Los Angeles with a model of civic excellence that they could emulate—indeed, that they would have to emulate" (Schmidt 2005; Kramer 2007; Bevan 2011). To achieve that end, Parker employed radio, television, and social conduits, such as African American clergy. He worked closely with the makers of the television series *Dragnet* to accurately reflect the daily workings of the LAPD and to broadcast in a fictionalized form the very emulatory model of policing he cherished.

When Parker's attention turned to the ghettoized ranks of black Angelenos, however, he took a different tack. Such residents were "statistically more likely," he held, to engage in criminal activity, and they were met with the full force of the LAPD and its innovative tactics, such as the use of police cruising. In the wake of the 1965 Watts rebellion, which rocked the black South Central section of the city, Parker made clear the limits of his emulatory strategy. That softer mode of policing was intended for the virtuous middle class; the ghetto deserved stricter social control. "This is the lesson that we refuse to recognize, that you can't convert every person into a law-abiding citizen," Parker lamented after Watts, "If you want any protection in your home and family in the future, you're going to have to stop this abuse, but you're going to have to get in and support a strong police department" (Schmidt 2005). Watts marked an abrupt ending to the Parker regime and signaled the beginning of a new era, where cities would become firmly associated in the popular imagination with blackness, crime, and danger.

Parker and other urban leaders, such as Chicago's mayor Richard J. Daley, were upfront about how they viewed the role of the police department and its duty to protect social order against ghetto discontent. In April 1968, Daley would issue his infamous "shoot to kill" order to discourage looting and arson after the assassination of Martin Luther King Jr. He would marshal the full force of his police department again later that summer in an effort to crush street demonstrations at the Democratic National Convention (Kusch 2008). Tapping into public anxiety over successive long summers of urban rioting, Richard Nixon entered the White House promising to restore "law and order" to the nation. Under Nixon, the FBI and local police forces would coordinate and intensify efforts to infiltrate and repress growing black power militancy.

Out of this postwar transformation, race emerged as the dominant symbolic language for understanding American inequality. If "white" became a synonym for middle class, suburban, law abiding and virtuous, property owning, hardworking, and self-governing, then "black" came to function as a euphemism for poor, urban, criminal and dysfunctional, dispossessed, lazy, and dependent. Contemporary antiracist discourse contests these pejorative connotations of blackness but obscures as much as it reveals about the actual historical interests that propelled the expansion of more aggressive modes of policing, from Nixon's initial pronouncement of the War on Drugs through the militarization and pretext policing that lay at the heart of urban revanchism, the literal taking back of the city by tech workers, creative entrepreneurs, real estate developers, and transnational corporations that began in the 1980s.

Policing the Revanchist City

The expansion of the carceral state and more aggressive policing of urban minority communities coincided with the rollback of the welfare state at the national level and the almost universal pursuit of urban downtown redevelopment as an antidote to the decline of the manufacturing sector in many US cities. The ramping up of the War on Drugs during the Reagan-Bush years coincided with class war at the urban level in an era where the aggressive removal of the urban poor from the inner city was central to the new model of real estate and tourism-driven growth (Gordon 2005; Sharp 2014). The late geographer Neil Smith characterized this historical process in terms of the revanchist—derived from the French word for revenge—city to describe the literal retaking of power by the ruling class under neoliberal urbanization.

While the postwar transformation of the urban landscape created physical distance between the new middle class and those left ghettoized in the inner-city core, the taking back of the city through gentrification and real estate speculation brought these disparate classes into direct confrontation—with middle-class urban pioneers, house flippers, large real estate developers, and tourists on one side and old ethnic neighborhoods, the unemployed, the itinerant poor, sexual minorities, and countercultural spaces on the other. "This revanchist antiurbanism," Smith holds,

represents a reaction against the supposed "theft" of the city, a desperate defense of a challenged phalanx of privileges, cloaked in the
populist language of civic morality, family values and neighborhood
security. . . . More than anything the revanchist city expresses a race/
class/ gender terror felt by middle- and ruling-class whites who are suddenly stuck in place by a ravaged property market, the threat and reality
of unemployment, the decimation of social services, and the emergence
of minority and immigrant groups, as well as women, as powerful urban actors. It portends a vicious reaction against minorities, the working class, homeless people, the unemployed, women, gays and lesbians,
immigrants. (Smith 1996)

The process of revanchism has occurred in fits and starts, achieving more success in some cities than in others, but securitization has been at the heart of this
process, ensuring the safe passage of more upwardly mobile residents and visi-
tors as a prerequisite to growth.

Pacification of the poor, architectural fortressing, and renewed processes of
enclosure have produced a new central-city landscape, where class contradictions
are managed through manifold technologies of policing, surveillance, and social
accreditation that permit ease of movement across urban space for those of means
while regulating and constricting the poor—a new urban landscape defined by
helipads and Uber Black, artisanal grocers, boutique fitness clubs, private roads,
dog parks, and relentless condo tower construction for the investor class and renascent bon vivant, and "bum-proof" benches, ankle monitors, stress policing,
the demolition of public housing, water shutoffs, ubiquitous closed-circuit cameras, and check-cashing centers for the working-class enclaves. One immediate
casualty of this new urban warfare, as Mike Davis reported, was the elimination
of the very notion of the public. "The universal consequence of the crusade to
secure the city is the destruction of any truly democratic urban space," Davis wrote
in 1992, "The American city is being systematically turned inward. The 'public'
spaces of the new megastructures and supermalls have supplanted traditional
streets and disciplined spontaneity" (Davis 1992). These processes of urban fortressing were further entrenched in the wake of the terrorist attacks on September 11, 2001, which precipitated increased federal and state spending on policing
and surveillance programs under the pretext of enhancing national security. This
war on the public, and the privatization of social services, has created new opportunities for profit making and philanthropy and made already vulnerable segments of the working class even more desperate, stripped of the basic social wage
guarantees of previous generations, ensuring a ready and cheap reservoir of ser-
vant labor (Johnson 2015).

In a rather cruel historical twist, the liberal black political elite who governed many American cities throughout the cycle of manufacturing decline and "post-industrial" renaissance also presided over these processes of neoliberal fortressing and hyperpolicing. The carceral buildup of the late War on Drugs era was not merely the handiwork of conservative Republicans. Rather, mass incarceration was produced by various constituencies—black and white; urban, suburban, and rural; liberal and conservative; new Democrats; black nationalists; victims' families; drug rehabilitation clinicians, social workers, and community activists—who supported laws that were more punitive, expanded police patrols, increased funding for prison construction, and the like. Some supported these policies for staunchly ideological reasons, while others did so out of desperation, seeing punishment as the only plausible antidote to worsening crime, drug trafficking, and deteriorating neighborhoods, especially as the tangible benefits of social democracy were no longer part of the lived experiences and popular memory of millions of Americans. The roots of this dilemma lie in the Cold War liberal turn away from public works and redistributive public policy and toward civil society and cultural solutions to urban poverty. The complex role of black elites and black popular constituencies is neglected in most accounts of the carceral buildup, and the fact of multiracial support for policing and incarceration remains a formidable barrier to the kinds of reforms promoted via Black Lives Matter protests.

In the two decades after the upheavals of 1968, black political incorporation became a reality, with most major American cities electing black mayors and often majority-black city councils. These black-led cities, however, would inherit a number of well-known constraints on their capacity to govern, such as declining tax bases, population loss, capital flight, declining federal investment, worn infrastructure, and worsening social conditions (Reed 1999; Arena 2011; Johnson 2016b). The class-diverse black ghettoes of the mid-twentieth century, to which all blacks were relegated regardless of income or educational attainment, provided the spatial-demographic basis for black power demands for indigenous control. Such urban zones, however, would undergo dramatic transformation during the 1970s and 1980s, giving way to the hypersegregation of the black poor (Wacquant 2010). Within this difficult context, citizens and civic leaders made policy choices that were even more difficult, with some blacks supporting anticrime measures because of idiosyncratic political beliefs (e.g., cultural nationalism, noblesse oblige, temperance, and others) and others doing so because of specific constituent or class interests (e.g., as homeowners, business owners, clergy, health-care professionals, victims' families, and block clubs).

James Forman Jr. offers a highly textured account of how and why some residents, politicians, and activists in Washington, D.C., supported a politics of incarceration during an era of black political control (Forman 2017). In his study, we find divergent and historically discrete motives for black support of various anticrime and policing policies. Black civil rights activists in Atlanta during the 1940s and the District of Columbia in the 1960s demanded the hiring of more black officers as a remedy to police brutality. During the 1970s, black nationalists opposed marijuana legalization in the District because they viewed it as a "gateway" drug to more debilitating addictions. Some black judges insisted on harsh punishment for black violent offenders out of a moral obligation to black victims, who for too long were denied adequate police protection or court justice under Jim Crow. These decisions were made with an eye toward what might be done to reduce addiction, theft, and violence within a context of limited choices. The stories Forman presents contradict contemporary antiracist sloganeering and analyses that portray the problems of policing and mass incarceration in stark black-and-white terms. Instead, he gives a more nuanced historical appreciation of why certain constituencies supported policies that would eventually have a disastrous effect on black incarceration rates. He also illustrates, through a close analysis of attitudes toward policing in black professional and working-class neighborhoods, that there are distinct class experiences of policing, with working-class blacks more likely to be subjected to intensive and routine police surveillance and arrests.

Forman's work presents us with a political paradox that remains instructive in this era of resurgent liberal identity politics: that black political control did not protect black District residents from the escalating problems of crime and policing. Rather, within the all-black context of the District, specific historical constituencies combined to produce measures that had unintended consequences, and efforts to protect victims and reduce drug crime and violence contributed to mass incarceration. Racial affinity and ascriptive status should not be mistaken for political constituency, and an understanding of the granular interests and shifting political positions constituting black life will be crucial to any success that police-reform forces hope to achieve going forward. Former New Democratic black mayors such as Adrian Fenty in Washington, D.C., C. Ray Nagin in New Orleans, and Stephanie Rawlings-Blake in Baltimore presided over a period of urban revanchism where the interests of capital were prioritized over genuinely public education and the safety, peace, and quality of life in black working-class neighborhoods. Alongside black contractors and school privatization advocates, such black leadership has played a crucial role in legitimating neoliberalization by providing it with a multiracial countenance. In cities such as Baltimore and Chicago, which possess integrated police forces and city administrations, massive antipolicing protests have forced legal prosecution of police, officer suspensions, and token firings, and some increased transparency. Street demonstrations against overpolicing, however, have also been countered with the mobilization of

more centrist black political elements, which have called for modest technical reforms to correct police abuse, such as standard-issue body cameras, as well as
advancing private charitable projects and volunteer mentoring as solutions to poverty (Johnson 2016a). In large and complex urban areas, where black power has
long been institutionalized and entrenched, analyses and political strategies that
ignore the existing class relations and interests shaping incarceration and the
policy-making arena will do little to advance the kind of substantive reforms
touted by the most progressive elements of antipolicing protests.

What Is to Be Done?

It is crucial for those of us on the labor Left not only to advance assertive working-
class-centered and anticapitalist politics but also to insist that those issues commonly discussed as uniquely black concerns—policing, incarceration, predatory
lending, and discrimination—are in fact broader working-class issues. Although
it is common to hear liberal academics and activists argue that we should think
in terms of racial disparities rather than class inequality, race and class are, as Barbara Fields once noted, "concepts of a different order"; they are not interchange-
able as such (Fields 1982). Moreover, the predicament of blacks since the formal
end of Jim Crow segregation has risen and fallen with that of the wider working
class. Whether measured in terms of stagnant wages, increased job insecurity,
mortgage foreclosures, or lack of adequate health care, the worsening economic
conditions experienced by blacks over the last few decades are a direct consequence of neoliberalization and the decimation of the public sector, which was a
major force in the expansion of the black middle class from the New Deal through
the black urban regime era. The first step here is to think about class in terms of
the social relations of production and not simply according to those indicators
of income, wealth, or education used by social scientists and pollsters. When we
think of class in terms of social power, both within the production and circula-
tion of commodities and throughout society as a whole, a different understanding of society emerges, along with a new horizon of political possibilities.

The postwar economic boom and Cold War anticommunism expunged the
language of workers and the working class from popular and political debate in
favor of the middle class and offered up the underclass as its antithesis. For decades thereafter, most Americans would come to define themselves as middle class
even when their actual role in the economy and their consumer capacity fell short
of this aspirational identity in real terms. Over time, politicians likewise retooled
their appeals away from populist overtures to the "working man" and toward
the new middle class or, at best, "working families," all the while criticizing the

excesses of the wealthy and the moral depravity of the desperately poor. Neither criticism carried real consequences for candidates, by the way, since the donor class understood the difference between campaign stumping and the machinations of government, and the "underclass" was not a real constituency and did not matter electorally. Appealing to the middle class has provided a safe and soft target for the campaign speeches and policy prescriptions of both conservative Republicans and New Democrats. If the middle class came to be understood as white, suburban, law abiding and virtuous, affluent, property owning, hardworking, autonomous, and Republican, the underclass was black and brown, urban, poor, criminal and dysfunctional, dispossessed, lazy, dependent, and apathetic. Challenging these myths of class that have come to dominate American politics, and coming to terms with the landscape of power we now inhabit, should be central tasks of the contemporary Left. Moreover, understanding the making of the consumer society, its contradictions and unique historical character, and how it gave rise to the current carceral state should help us clarify the underlying class relations that are codified in black and white but are not reducible to those identities. Trump's ascendancy has emboldened extreme right-wing, racist elements, but it is unlikely that a strong left opposition can be built by embracing the same logic of identitarianism.

Trump's version of "law and order" conservatism is a crudely stitched, Frankenstein's monster combination of the worst racist and authoritarian stances used by the Right over the last half century. Trump has legitimated a few decades' worth of repressive policing strategies, which guarantee a level of security for the middle class and capital but at the cost of mass warehousing, social disruption, wrongful convictions, police abuse, and disenfranchisement for the most vulnerable segments of the working class. How do we reverse this state of affairs? More precisely, how do we roll back the carceral state, which is not an exception to the market system but rather a central dimension of capital accumulation in our times? What role might labor play in creating forms of public safety that are more just?

The Black Lives Matter protests during the waning years of the Obama administration, and the flurry of national demonstrations against white nationalism and Confederate monuments, ICE family separations and deportations, and the daily outrages stoked by the Trump regime, have been crucial to politicizing different social layers. Such political momentum has generated much-needed public debate, intensified local political work and coalition building, and sparked renewed attention to electoral politics by the Left, with growing numbers of pro-labor, socialist, and progressive left candidates running for office. At the local level, activists have already posed creative alternatives to policing and mass incarceration, such as rerouting public spending on local police departments toward afterschool programs, neighborhood youth centers, and public-works jobs.

Achieving concrete reforms, however, requires legislative majorities, in local city councils, state assemblies, and Congress. Many established civil rights and criminal justice organizations have been working to achieve concrete policy reforms for years. Some Black Lives Matter forces, however, have been less likely to pursue formal political avenues, given the prevalence of anarchistic sensibilities and an understandable aversion to bourgeois state institutions. At the time of this writing, such reforms constitute a horizon of struggle for activists, but there is little evidence that antipolicing forces have achieved the requisite public support to turn these agenda demands into public policy. How might such forces build popular support?

Struggles to demilitarize police departments and to roll back the carceral state will not succeed in the grandest terms set out by activists if they do not turn public opinion against underclass views of the poor and the equally extensive commitments to capital that persist in our times, despite the growing popularity of left politics. For decades, many Americans have made peace with aggressive policing as a necessary evil. The small victories of local and state-based organizations fighting for decarceration, the worsening conditions of the middle class, and the wide impact of the opioid epidemic, however, have all combined to unsettle, if not overturn, conventional thinking about whether we should address problems such as addiction, mental health, and inequality through punishment. The view that the poor are somehow different from the rest of us and deserve discipline rather than public assistance is a core pillar of the current policing order, a popular mythology that activists should work to demolish. As the favorable public opinion for police and support for Trump's brand of racism and victim blaming attest, there is still considerable work to be done. Unions could play a crucial role here in creating the space for honest talk about inequality, how it is produced, and why we should think about the poor as the most submerged segments of the working class, as contingent workers, undocumented workers, informal workers, and ruined workers. I am not suggesting merely training officers to be more sensitive, preaching against "classism," or asking whites to "check their privilege," which are all modes of liberal antiracism as therapy that dominate certain corners of the Left. Instead, I am suggesting something more sustained and difficult: the tedious work of building popular support for notions of public safety that are predicated not on crime and punishment but on the universal guarantee of economic security and freedom from compulsory wage labor and the struggle to afford life's necessities. That task entails contesting liberal thinking about class, middle-class commitments to capital and the dogma of work, and pejorative views of the black and brown poor, which are all ideological facets of the Cold War suburban dream of limitless growth and cornucopic mass consumption.

Mass incarceration and aggressive policing were built from the ground up, at the level of local and state legislation and with the consent of a wide array of constituencies. Decades of antipolicing activism; civil rights campaigns to exonerate the wrongfully convicted and secure restitution for victims of police torture and redress for racism in the criminal justice system; and contemporary Black Lives Matter demonstrations have charted a path toward a more just order, but they have also revealed the limits of protests and antiracism as strategies. Meaningful reform must build support where it does not now exist, and that might mean speaking across the inherited geopolitical boundaries set in place by the postwar transformation. It would seem that central labor councils might also play a significant leadership role in advancing local struggles, inasmuch as they can leverage local police unions, which have often been the most recalcitrant forces blocking reforms and demands for greater citizen oversight of law enforcement. Beating back the reactionary forces Trump represents, entrenched blocs of capital, and disgruntled citizens and alt-right elements will require the construction of a different Left, one that is not driven so much by mass protests, social media debates, memes, and online sloganeering but anchored in the moil of everyday life and felt needs of the vast majority of Americans and focused on the mobilization of the working class as a class for itself. To that end, the most progressive unionists have an important role to play in challenging reactionary attitudes in their midst, creating space for critical thinking about class and capitalism, and amassing support for local and state-level campaigns that might dismantle the carceral state.

References

Adams, Thomas Jessen. 2014. "The Theater of Inequality." nonsite.org, August 12. https://nonsite.org/feature/the-theater-of-inequality.

Adamson, Christopher. 1984. "Toward a Marxian Penology: Captive Criminal Populations as Economic Threats and Resources." *Social Problems* 31(4): 435–458.

Arena, John. 2011. "Bringing in the Black Working Class: The Black Urban Regime Strategy." *Science and Society* 75(2): 153–179.

Bevan, Robert. 2011. "Screening the L.A.P.D.: Cinematic Representations of Policing and Discourses of Law Enforcement in Los Angeles, 1948–2003." PhD diss., University College London.

Chiricos, Theodore G., and Miriam A. Delone. 1992. "Labor Surplus and Punishment: A Review and Assessment of Theory and Evidence." *Social Problems* 39(4): 421–446.

Cohen, Lizabeth. 2004. *A Consumer's Republic: The Politics of Mass Consumption in Postwar America*. New York: Vintage Books.

Davis, Mike. 1992. *City of Quartz: Excavating the Future in Los Angeles*. New York: Vintage.

Donato, Marla. 2017. "Pulling Back the Curtain on Police Officers' Suicides." CityLab, May 22. https://www.citylab.com/solutions/2017/05/pulling-back-the-curtain-on-police-officers-mental-health-needs/527505/.

Ellin, Nan, ed. 1997. *Architecture of Fear*. New York: Princeton Architectural Press.

Fields, Barbara. 1982. "Ideology and Race in American History." In *Region, Race, and Reconstruction: Essays in Honor of C. Vann Woodward,* edited by Morgan Kousser and James M. McPherson, 143–177. New York: Oxford University Press.

Forman, James, Jr. 2017. *Locking Up Our Own: Crime and Punishment in Black America.* New York: Farrar, Straus and Giroux.

Frase, Peter 2014. "When Will They Shoot?" *Jacobin,* August 17. https://www.jacobinmag.com/2014/08/when-will-they-shoot/.

Gilmore, Ruth Wilson. 2007. *Golden Gulag: Prisons, Surplus, Crisis, and Opposition in Globalizing California.* Berkeley: University of California Press.

Gordon, Todd. 2005. "The Political Economy of Law-and-Order Policies: Policing, Class Struggle, and Neoliberal Restructuring." *Studies in Political Economy* 75 (Spring): 53–77.

Graham, Stephen. 2010. *Cities under Siege: The New Military Urbanism.* London: Verso.

Hall, Stuart, Chas Critcher, Tony Jefferson, John Clarke, and Brian Roberts. 2013. *Policing the Crisis: Mugging, the State and Law and Order.* London: Palgrave-Macmillan.

Harvey, David. 2008. "The Right to the City." *New Left Review* 53 (September–October): 27.

Jackson, George. 1996. *Blood in My Eye.* Baltimore: Black Classics Press. Reprinted, 1996.

Jackson, Kenneth T. 1985. *Crabgrass Frontier: The Suburbanization of the United States.* New York: Oxford University Press.

Johnson, Cedric G. 2015. "Working the Reserve Army: Proletarianization in Revanchist New Orleans." nonsite.org, September 4. https://nonsite.org/article/working-the-reserve-army.

Johnson, Cedric G. 2016a. "Afterword: Baltimore, the Policing Crisis and the End of the Obama Era." In *Urban Policy in the Time of Obama,* edited by James DeFilippis. Minneapolis: University of Minnesota Press.

Johnson, Cedric G. 2016b. "The Half-Life of the Black Urban Regime: Adolph Reed, Jr. on Race, Capitalism and Urban Governance." *Labor Studies Journal* 41(3): 248–255.

Johnson, Cedric G. 2017. "The Panthers Cannot Save Us Now: Anti-policing Struggles and the Limits of Black Power." *Catalyst* 1(1): 56–85.

Johnson, Jenna. 2016. Trump: Racial Divisions Have Gotten Worse, Not Better," *Washington Post,* July 8. https://www.washingtonpost.com/news/post-politics/wp/2016/07/08/donald-trump-racial-divisions-have-gotten-worse-not-better/?utm_term=.4b91ea6ccd14.

Jones, William P. 2013. *The March on Washington: Jobs, Freedom, and the Forgotten History of Civil Rights.* New York: W. W. Norton.

Katznelson, Ira. 2005. *When Affirmative Action Was White: An Untold History of Racial Inequality in Twentieth-Century America.* New York: W. W. Norton.

King, Shaun. 2016. "White men killed more American police than any other group this year, but conservatives won't address the facts," *New York Daily News,* May16. https://www.nydailynews.com/news/national/king-cops-killed-white-men-conservatives-silent-article-1.2632965.

Kramer, Alisa Sarah. 2007. "William H. Parker and the Thin Blue Line: Politics, Public Relations and Policing in Postwar Los Angeles." PhD diss., American University.

Kusch, Frank. 2008. *Battleground Chicago: The Police and the 1968 Democratic National Convention.* Chicago: University of Chicago Press.

Labor Beat. 2015. "Unions and the Police." Video posted December 27. https://www.youtube.com/watch?v=6j0e5Lv2xKE.

Landry, Bart. 1987. *The New Black Middle Class*. Berkeley: University of California Press.

Larimer, Sarah. 2016. "Rudy Giuliani: Black Fathers Need to Teach Kids 'the Real Danger to Them Is Not the Police.'" *Washington Post*, July11. https://www .washingtonpost.com/news/post-nation/wp/2016/07/10/rudy-giuliani-black -fathers-need-to-teach-kids-the-real-danger-to-them-is-not-the-police/?utm _term=.23e5ea0e82d7.

Levine, Rhonda F. 1988. *Class Struggle and the New Deal: Industrial Labor, Industrial Capital, and the State*. Lawrence: University Press of Kansas.

Lewis, Nathaniel. 2018. "Mass Incarceration: New Jim Crow, Class War, or Both?" People's Policy Project, January 30. https://peoplespolicyproject.org/2018/01/30 /mass-incarceration-new-jim-crow-class-war-or-both/.

Linebaugh, Peter. 2003. *The London Hanged: Crime and Civil Society in the Eighteenth Century*. London: Verso.

Lopez, Leslie. 2016. "'I Believe Trump like I Believed Obama!' A Case Study of Two Working-Class 'Latino' Trump Voters: My Parents." nonsite.org, November 28. https://nonsite.org/editorial/i-believe-trump-like-i-believed-obama.

Low, Setha. 2004. *Behind the Gates: Life, Security and the Pursuit of Happiness in Fortress America*. New York: Routledge.

Marx, Karl. 1867. *Capital*, volume1. New York: Penguin Books.

Morin, Rich, Kim Parker, Renee Stepler, and Andrew Mercer. 2017. *Behind the Badge: Amid Protests and Calls for Reform, How Police View Their Jobs, Key Issues and Recent Fatal Encounters between Blacks and Police*. Pew Research Center, January. http://www.pewsocialtrends.org/2017/01/11/behind-the-badge/.

Neocleous, Mark. 2000. *The Fabrication of Order: A Critical Theory of Police Power*. London: Pluto Press.

Nickeas, Peter. 2018. "Chicago Officer Kills Himself in Police Station Parking Lot, Officials Say." *Chicago Tribune*, July 10. http://www.chicagotribune.com/news /local/breaking/ct-met-chicago-police-suicide-20180709-story.html.

O'Connor, Lydia. 2016. "Rudy Giuliani Says Black Parents Need to Teach Their Children to Respect Police." *Huffington Post*, July 10. https://www.huffingtonpost.com /entry/rudy-giuliani-dallas-shooting_us_5782a9b5e4b0344d514fd28e.

O'Hara, Andy. 2017. "It's Time We Talk about Police Suicide." The Marshall Project, October 3. https://www.themarshallproject.org/2017/10/03/it-s-time-we-talk -about-police-suicide.

Palmer, Bryan D. 2016. "Teamsters and Cops." *Jacobin*, July 15. https://www.jacobinmag .com/2016/07/police-brutality-philando-castile-unions-teamsters-labor.

Parenti, Christian. 2016. "Listening to Trump." nonsite.org, November 17. https:// nonsite.org/editorial/listening-to-trump.

Pattillo, Mary. 1999. *Black Picket Fences: Privilege and Peril among the Black Middle Class*. Chicago: University of Chicago Press.

Reed, Adolph, Jr. 1999. *Stirrings in the Jug: Black Politics in the Post-segregation Era*. Minneapolis: University of Minnesota Press.

Reed, Touré F. 2015. "Why Liberals Separate Race from Class." *Jacobin*, August 22. https://www.jacobinmag.com/2015/08/bernie-sanders-black-lives-matter-civil -rights-movement.

Reed, Touré F. 2018. "Between Obama and Coates." *Catalyst* 1: 8–54.

Satter, Beryl. 2010. *Family Properties: How the Struggle over Race and Real Estate Transformed Chicago and Urban America*. New York: Picador.

Schmidt, Ronald J., Jr. 2005. *This Is the City: Making Model Citizens in Los Angeles*. Minneapolis: University of Minnesota Press.

Schor, Juliet B. 1992. *The Overworked American: The Unexpected Decline of Leisure*. New York: Basic Books.
Sharp, Elaine B. 2014. "Politics, Economics, and Urban Policing: The Postindustrial City Thesis and Rival Explanations of Heightened Order Maintenance Policing." *Urban Affairs Review* 50(3): 340–365.
Smith, Neil. 1996. *The New Urban Frontier: Gentrification and the Revanchist City*. London: Routledge.
Smith, Neil. 2009. "Revanchist Planet: Regeneration and the Axis of Co-evilism." *Urban Reinventors* no. 3 (November): 1–18.
Smith, Preston H., II. 2012. *Racial Democracy and the Black Metropolis: Housing Policy in Postwar Chicago*. Minneapolis: University of Minnesota Press.
Sobol, Rosemary, and Zak Koeske. 2018. "Days after Cop Committed Suicide at South Side Station, another Officer Collapses and Dies There." *Chicago Tribune*, July 11. http://www.chicagotribune.com/news/local/breaking/ct-met-police-deaths-roseland-20180710-story.html.
Wacquant, Loïc. 2009. *Punishing the Poor: The Neoliberal Government of Social Insecurity*. Durham, NC: Duke University Press.
Wacquant, Loïc. 2010. "Class, Race and Hyperincarceration in Revanchist America." *Daedalus* 140(3): 74–90.
Washington Post. 2017. "Police Brutality Is No Joke, Mr. President." Editorial, July 31. https://www.washingtonpost.com/opinions/police-brutality-is-no-joke-mr-president/2017/07/31/f584c174-7622-11e7-8f39-eeb7d3a2d304_story.html?utm_term=.6c66a81c6940.
Whitehouse, David. 2014. "Origins of the Police." *Works in Theory* (blog), December 7. https://worxintheory.wordpress.com/2014/12/07/origins-of-the-police/.
Wiese, Andrew. 2006. "'The House I Live In': Race, Class and African American Suburban Dreams in the Postwar United States." In *The New Suburban History*, edited by Kevin M. Kruse and Thomas J. Sugrue. Chicago: University of Chicago Press, 99-1999.
Zweig, Michael. 2000. *The Working Class Majority: America's Best Kept Secret*. Ithaca, NY: ILR Press/Cornell University Press.

Part IV

LABOR STRATEGIES AND RESPONSES

10

GOING SOUTH: HOW SOUTHERN ORGANIZING WILL DETERMINE THE FUTURE OF THE LABOR MOVEMENT

MaryBe McMillan

In this time of rising inequality, working people need the bargaining power of unions more than ever, yet sustained attacks on workers' right to organize, combined with geographically shortsighted organizing by labor leaders, have left many workers without the option of joining a union. This chapter makes the case that our ability to raise wages, protect labor rights, and improve working conditions across the nation depends largely on increased efforts to organize working people in the South. Population growth, job expansion, and political influence all point to the importance of the South as a driver of our nation's economy and its politics.

In this race to the bottom to see who can pay workers the least, companies are flocking to the South, and as they move south, wages tend to go south, too. Between 1980 and 2013, the number of auto industry jobs in the South increased by 52 percent, while those in the Midwest fell by one-third. At the same time, Alabama, South Carolina, and Tennessee each saw a rise in manufacturing jobs of over 100 percent, while Ohio, Wisconsin, and Michigan lost from one-third to one-half of their manufacturing jobs (Meyerson 2015). Six of the top ten metropolitan areas experiencing the most job growth in 2016 were in the South (Portillo 2017).

The South is gaining not just jobs but also population and political influence. Thirty-eight percent of the nation's population live in the South—almost as many people as live in the Northeast and Midwest combined (US Census Bureau 2018). After the 2010 census, the South gained eight congressional seats, while the Northeast lost five (Burnett 2011). After the 2020 census, the South is projected to gain another five seats, while the Northeast and Midwest are projected to lose a combined nine seats (Tippett 2017). In 2016, the South delivered over half the Electoral College votes that propelled President Trump to victory (Kiersz 2016), and prior to the 2018 midterm election, representatives from the South made up 45 percent of the Republican caucus in the US House of Representatives and chaired twelve out of twenty-one House committees (Haas 2017).

Changing our nation's policies and politics depends on changing the South. The right wing has long understood the importance of the South. Nancy MacLean's book *Democracy in Chains* (2017) documents how, decades ago, a conservative pundit in the South developed a long-term strategy funded by the Koch brothers that has led to both the rightward shift in our nation's politics and increased attacks on organized labor. Using this strategy, conservative politicians, with the help of the American Legislative Exchange Council (ALEC), have spread the South's repressive policies, such as voter suppression, mass incarceration, and "right-to-work," around the country.

For decades, southern states have been dealing with right-to-work and restrictions on public-sector bargaining—challenges now faced by unions in the Midwest and elsewhere. This chapter will explore how organizers in the South have overcome those challenges and what lessons the South offers for labor leaders across the country about how we build a strong working people's movement not limited by the walls of the workplace or the inadequacy of our labor laws.

A Southern Perspective

Although I am trained as a sociologist, I write this chapter primarily from the perspective of a labor leader who is working to build a movement in a state that has been right-to-work for over seventy years. Right-to-work is all organizers have ever known in North Carolina and in most of the South. When I have listened to labor leaders' outrage about states like Wisconsin and Michigan passing anti-union laws or the Supreme Court ruling in *Janus v. AFSCME*, I have often wondered, where is the outrage about the lack of worker freedom in North Carolina and other states that have long been right-to-work and have denied our public employees the right to bargain collectively?

Consider that in 2011, when then governor Scott Walker of Wisconsin launched his attack on collective bargaining rights, the labor movement around the country and around the globe rallied in support of Wisconsin's public employees. What if, decades ago, the labor movement had rallied in support of bargaining rights in North Carolina or Virginia? If that had happened, maybe working people would not have had to fight attacks on bargaining rights in Wisconsin and Iowa or right-to-work in Michigan and Missouri. Maybe our country would not have elected Donald Trump as our president. But here we are, and now, ironically, labor leaders around the country are looking to the South to find out how to fight back and build strong unions in a hostile legal and political climate. By heeding the lessons of the South and, as I will argue later, by investing resources in the South, labor leaders can successfully fight back and change our country's policies and our politics.

When working people stand up, and when community allies and people of faith stand with those workers, victory is possible—even in the unlikeliest of places. North Carolina has long been one of the least unionized states in the country, but in recent years, unions have made headlines for achieving several significant victories in the state. In 2004, the Farm Labor Organizing Committee (FLOC) made national news by winning a historic three-party collective-bargaining agreement with the Mount Olive Pickle Company and the North Carolina Growers' Association that covered 8,000 farmworkers—the largest collective bargaining agreement in North Carolina history (Reyes 2004). Then, in 2008, after a fierce fifteen-year struggle, workers at Smithfield Packing in Tarheel, North Carolina, won a union at the world's largest pork-processing plant in what became one of the United Food and Commercial Workers (UFCW) Union's largest victories ever (Bacon 2008). And in 2016, adjunct faculty at Duke University in Durham, North Carolina, organized with the Service Employees International Union (SEIU) and formed the first faculty union at a major private university in the South. This effort resulted in a groundbreaking first contract that guaranteed job security through multiyear teaching engagements and secured pay raises for the lowest-paid faculty of 46 percent over three years (Stancill 2017).

Four Strategies for Success

My experience in North Carolina indicates that there are at least four strategies needed for successful organizing in the South or, more generally, organizing in right-to-work states with hostile political climates. First, we need a moral economic message that can move people to action and must use that message to organize constantly—both internally and externally. Second, we must unite and organize with our allies to create a broad, diverse movement that is rooted in our local communities. Third, we must address issues of race and gender equality. Finally, we must work to change the political climate through long-term base building, not just through short-term electoral strategies.

For decades, organizers in the South have held onto the faith that, despite long odds and a long fight, working people can win, and that the way we win is by building a movement. Labor leaders in the South learned a long time ago what others around the country are just beginning to understand: unions cannot win in a right-to-work, anti-union climate by ourselves. That is why, across the South, strong coalitions have formed among labor, faith, and civil rights groups; a new solidarity is developing among black, white, and brown workers; and unions are experimenting with innovative, nontraditional organizing.

Start Small, Dream Big

From over a decade of working with union members, I have learned that by uniting working people around a moral economic message, and by constantly and creatively organizing, we can triumph over divisiveness and build both strong unions and a growing movement for shared prosperity. I have also learned that to build such a movement, we must start small and dream big. That means we begin by motivating one person at a time to join us—first in the workplaces we represent and then by reaching out to organize new workers in new ways. Starting small also means building power locally, one community at a time.

Most importantly, as we are building this movement person by person, workplace by workplace, and community by community, we cannot lose sight of the larger dream of a country where there is truly justice and freedom for all. Our organizing should be guided by a long-range vision of building lasting power for all working people, and to be successful, that vision must include a strategy to organize working people in the South. If we build a strong labor movement in the South, we can improve conditions for working people everywhere.

That movement must start with a compelling message. We have no movement unless we move people. That means changing the way people think and growing our ranks. Our ability to motivate people depends on how we talk about our issues and goals. Scholars use the term "movement frame" to describe the way leaders message around issues (Benford and Snow 2000). Gamson (1992) outlines three components of a successful frame: identity, injustice, and agency. The labor movement can frame issues in a way that is salient to all three, especially around identity. Numerous pundits and union leaders have discussed how political candidates and parties framed issues in the 2016 election. Generally, the debate has revolved around how much Democrats or the Left should focus on economics versus "identity politics" (Lynch 2016). This debate poses a false dichotomy because to talk about economic issues draws on our common identity as workers.

While few may relate to a conversation about social class and class consciousness, most people can identify with the need for a job and to make a living. Most Americans believe in fair pay for a day's work, that our employers should provide safe working conditions, and that we should have some reasonable time off to spend with our families. A message of economic fairness can unite people re-gardless of profession, race, or gender. By using the economic message as the opening line, we can invite people into a conversation that can connect the dots between wages and immigration reform, and between poverty and mass incar-ceration, a conversation that over time can transform the way people think about race, gender, and cultural differences.

A message rooted in economic fairness provides not only the common ground to bridge differences, but also a foundation for talking about injustice and in-equality. Millions of Americans are underemployed, wages have stagnated, and income inequality has reached staggering proportions, and yet these are not the issues we hear about each day in the news. Economic insecurity in this country has become normalized so that as we sink lower and lower in this race to the bot-tom, we have become a country of lowered expectations. Desperate workers ig-nore safety violations and risk their lives for a job that barely pays the bills. Com-munities give away millions in tax incentives to companies for a handful of jobs that may not pay a living wage. Democrats shy away from policies that do not appear business-friendly, while progressives write off unions as irrelevant. Voters seem resigned to choosing between the lesser of two evils at the ballot box, and, for the most part, Americans seem to accept this as inevitable.

To motivate people to fight back, we must raise expectations so that it is not okay for people to work full-time and live in poverty; it is not seen as normal for people to work two or three jobs to make ends meet; and it is not acceptable to spend most of one's life at a job and have little or no retirement savings at the end. Working people must expect better, especially in the South. One way to shift the conversation and raise expectations is to take the moral high ground and call out corporate greed as immoral and unjust. People working full-time and living in poverty, CEOs earning 400 times what workers make, and working people cre-ating the wealth but not getting our fair share are all wrong, plain and simple. To fight back, people must know it is right to stand up for what we deserve, that it is okay to stand together with our co-workers to ask for better, and that any attack on our right to do so is unjust. Labor cannot let corporate America and conser-vative politicians define fair pay as a radical idea when instead it is a moral princi-ple that most Americans believe in.

The Moral Monday movement that united diverse groups in North Carolina to fight back against an extremist legislature shows the importance and effective-ness of taking back the moral frame from the Right (McClain 2014). A moral mes-sage transcends partisan politics to frame the discussion as right or wrong, not Right or Left, and part of that message is that we can do better. Workers must understand that massive inequality is not inevitable and that together we can change it. That message is a major component of the AFL-CIO's Common Sense

Economics education program because too often when people look at inequality, the problem can seem so overwhelming that they feel powerless to change it. Too many Americans believe nothing they do will make a difference, that voting in an election or calling their lawmaker will not change anything. To counter that, we must provide hope that collective action will indeed make a difference, and, equally important, we must give people opportunities to take action.

Organize, Organize, Organize

Through our local unions, we can demonstrate that solidarity and action can win victories in the workplace and beyond. We can move people with a compelling moral message about economic fairness. To spread that message, we start by using it to organize more members in the workplaces we represent. A powerful movement starts with strong local unions, and, despite right-to-work, organizers have built locals with high membership rates in the South. One national union has an average membership rate of 85 percent in its southern locals.

That union and others have grown their membership by focusing on internal worksite organizing—something that is critical for labor in a right-to-work environment. Worksite organizing and the economic fairness message should touch workers on the job from their first day until their last one. Workers must know their union is fighting for them and that together we can make a difference. In newsletters, e-mails, and bulletin boards, communications should provide information to both members and nonmembers that the bargaining committee is fighting for a good contract, that the union representative won someone's job back, and that union leaders are lobbying lawmakers for policies to benefit their industry. Workers want and need to know who their union leaders and stewards are. They should hear regularly from those leaders and representatives, and if a worker is not yet a member, someone should ask that person to join and keep asking.

Successful unions in the South have learned this lesson and worked to turn members into organizers. Few locals in North Carolina have staff organizers, and many do not have full-time officers. For unions to be effective, they cannot rely on elected leaders and staff to do all the organizing and instead must create a culture where stewards and rank-and-file members feel a responsibility to organize and mobilize. To create that culture requires constant organizing, a worksite mobilization structure, and an accountability system. The United Steelworkers have worked to create that kind of culture in their locals in the South with a campaign called "Wrong Not to Belong." In addition to promoting that slogan in a visible way with t-shirts and stickers, the campaign also involves local leaders regularly comparing lists of dues-paying members to lists of those who are eligible for membership and then developing a strategy to recruit nonmembers to join. Leaders and staff then report frequently on the number of new members signed.

Other affiliates have developed similar strategies. By posting a list of nonmembers, working with stewards to map out shifts and departments, and making assignments for who will talk to whom, locals create a mobilization structure that not only can result in new members, but also allows for rapid-response mobilization around legislative fights, contract issues, or get-out-the-vote efforts. Because we should always be focused on the long-term goal of building power, internal organizing should be seen not simply as a way to grow members, but also as an opportunity to grow activists who will be engaged and ready to act around issues and campaigns. As unions around the country renew their focus on worksite organizing, it is a chance to hone our message, strengthen our unions, and build a mobilization structure to help us win not just in the workplace but also at the ballot box and at the state capitol.

We can build strong locals with high membership rates under right-to-work, but we cannot stop there—we must keep growing this movement by organizing working people wherever they live, whatever they do. To build the labor movement we need in the South and in the nation, we must think outside the box, reach a broader audience with our message, and organize more working people into unions and other labor organizations. In the South, where it has long been difficult to organize unions, workers have learned that they cannot be deterred by the loss of a National Labor Relations Board (NLRB) election. For example, with the help of the United Auto Workers, workers formed a minority union at the Volkswagen plant in Chattanooga, Tennessee. Similarly, the United Electrical Workers (UE) and others have organized public employees in states with no public-sector bargaining rights, and through public pressure on elected officials, they have been able to win wage increases and policy changes.

Innovative strategies are necessary to bring justice to workers who have few legal protections. That is certainly true for farmworkers, who are excluded from the National Labor Relations Act. The Farm Labor Organizing Committee (FLOC) won better wages and treatment for farmworkers who pick cucumbers by targeting not farmers but Mount Olive Pickle, the corporation that bought the produce, because the company controlled the price paid for the cucumbers and the wages paid to workers. In addition to launching a boycott of Mount Olive products, FLOC personalized the campaign by focusing on the company's CEO and identifying pressure points to persuade him to come to the bargaining table. After FLOC determined that the CEO of Mount Olive was a deacon in his local Methodist church, the union focused on getting congregations and, ultimately, the national church governing body to pass a resolution in support of the campaign. The CEO agreed to negotiate with the union and the North Carolina Growers Association soon after the national Methodist Church passed the resolution. FLOC's strategy shows the necessity of sometimes rethinking the traditional employer relationship and the importance of enlisting community support for labor struggles.

Similarly, after two failed union elections and over a decade of corporate union busting, the UFCW campaign at Smithfield Packing in Tar Heel, North Carolina, turned a corner after the union hired a full-time community organizer to gain the support of faith and community leaders in pressuring the company to respect workers' right to organize. While waiting for the appeals of the last NLRB election to go through the courts, UFCW's community organizer regularly engaged other unions and community allies by organizing petition drives, letters of support, shareholder actions, and informational pickets outside grocery stores in multiple states. With a full-time focus on community outreach, UFCW kept up pressure on the company for over two years. With that pressure and a litigation strategy, workers were able to get a neutrality agreement for a truly fair election, which the union won in 2008.

Address Race and Gender Inequality

Both FLOC's campaign with Mount Olive Pickle and UFCW's campaign at Smithfield Packing combined the fight for workplace justice with the fights for immigration reform and civil rights. As unions think creatively about both new ways and new workers to organize, our movement must prioritize reaching out to those workers who need a union the most. Not surprisingly, those workers who earn the lowest wages and are the most exploited are most often workers of color. With the South home to the majority of African Americans in the country and an increasing number of immigrants, the success of the southern labor movement depends on organizing workers of color and fighting for racial and gender equality.

A consistent reason given for the failure of Operation Dixie, which was launched to organize workers in the South in the 1940s, is that rather than focusing on organizing African American workers who were receptive to the union, the effort focused on organizing mostly white workers in the textile industry, who were more resistant to organizing efforts (Fones-Wolf and Fones-Wolf 2015). In contrast, the Food, Tobacco, Agricultural, and Allied Workers of America (FTA) in the 1940s helped predominantly African American workers win a campaign at RJ Reynolds Tobacco Company in Winston-Salem, North Carolina (Korstad 2003). African American women in the factory led a strike and spearheaded the organizing campaign to improve working conditions and challenge racial discrimination in the plant. The workers were successful not only in organizing the factory but also in electing an African American alderman for the city and paving the way for the growth of an African American middle class.

Polls have shown that people of color continue to be more receptive to unions (Ramirez 2012). Both history and current campaigns such as SEIU's Fight for $15 show that linking the fights for labor rights and civil rights helps bring working people and community allies together as a powerful force for change. At a time when racist rhetoric has become commonplace in our politics and workers of color are among the most exploited, labor organizers must address racism in the workplace, the country, and in our unions.

Building a movement does not mean simply moving people who agree with us to action. It also means changing attitudes. Unions shape policies to reduce discrimination, but more than that, unions are uniquely situated to challenge racist and sexist beliefs, because they bring diverse people together around a common identity and can foster transformative conversations that change biases.

For this reason, I believe it is also important that our movement continue to find new ways to reach the white working class and engage them in conversations about racial equality and economic justice. Through its canvassing program, Working America, the community affiliate of the AFL-CIO, has successfully organized moderate white voters who do not belong to a union by having such conversations at the door. By talking about economic fairness, Working America has changed people's attitudes about immigration reform and other divisive issues and motivated them to take political action. Over several years in North Carolina, Working America has added over 40,000 members to our movement—members who have mobilized around legislative fights and supported labor-endorsed candidates all because someone reached out to them with a message of economic fairness and asked them to act.

Build Political Power Locally and Statewide

To grow our movement, we need to organize more workers into unions, but we must do much more than that. We must organize those who do not have a union into alternative organizations like Working America. We must organize voters to elect worker-friendly candidates, organize constituents to demand better legislation, and, ultimately, organize the working class into a broad, diverse movement for economic justice. The target can no longer be a specific workplace; it must be a community. To win the hearts and minds of people in the workplace, we must win over their friends, their families, and their neighbors. To change what happens in Congress or the state capitol depends on changing what happens in lawmakers' home districts. The future of our movement will be determined not by what happens in Washington, D.C., but by what happens in the places working people call home.

The idea of building power locally is not new. The AFL-CIO launched a "Union Cities" program in the late 1990s and has revived it since then. The idea behind "Union Cities" is that unions working together to mobilize their members and community allies in direct action can influence local ordinances and politics to help create jobs, raise wages, and empower working people (Moberg 2001). AFL-CIO central bodies serve as hubs for these local efforts. Central bodies, which are the local groups of affiliated unions such as state federations, area labor federations (ALFs), and central labor councils (CLCs), coordinate and drive the local work, especially candidate endorsements and get-out-the-vote efforts. A major focus of "Union Cities" has been electing worker-friendly candidates, including union members, to local office—something that unions can do more easily as union membership grows.

Just as unions work together locally to elect candidates they endorsed, they should join forces to win organizing campaigns in the workplace. State federations, area labor federations, and central labor councils can play significant roles in organizing (Fletcher and Gapasin 2008). Rather than building relationships from scratch, unions can call on AFL-CIO central bodies to leverage longtime relationships they have with community partners, area media, and local elected officials. Central bodies can also mobilize other unions in the area to show solidarity. For example, our state federation mobilized organizers from multiple unions to make house calls to potential members for the faculty union campaign at Duke University. Our organization also housed the community organizer who worked for UFCW on the campaign at Smithfield Packing, and we helped that organizer make connections with faith and community leaders.

Larger state federations and CLCs around the country have added staff to do strategic research on organizing targets, hired organizers to lend to affiliates for campaigns, and established organizing roundtables where affiliates not only share best practices but also collaborate on campaigns. When affiliates ask for help and provide resources, central bodies can do even more to support organizing and grow our movement.

To make progress in the South and build power, investment in state federations and central bodies is essential. In an anti-union environment, it takes real effort to garner community support, build relationships, and sway public opinion. By helping affiliates research and identify geographic areas with multiple organizing targets, the central body can coordinate union efforts to work together to build community relationships, educate the public about unions, and engage in local political struggles. For example, if an auto plant is near a poultry processor, unions at both can work together to develop a strong coalition of support and build a lasting infrastructure that can support ongoing campaigns.

The central body can work with affiliates to map relationships and do a power analysis of the whole community: Who goes to which church? Who has family members in the targeted workplace? Who has sway with local politicians? Who or what could influence the CEO of the targeted workplace? By bringing working people and organizations together in their communities, we can alter the power structure and win gains for workers.

Using this model in Durham, North Carolina, our state federation and the local CLC helped bring together unions, allies, and sympathetic elected officials to support union organizing on the Duke University campus and to elect a worker-friendly mayor and city council. After accomplishing that, local unions and allies created the Durham Workers Assembly, which is working with city officials to establish a workers' rights commission that, given our state's prohibition against public-sector collective bargaining, is a model for other cities of how unions and worker organizations can engage with elected officials on workplace issues (Baumgartner Vaughan 2018). The Workers Assembly is also starting a "Durham is a Union Town" campaign and exploring ways to work together to expand union membership in the city.

Organize the South, Change the Nation

By spreading a moral economic message, building strong local unions, organizing new workers, and coming together to organize and build power in communities, we can fight back and change policies. As labor leaders across the country look to the South for strategies for fighting back under right-to-work, the question may arise, if these strategies really are successful, then why are there not more unions in the South? I argue that we would have more unions in the South if labor leaders took the long view and made significant and lasting investments in southern organizing.

A critical lesson for labor leaders is that the South is a reflection not of our nation's past but of its future. That is true now and it was true in the 1940s when the Congress of Industrial Organizations (CIO) launched Operation Dixie. Both union organizers and company owners knew that increased union density in the South could increase support for New Deal liberalism and impact labor relations around the nation (Fones-Wolf and Fones-Wolf 2015). Operation Dixie, however, failed to yield substantially more CIO members in the South. Historians cite several factors that contributed to the project's lack of success, including anticommunism, racism (in society and within unions), fundamentalist religion, and fierce employer opposition (Fones-Wolf and Fones-Wolf 2015). In addition, some cite the lack of a long-term view of social change among CIO leadership as another reason for Operation Dixie's failure (Griffith 1988).

Such shortsightedness continues to plague the labor movement. While union organizing in the South has increased and the AFL-CIO passed a resolution at its 2013 national convention to develop a "Southern organizing strategy," labor leaders have not developed a concerted, coordinated plan to organize working people in the South in a systematic, purposeful way. As a result, some of our nation's most populous states, such as North Carolina and Georgia, are also the least unionized, and the South continues to push our politics and our policies rightward.

Keep Sight of the Dream

For too long, many unions have focused on short-term political wins in a few states rather than building a grassroots movement around the country. The focus on political deals and electoral wins has also meant that too many unions in non–right-to-work states lost their focus on internal worksite organizing—something essential not only to survival in a post-*Janus*, increasingly right-to-work world but also to get-out-the-vote efforts and legislative mobilization. As unions devote more resources to super PACs and political campaigns, there are fewer resources available to organize new members, mobilize existing members, and build the labor movement's own internal structure—a structure that, while not perfect, is critical to winning victories in the workplace and beyond. Working people will never be able to match the amount of money available to the Koch Brothers, CEOs, and Wall Street bankers, and even if labor could raise equal amounts, we cannot expect to strengthen our democracy by putting more money into politics and fueling the rising campaign costs that keep working people out of elected office.

If our goal is not simply resistance but systemic change, then we as leaders cannot focus only on short-term electoral wins. Likewise, we must also stop conflating rallies and mass protests with building lasting power. Protest is necessary but not sufficient to build a movement. Marches and protests in Washington, D.C., and our state capitals can motivate and inspire, but to grow and sustain a movement, we have to inspire those back home by hosting town halls, holding our local legislators accountable, recruiting good candidates for the next election, and most of all by organizing conversations in our neighborhoods, our workplaces, and our community centers to move people to action. Start small and dream big—by changing individuals, we change our culture and our country.

I believe that in this moment of increasing inequality and divisiveness, a strong and vibrant labor movement is the only force that will transform our economy into one that works for all of us. Unions change the dynamics of the workplace and shift the direction of our policies, and they do that by changing people. I have seen workers who had lost hope become energized leaders, I have heard white union members who once ranted about "illegal aliens" speak out for the Dreamers, and I have talked to union members who were diehard activists in their political party but now vote based on labor's endorsement, not party affiliation.

Unions are transformative and, according to polls, more popular than they have been in years (Swift 2017). No unionist wants a right-to-work law, but "right to work" can never mean "right to surrender," especially when so many working people want and need a union. As organizers in the South have shown for decades, it is possible to organize and build strong unions anywhere. We are at a critical moment when labor leaders have an opportunity to reinvent and rebuild our movement; yet too many seem to have lost faith in our ability to organize and thrive.

At a time when it seems that our movement has lost its faith, I know just where to find it. The South is the land of revival, it is where people get born again, and it is where, for decades, working people have taken a leap of faith to organize in some of the toughest conditions around. We persist because, as an underdog, as we have been in the South for so long, we are motivated not from fear of all we can lose but by hope of all we can gain. That is perhaps the most important lesson our movement can learn from the South. We must organize not out of fear but out of hope.

The labor movement can grow and thrive, but to do so, labor leaders must believe that success is possible. So now is not the time for those of us in the labor movement to hang our heads and hunker down. It is time to stand up and show working people across this country that the labor movement is on their side; that the collective strength of a union can win good wages; that our political power as a movement can keep good jobs here, and that our families and our neighbors coming together will save the working class. It is not Donald Trump or Bernie Sanders, and it is not either political party or yet another super PAC. The only way we move this country forward is by uniting and building a bigger, bolder labor movement. If we start small, dream big, and never lose sight of the dream of shared prosperity for all of us, we can do just that.

References

Bacon, David. 2008. "Unions Come to Smithfield." *American Prospect*, December 17. http://prospect.org/article/unions-come-smithfield.
Baumgartner Vaughan, Dawn. 2018. "Is Durham a Union Town? Labor Groups Hope So." *Herald Sun*, February 2. http://www.heraldsun.com/news/local/counties/durham-county/article197987319.html.

Benford, Robert D., and David A. Snow. 2000. "Framing Processes and Social Movements: An Overview and Assessment." *Annual Review of Sociology* 26:611–639.

Burnett, Kristin D. 2011. "Congressional Apportionment." *2010 Census Briefs*, November. https://www.census.gov/prod/cen2010/briefs/c2010br-08.pdf.

Fletcher, Bill, Jr., and Fernando Gapasin. 2008. *Solidarity Divided: The Crisis in Organized Labor and a New Path toward Social Justice.* Berkeley: University of California Press.

Fones-Wolf, Elizabeth, and Ken Fones-Wolf. 2015. *Struggle for the Soul of the Postwar South: White Evangelical Protestants and Operation Dixie.* Urbana: University of Illinois Press.

Gamson, William A. 1992. "The Social Psychology of Collective Action." In *Frontiers in Social Movement Theory*, edited by Aldon D. Morris and Carol McClurg Mueller, 53–76. New Haven, CT: Yale University Press.

Griffith, Barbara S. 1988. *The Crisis of American Labor: Operation Dixie and the Defeat of the CIO.* Philadelphia: Temple University Press.

Haas, Karen L. 2017. "List of Standing Committees, One Hundred and Fifteenth Congress." http://clerk.house.gov/committee_info/scsoal.pdf.

Kiersz, Andy. 2016. "Here's the Final 2016 Electoral College Map." *Business Insider*, November 28. http://www.businessinsider.com/final-electoral-college-map -trump-clinton-2016-11.

Korstad, Robert. 2003. *Civil Rights Unionism: Tobacco Workers and the Struggle for Democracy in the Mid-Twentieth-Century South.* Chapel Hill: University of North Carolina Press.

Lynch, Conor. 2016. "Identity Politics vs. Populist Economics? It's a False Choice— Liberals Need to Look in the Mirror." *Salon*, December 3. https://www.salon.com /2016/12/03/identity-politics-vs-populist-economics-its-a-false-choice-liberals -need-to-look-in-the-mirror/.

MacLean, Nancy. 2017. *Democracy in Chains: The Deep History of the Radical Right's Stealth Plan for America.* New York: Viking Press.

McClain, Dani. 2014. "How the Moral Mondays 'Fusion Coalition' Is Taking North Carolina Back." *The Nation*, July 2. https://www.thenation.com/article/how-moral -mondays-fusion-coalition-taking-north-carolina-back/.

Meyerson, Harold. 2015. "How the American South Drives the Low-Wage Economy." *American Prospect*, July 6. http://prospect.org/article/how-american-south-drives -low-wage-economy.

Moberg, David. 2001. "Union Cities." *American Prospect*, December 19. http://prospect .org/article/union-cities.

Portillo, Ely. 2017. "Charlotte Had Fourth-Fastest Job Growth in U.S. Last Year, Study Says." *Charlotte Observer*, July 5. http://www.charlotteobserver.com/news /business/biz-columns-blogs/development/article159666734.html.

Ramirez, Rosa. 2012. "Poll: Minorities View Labor Unions More Favorably." *The Atlantic*, October 16. https://www.theatlantic.com/politics/archive/2012/10/poll -minorities-view-labor-unions-more-favorably/429102/.

Reyes, Teófilo. 2004. "8000 'Guest Workers' Join Farm Union in North Carolina." *Labor Notes*, September 30. http://www.labornotes.org/2004/09/8000 -%E2%80%98guest-workers%E2%80%99-join-farm-union-north-carolina.

Stancill, Jane. 2017. "Duke Faculty Members Win Big Raises in Historic Union Agree-ment." *News and Observer*, July 12. http://www.newsobserver.com/news/local /education/article160915224.html.

Swift, Art. 2017. "Labor Union Approval Best since 2003, at 61%." Workplace, August 30. http://news.gallup.com/poll/217331/labor-union-approval-best-2003.aspx.

Tippett, Rebecca. 2017. *2020 Congressional Reapportionment: An Update.* Carolina Population Center, December 21. http://demography.cpc.unc.edu/2017/12/21/2020-congressional-reapportionment-an-update/.

US Census Bureau. 2018. "US Population Growth by Region." https://www.census.gov/popclock/data_tables.php?component=growth.

BETWEEN HOME AND STATE: CARE WORKERS AND LABOR STRATEGY FOR THE NEW OPEN-SHOP ERA OF TRUMPLANDIA

Jennifer Klein

With changes to the US Department of Labor, US Supreme Court, National Labor Relations Board, Department of Health and Human Services, and many other parts of the regulatory state, liberals and conservatives alike have proclaimed the Trump era the apocalyptic end of organized labor in the United States. Indeed, conservatives have certainly pressed ahead full steam to make it so. Unions are losing much of the legal grounding on which they have stood for the last eight decades. Nonetheless, the savvier unions have found new footing, building foundations for unions to move from life support to fighting offense. From the Supreme Court's 2014 *Harris v. Quinn* decision to its 2018 ruling in *Janus v. AFSCME*, federal courts have inserted themselves into labor relations in the most aggressive, pro-employer way since the late nineteenth century. Surprisingly, unions that have long balanced on the edge of public and private, of exclusion from the law, of hostility from courts, and of inclusion in the welfare state have some creative responses.

Care-worker unionism is one of those movements leading the way. For the last two decades, home health care has been one of the fastest-growing occupations in the United States, adding hundreds of thousands of positions at a steady clip. The workforce tripled between 1989 and 2004, with those who can be officially counted numbering well over two million workers by the end of that period. The US Bureau of Labor Statistics correctly projected rapid employment growth in home health-aide jobs for the next decade (US Bureau of Labor Statistics 2008a, 2008b, 2011; Howes, Leana, and Smith 2012, 81). Alternatively called personal attendants, home aides, and home-care workers, they are America's frontline caregivers, who perform intimate daily tasks—such as bathing bodies, brushing teeth, putting on clothes, and cooking meals—that enable elderly or disabled people to live decent lives at home. They typically have earned hourly wages lower than those of all other jobs in health care (well below a living wage) and historically have labored without security of employment, medical or retirement benefits, workers' accident compensation, or even sufficient hours (Crown, Ahlburg, and MacAdam 1995; Burbridge 1993; Dawson and Surpin 2005).

They labor in private spaces, meeting individual and family needs, but how they do their jobs is anything but private: theirs is a story of political economy that reflects the major shifts in work and welfare that define contemporary America. Home-care aides make up a vast workforce—much larger than those of the iconic auto and steel industries. Their lives tell us much about the shifting relations between home and market, state and family. Their fate links together some of our most challenging social issues: an aging society and lack of a national long-term-care policy; the rise of a vast medical-industrial complex; the neoliberal restructuring of public services; the crisis of domestic labor and decline of family income; new immigration and systemic racial inequality; the expansion of the service economy; and the precariousness of the American labor movement.

Remarkably, at the end of the twentieth century, home care became a pivotal sector in which unions experimented with new tactics. These workers transformed organizing strategy, union demands, and the very nature of collective bargaining. Since the job stood outside New Deal labor laws, unionization had to take shape apart from that framework. Union activists also had to take account of the complex interpersonal relations essential to care work. They had to enter into alliances with the receivers of care (who have labeled themselves "consumers"). Even though they labored in private homes and had no legal standing as employees, they turned the public welfare state itself into a terrain of social struggle. Workers themselves stepped forward, "out of the shadows" as they have put it, to transform labor standards by compelling states to recognize long-term care as public labor. By 2010, over 400,000 home-care workers had joined unions.

Just as they began to change the terms of such previously "invisible," low-wage work, bringing the labor, the provision, and the clients of care into the public light of day, new attacks on the welfare state coalesced—precisely around the ideological meanings of such labor and the blurred boundaries between public and private it implied. As sociologists Daniel Beland and Brian Gran write, "The redefinition of the boundaries between public and private social policy has become a major economic and political issue in most advanced industrial societies" (Beland and Gran 2008, 2). In particular, these attacks emphasize the privatization of benefits and the privatization of risk—the very opposite of the underpinnings of "social security." Indeed, having built up varying degrees of economic and political power, as well as economic gains, especially through key alliances that together defended public services and the social public budget, home-care workers and their unions became the direct target of an anti-labor and anti–welfare-state counteroffensive launched by conservative groups through the courts and Republican state electoral gains since 2010. The 2014 Supreme Court case *Harris v. Quinn* aimed to push care workers and recipients back into the shadows, where social rights do not penetrate. State retrenchment will be facilitated through reprivatization of the labor of the welfare state.

The litigation strategy pried open space for militant action by arch-conservative groups, including directly contacting workers to dissuade them from union membership. The direct-action strategy enabled them to insert another obstructive wedge between unions and state government, while anti-union forces waited for another "agency fee" public-sector-union case to work its way back to the US Supreme Court. Yet, because home-care unionism emerged from community organizing and poor people's movements, these workers already knew nothing would be won without a fight, and, as stigmatized workers taking care of stigmatized people, unionism meant more to them than a few more dollars an hour.

Defining Home-Care Unionism

In our book *Caring for America: Home Health Workers in the Shadow of the Welfare State* (Boris and Klein 2012) and in a number of articles (see Boris and Klein 2007, 2010, 2014), Eileen Boris and I have demonstrated that government has had a central role in creating labor markets in human and social services. Not only did particular US social and employment policies over the latter half of the twentieth century foster the creation of new occupations, funded by the state, they have also actively channeled particular workers into these jobs, especially poor and minority women, deploying and perpetuating gender and racial inequality. The beneficiaries of the services, the structure of the industry, and the terms and conditions of the labor were all products of state intervention (Boris and Klein 2012).

Given this structure of home care, it was never enough just to win collective-bargaining rights with individual vendor agencies. To make economic gains, the union had to go to government. Illinois provides a good case example, since it ultimately became a defendant in the fateful Supreme Court decisions *Harris v. Quinn* and *Janus v. AFSCME*. Illinois ran home-care services through two different agencies, the Department of Aging and the Department of Rehabilitative Services. The Department of Aging contracted with vendors, for-profit or nonprofit private agencies that hired workers and sent them out to work in the homes of elders. People under sixty received similar assistance from the Department of

Rehabilitative Services (DORS), funded in good part by Medicaid after 1984. In keeping with the disability-rights ethos of independence, DORS relied on a different model: clients hired their own providers, who could be family or friends, but DORS claimed to be a co-employer and set wages—typically at the minimum wage. Regardless of which mode of provision they worked under, workers had no hospital or medical insurance, no paid vacation, no compensated sick days, no life insurance, and no compensation for time spent traveling to and from clients' homes, often on long bus and subway rides. With no common worksite, they perceived themselves alone and isolated (Boris and Klein 2012).

Emerging in the 1980s, Chicago's home-care Local 880 of the Service Employees International Union (SEIU) pursued innovative tactics and new allies. They not only reached out to workers in casual or service sectors but also experimented with new structures of representation and distinct forms of unionism. They had to devise legal and political strategies for an era in which governments denied they were the employer responsible for poverty wage rates or twelve-hour shifts, the National Labor Relations Board (NLRB) election often was a dead end, and courts refused coverage under the Fair Labor Standards Act (FLSA). Before caregivers were even able to bargain for better conditions, they had to see themselves as workers and fight for recognition as such by the public, the state, and the very users of their services. They had to seek the right to organize in the first place. Political brokering with the state thus became an important part of home-care unionism. They had to gain "visibility" and "dignity," which became two key words both in their self-presentation and in media representations of home-care providers. Home-care workers and their allies among consumers had to challenge representations of self-sacrificing workers and helpless consumers, as well as the stigmatization of dependency, whether on other human beings or on the state.

Victories in the 1990s and early years of the twentieth century were the culmination of a thirty-five-year struggle that began with the surge in public-sector unionism in the mid-1960s. Home-care unionism benefited from a surge of organizing among poor, black, Latina, and immigrant women. Mirroring home care's hybrid origins, home-care unionism had roots in the welfare-rights movement and in the dynamic growth in hospital and health-care unionism in the latter decades of the twentieth century. The movement drew lessons from domestic workers in New York and San Diego; farmworker unionism in California; public-sector militancy bound up with political struggle around state budgets in many cities; and the community organizing of groups like the Association of Community Organizations for Reform Now (ACORN). Local 880 in fact began as an ACORN chapter that sought to create solidarities out of the social structures inhabited by the poor.

Through persistent political action and mobilization with clients, Illinois finally agreed to take on the role of employer and engage in collective bargaining. By using collective bargaining, the state, workers, agency employers, and clients/consumers worked out a functional arrangement that, to a good degree, reduced labor turnover and provided more reliable social welfare support services (Boris and Klein 2012, chap. 6). Illinois officials decided that, in order to provide a consistent and essential service to its citizens, it would have to recognize its own role as "co-employer" of the actual hands-on providers of the service—the home-care workers. While the state seeks "to preserve customer autonomy whenever possible," notes the Illinois official statement, "it does not diminish the State's interests in the effective provision of services." According to state officials, "personal assistants" perform services outlined in a "state-created plan." While an individual or family may select an individual care provider, the department establishes the qualifications, approves the person for hiring, has the "customer" and worker sign a department-drafted agreement detailing responsibilities, and conducts an annual review of the worker's performance. The state pays the worker's salary and withholds Social Security and state and federal income taxes. "Customers neither pay their personal assistants nor may they vary the wage rate established by the state." The state legislature ultimately determined to recognize the "personal assistants" and "homemakers" as public workers under the Illinois Public Labor Relations Act for the purposes of bargaining over wages, working conditions, training and safety, benefits, and establishing a grievance procedure to resolve disputes. Recognizing both the structural realities of the sector and the fact that isolated solo workers still constitute a "workforce," state officials decided that "to effectively coordinate with this widely dispersed workforce, the State gives personal assistants the option to elect a union to negotiate with the State" and that this would be "the best way to ensure a workforce that will meet the needs of the State's most vulnerable residents in a professional and effective manner" (Brief for Respondent [Pat Quinn, Governor of Illinois], Harris v. Quinn, 134 S. Ct. [2013], at 1–8); Harris et al. v. Quinn, 573, U.S. __ [2014]).

Consequently, while union membership fell in manufacturing and other private-sector enterprises, publicly subsidized home health care, and subsequently child care, became one of the few areas of union growth and substantial union density. Having honed a set of organizing and political strategies in Illinois, SEIU and other unions began to spread this model to other states, including Oregon, Washington, Maryland, New Jersey, Massachusetts, Missouri, and Connecticut. The spread of unionization not only resulted in higher wages (in Illinois, wages rose from $7 an hour in 2003 to $13 in 2014), coverage under state worker compensation programs, safety training, a grievance procedure, and health benefits for the workers but also, where the union had real clout, in more hours of service for the clients and due process rights, such as hearings if the workers faced termination of benefits (Brief for Respondent 2013, 7).

The Right Mobilizes a New Front against Public Labor

This set of successes caught the attention and raised the alarm of conservative opponents of organized labor and the welfare state. Partly owing to its innovative strategies of linking unionism and the welfare state, and partly owing to home care's legal limbo (lacking legal recognition as "real work"), home care became an ideological arena in which a coalition of political conservatives, business associations, and anti-labor interests organized to stage a new assault on public-sector unionism and labor rights. This anti-union coalition has turned to the courts to undermine the gains care workers made through organizing within the welfare state.

Beginning with two lawsuits, filed in Illinois and Wisconsin in 2010, a group known as the National Right to Work Legal Defense Foundation (NRWLDF), supported by a who's who of conservative think tanks (e.g., the Cato Institute, the Mackinac Center for Public Policy, and the Pacific Legal Foundation) sought to dislodge state-level executive orders and legislative mandates conferring collective bargaining rights. They did so by shifting the focus from employment law to First Amendment grounds (particularly so that they could make a constitutional argument the US Supreme Court could later take up). They generated three interlocking claims. First, by opening the door to unionization through political means, states had designated representatives for personal care providers, thereby denying them the right to choose their own political representatives. This is an alleged violation of the First Amendment. Second, there is no employee-employer relationship between the care providers and any employer, and thus such representation has nothing to do with collective bargaining or labor standards. Third, this lack of an employee-employer relationship means the state has no right to authorize unions as the representatives of care workers in negotiations with state oversight authorities. William L. Messenger, staff attorney for the NRWLDF, wrote, "Providers are simply a group of citizens who receive monies from a government program"—in other words, they are not really workers at all! (Boris and Klein 2010; Brief for Plaintiffs, Harris v. Quinn, 134 S. Ct. [2013]). Indeed, the NRWLDF carefully constructed the case to imply as much by choosing six plaintiffs who cared solely for family members and suggesting that they represented the vast majority of the two million other workers in the field.

One of the intellectual genealogies of this argument stems from the work of libertarian legal scholar Sylvester Petro, who argued that unions in the United States were coercive institutions with authoritarian leadership. Petro insisted that "labor solidarity was not a social fact but a creation of undemocratic laws that allowed unions to politicize the workplace." He contrasted mandated collective bargaining with "freedom of individuals to dissent from or avoid membership in labor organizations" and the protection of their "right to work." According to Joseph McCartin and Jean-Christian Vinel, Petro applied this "rights discourse" to public-sector unions and became one of the nation's most effective critics of public-sector unionism; indeed, in 1973, he created an entire new center at Wake Forest University Law School in North Carolina that was dedicated to developing conservative legal thought on "right to work" doctrine and identifying the corruption of public-sector bargaining. Petro argued that public-sector unionism undermined government sovereignty and popular sovereignty and therefore First Amendment freedom of expression and association (McCartin and Vinel 2012, 232–244).

Petro had a chance to put these ideas into play with the 1977 Abood v. Detroit Board of Education case. Petro argued that public-sector union activity was inseparable from politics. Virtually all the things such unions did were inherently political acts, and thus any money paid (even if only fair share fees and not full dues or Committee on Political Education [COPE] funds) would be put to political uses. The compulsion to make payments to unions therefore represented a violation of a worker's constitutional rights. The ruling in the *Abood* case stated that, while the union had to represent everyone, it is unconstitutional to require a public employee to join a union (although in fact there were no union-shop agreements in any state or city). The union, however, could require covered workers to pay agency or "fair share" fees to support collective bargaining, since workers would reap the benefits of the contract, a ruling that the justices saw had a number of precedents. Nonetheless, workers could opt out of having a portion of their fees used for political activities (McCartin and Vinel 2012, 237, 240–248).

In 2013, NRWDLF got the US Supreme Court to agree to hear the home-care workers' case *Harris v. Quinn* on First Amendment grounds; at the same time, the group also asked the Court to look more broadly and overturn the forty-year-old *Abood v. Detroit Board of Education* precedent that stands as one of the foundations for public-sector unionism and collective bargaining. Contrary to the actual history of home-care service, the petitioners represented the home as private and the state as interfering in what allegedly had always been the nonmarket, nonwage private sphere. It redirected the state's interest into a question of private interests: the family versus the union.

The conservative majority on the US Supreme Court agreed and, in a decision written by Justice Samuel Alito, handed down what an essay in the magazine *The*

Nation called "one of the most anti-labor rulings flung from the bench in recent years" (Boris et al. 2014). In *Harris v. Quinn*, the Court ruled that home-care workers paid through Medicaid do not have to pay fair share fees to support collective bargaining, because they are not bona fide public employees. Since Alito could not at the same time claim they are not workers and vacate Abood's precedent for public-sector workers' collective bargaining, he invented a new category, calling the workers "partial public employees." In doing so, he could again demote their status as real workers, while also signaling to right-wing groups that he was ready to overturn Abood if they brought a real public-sector workers case to the Court.

The decision colludes in misidentifying care workers as "just moms" and thereby denies women working in the home the same rights as other employees, returning unionized personal attendants to the status of household workers still excluded from the National Labor Relations Act. By dismissing the decades-long struggle of African American, Asian, Latina, and immigrant women for recognition as workers, *Harris v. Quinn* reduces a state-regulated labor market to individualized acts of love and obligation, furthering the agenda of well-funded anti-union forces. The Court deliberately chose to ignore the ways in which home care is a business sector comprised of a modern, globalized service workforce. Writing for the dissenting minority, Justice Elena Kagan concluded, "The [Court's] majority robbed Illinois of . . . choice in administering its in-home care program." Such a ruling subverts the state's determination of these labors as being of the utmost public interest (Harris v. Quinn; Harris v. Quinn, dissent, at 6–7, 4, 8; Boris and Klein 2014).

In the eyes of the Court's conservative majority, the home is a private place that a union has no business invading. "Personal assistants spend all their time in private homes," Justice Alito wrote. Union organization therefore "does not further the [public] interests of labor peace." The Harris decision aims to insulate the home from law and labor standards, reprivatize care, and thereby eliminate the need for and legitimacy of unions. The emphasis on the imperative of separating what is private from what is public is anxiously woven throughout the majority opinion. "Today's decision is good news for our nation's families, who are now protected from a disturbing union scheme to turn private homes into unionized workplaces," said Sen. Lamar Alexander (R-TN), the ranking member of the Senate Health, Education, Labor and Pensions Committee, adding, "The Supreme Court has preserved the First Amendment rights of dedicated parents like Pamela Harris." History, however, contradicts this view. The idea of the private, insular home, untouched by market or state, is a myth (Boris and Klein 2014).

Yet, through the potency of this myth, Justice Alito also opened the door to overturning the Abood precedent, affecting millions of other public-sector workers.

Alito brought in a number of tangential arguments to build the case that *Abood* violates the First Amendment. For legal scholar Joel Rogers, the First Amendment has also been used in cases "against the affirmative state" (Rogers 2014). By taking aim at the ambiguity of care labors (which seemed to hover between paid employment and unpaid familial obligations) and the workplace (both open to the market and seemingly closed to the purview of the state), conservatives had created a new route toward breaking the closed shop and a new front in the battle over "right to work."

Using the door Justice Alito opened, the Center for Individual Rights (CIR), a conservative group previously involved in anti–affirmative-action and evangelical cases and now making its move into antiunionism, backed a suit against teacher unionism that could fulfill the agenda of undermining public-sector bargaining. Once again, it involved "fair share fees" that cover the cost of collective bargaining. In Friedrichs v. California Teachers Association (2016), teachers from Orange County (a crucible of modern conservatism) who are not members of the union sued on the grounds of "forced fees and forced unionism." Using the language of the First Amendment and free speech, the CIR's lawyer claimed that this was a "regime of compelled speech . . . that benefits unions." The fact is that the Supreme Court had already ruled long ago that government employees are not required to pay for activities of the union that are not associated with collective bargaining, but conservatives have sought to muddy the waters by casting all union activities as politics. The CIR's president said, "We are seeking the end of compulsory union dues across the nation on the basis of the free-speech rights guaranteed by the First Amendment" (quoted in Clough 2015). Strategically, conservatives have known that if these fees are banned, it will create a crisis for public-sector unionism and make "right to work" the rule in the public sector (Savage 2015; Eidelson 2015). The Supreme Court agreed to hear the case in 2015–2016. While public-sector unions waited for the axe to fall, bizarrely enough they were spared by the fortuitous—and untimely—death of Justice Antonin Scalia, which left the Court deadlocked four to four when it decided the case.

Impact of *Harris v. Quinn*

That reprieve would only hold so long—as anti-union forces fished around for another case. More immediately, the consequences of *Harris v. Quinn* were roughly twofold. First, institutionally, the ruling hit the unions that already relied on agency fees—or unions wherein the largest units relied on them. Once the *Friedrichs* case was on the docket and the possibility loomed of a successor case, some unions stopped collecting agency fees. Others continued to collect agency fees but put them into an escrow fund. Strategically and ideologically, says Deborah Schwartz, vice president of the home-care division of SEIU Healthcare 1199 New England, "it changed the conversations we had to have with our membership"— and potential membership. Facing an existential threat, they now had to acknowledge that defense was not a sufficient strategy (Schwartz 2018). Instead, home-care unions have once again turned to aggressive campaigns that mix fleet-footedness on the ground with targeted litigation and ideological political education. Taking on the full frontal assault of the current right wing, they recognized, requires a fundamental ideological battle as well as a tactical one.

Second, emboldened by *Harris v. Quinn*, a well-organized Right is pushing a mass union disaffiliation drive among care workers. Emerging in the Pacific Northwest, where care workers and public workers had strong SEIU locals, the Freedom Foundation (FF) became an innovative player in escalating the movement against public-sector unions. A libertarian and "free-market" political group, the FF receives funding through the State Policy Network (backed by brothers Charles and David Koch), the Walton Family Foundation, and the M. J. Murdock Charitable Trust. In care work, it particularly targeted SEIU, with "drop campaigns," a direct-action strategy. For decades, anti-union management consultants and law firms had instructed employers on how to deploy union disruption and decertification tactics and had prepped employers for small and large battles, but now the Freedom Foundation went directly for the workers themselves. They launched a door-to-door canvassing campaign aimed at unionized home-care and child-care workers, already low-paid. Their operatives have been filing public records or Freedom of Information Act requests with states and counties to obtain the names and addresses of care workers. Going to workers' homes, FF canvassers in Oregon and Washington told workers they should exercise their constitutional right to refuse agency fees and union dues, ratcheted up their pitch by urging them to drop the union, and beseeched them to recapture both their hard-earned money and their "liberty and freedom." (Never mind that as women of color working in homes, they had never had much of either.) FF cadres claim to have knocked on more than 10,000 doors in Oregon and Washington. They used saboteurs who showed up to disrupt union training and meetings and created an aggressive podcast. In part, groups like the Freedom Foundation have gone after home-care and child-care workers because they believe they can easily dismiss the notion that they are workers. As one Freedom Foundation official described child-care workers, "those workers are basically babysitters." In addition, they are seen as the "low-hanging fruit," particularly because they are low-paid and poor. "They're knocking on doors," notes Mary Kay Henry, national president of SEIU, "saying 'Do you want to save $30 in dues to buy your kids' shoes?'" (Greenhouse 2016). But these workers are also targeted because conservatives know that SEIU is one of the largest unions in the country and that by hitting home-based care workers they can take out 25 percent of the SEIU membership in one fell swoop (Kelleher 2018; Greenhouse 2016).

Having used these activities as a testing ground, FF activists turned to the large buildings and state government plazas where public-sector employees worked, confronting them as they entered or left the buildings. In December 2015, FF activists dressed up as Santa Clauses on the plazas where state workers are employed and prodded workers to "give themselves a Christmas present" and reclaim their money that went to the union. Next up for them were teachers' unions and public schools (Greenhouse 2016).

Freedom Foundation activists are very explicit and open about their anti-union campaign. After all, what would be the point of discrediting unionism ideologically if you are unwilling to speak the name—and there is no subtlety to their language or objectives. "Labor bosses are the single greatest threat to freedom and opportunity in America today," wrote FF director Tom McCabe. His FF fundraising letter stated directly, "The Freedom Foundation has a proven plan for bankrupting and defeating government unions through education, litigation, legislation and community activation" (Greenhouse 2016; Freedom Foundation 2018).

They are more cagey about the deeper political agenda: reverse all progressive gains, destabilize public services and institutions, and bankrupt liberal-left coalitions. For example, in Washington State, the Freedom Foundation has aimed to reverse progressive gains such as higher minimum wage laws and, through defunding unionism, flip the state from Democratic to Republican: the Scott Walker model. In 2016, the Freedom Foundation, which is also an active member of the American Legislative Exchange Council (ALEC), "crossed the Columbia River," in the words of McCabe, and began moving beyond its original base in the Northwest. It is now in California. Meanwhile, ALEC and the State Policy Network kept the ball rolling through state "right-to-work" initiatives and laws.

For the Illinois union that was the plaintiff in the *Harris v. Quinn* case, SEIU Healthcare Illinois, Indiana, Missouri, Kansas (HCIIMK), home-care and childcare workers were the two biggest units at the time of the case. In 2014, the union had 91,000 to 92,000 members paying agency fees. Keith Kelleher, who was president of the union at that time, estimates that had they just decided to wait out the case, they easily could have lost half that membership. Instead, as soon as the Supreme Court accepted the case, the union launched a major sign-up campaign. Hundreds of staff and member organizers fanned out to "hit the doors," hold house meetings, and host membership events. As a result, they signed up another 16,000 workers in a twelve-month period. This meant that about 65 percent of the public home-care members signed up (Kelleher 2017). Kelleher wrote, "Let's not forgot how we got here. Gov. Rauner chose to use low-wage home healthcare workers, and their health insurance and economic security, as 'leverage' for his extreme anti-worker and political agenda" (SEIU Healthcare-Illinois, Indiana, Missouri, Kansas 2015).

Anti-union forces were not complacent, however. With the *Harris* ruling in hand, they, too, mobilized on the ground. The Illinois Policy Institute and the Liberty Justice Center intensified the pressure to roll back careworker unionism by targeting workers directly and by funding Illinois governor Bruce Rauner, who in turn has persistently tried to eliminate contract obligations and even legislatively mandated bargaining issues. The union has felt the effect, as membership numbers have dropped; there are now around 62,000 to 63,000 child-care and home-care workers in those units (Kelleher 2018). Consequently, as Kelleher acknowledges, to simply keep going on that path—sign up workers and expect agency fees and dues checkoff—is like running on a treadmill and expecting to get somewhere. With all the focus on the 2017–2018 Supreme Court's *Janus* case, Kelleher says, "Look: We've already been Janused. We've already been Friedriched" (Kelleher 2018).

Organized Labor's New Offense for the Open-Shop Era

Home care nevertheless had some crucial elements that could form the foundation for the fight back. Both their unionization and their gains were relatively recent. "We still had the institutional memory and the techniques [of active mobilization]," explains Kelleher, "Our people stick to the union because the process of unionization is still in recent memory." In addition, from its inception, home-care unionism was a form of unionism that was linked to issues of low-income communities of color. Since their earliest days as part of ACORN, Chicago home-care workers had been organizing around housing access, credit discrimination, redlining, and living-wage ordinances. They engaged in squatting in housing and direct action against utility shutoffs. They also regularly went to Springfield to lobby legislators and the governor to raise their wages, recognize the union, and guarantee client hours and due process hearings. They formed alliances with consumers with disabilities and marched on the state capitol and attended hearings together. They used political action to link better wages and better care (Kelleher 2017, 2018; Boris and Klein 2012, chap. 6).

Indeed, union officials and rank-and-file leaders from California, to Illinois, to Connecticut have argued that home-care workers are among SEIU's most politically active members. Deborah Schwartz, who worked with the SEIU home-care unit in Oregon and is now vice president of the Home Care Division in SEIU HealthCare 1199 New England, found that in both places, home-care workers had the highest degree of political activism. When I interviewed unionists from SEIU United Healthcare Workers West in the Bay Area and asked why hospital workers, who already had higher wages and good benefits, would want to hitch themselves to low-wage home-care workers, the answer I received—without hesitation—was that home-care workers knew how to be political: they showed up at Board of Supervisors hearings, they lobbied the state, and they pressured public authorities. Nationally, even though they earn a lower income, they give a higher percentage of their income to COPE funds and make more contributions.

For seventy-five years, home-care workers stood outside New Deal labor standards and labor rights and therefore had to be innovators out of necessity. Home-care workers have always had to fight a threefold battle: getting their labors recognized as real work; getting the home recognized as a workplace; and using collective action directed at the state to win improved conditions and security.

Given that its workforce has been primarily poor women and women of color—and is tied to the racialized legacies of servitude, segregated labor markets, and coercive welfare policy—home-care unionism (whether among Latinas in California, African Americans in Chicago, or people from the Caribbean in New York) has been intimately, and explicitly, bound up with civil rights and women's rights. And in their alliances with disability activists, as both groups fought against stigmatization, forced dependence, and invisibility, they also articulated their struggle as one of human rights. Consequently, in the current environment, home-care unions emphasize what has driven their movement all along. In Kelleher's words, "Our union is all about gender rights, workplace rights, civil rights and human rights" (Kelleher 2018).

In New England, SEIU 1199 decided there was no need to wait for the next anti-union Supreme Court ruling to drop on them; the hostile open-shop movement was already upon them. In Connecticut, the main anti-union aggressor SEIU and AFSCME face is the Yankee Institute. More generally, the aggressive direct action of the Freedom Foundation, the successes of ALEC's state-level right-to-work efforts, and now President Trump's hostile appointments to the NLRB and Department of Labor made clear that there was no more time to waste on purely defensive or rearguard actions. Wisconsin, Michigan, Indiana, and Iowa have passed "right-to-work" laws, as well as measures to limit collective bargaining. This was followed by West Virginia going "right-to-work" in 2016 and Missouri and Kentucky doing the same in 2017. In anticipation of the *Janus v. AFSCME* decision, *Labor Notes* soberly noted, "Life will change for unions in the 23 states that till now have rejected right-to-work laws" (Winslow 2017).

For home-care and child-care unions, the Trump regime poses two more existential threats: the elimination of the dues checkoff and the access to employee lists. Dues have been collected from federal Medicaid payments to states for workers caring for Medicaid recipients. The Department of Health and Human Services is planning a rule change on Medicaid regarding what is known as wage reassignment. States that allow union dues checkoff through this mechanism include Connecticut, Maryland, Massachusetts, Missouri, New Jersey, Oregon, Vermont, Washington, and Illinois. The impending rule change would mean the end of dues checkoff, which, for example, in Illinois would directly affect 20–25 percent of the union's membership. In a sector where workers are individually isolated, work is insecure, and caregivers shift jobs and homes regularly, loss of dues checkoff would be an enormous impediment. Second, the NLRB has put the Excelsior Underwear, Inc. 156 N.L.R.B. 1236 (1966) on its target list. Under this ruling, when a union has obtained a certain threshold of signed-up members, it is entitled to receive the list (often called the Excelsior list) of all employees, including those not in the union. The union could then visit and talk to all employees. Again, given the structure of home care, where there is no central workplace, the Excelsior list has been critical. These kinds of rollbacks strike at the heart of what made careworker unionism so successful over the last two decades: the ability to recast home-based work as the labor of the public welfare state and leverage its connection to state policies of care support.

Careworker unions will have to become nimble and creative again, and, given their history, they are confident they can do so. As Kelleher explained, well-entrenched labor unions have become bound to the mechanisms of state dependence, such as NLRB certification and dues checkoff. Unions, however, existed before there was dues checkoff. In Chicago, women built a strong, militant union that produced results long before there was state recognition. In the 1980s, when the union was connected to ACORN, it built power by recruiting members through door-to-door canvassing, house meetings, and the development of leaders for specific actions. From the get-go, it mobilized members for electoral campaigns to gain access to political power (Kelleher 1985; Tait 2005; Brooks 2005). It would "build an organization first" that could maintain itself during workplace campaigns that could take years. Members paid dues from the moment they signed up, well before the union had a contract or certification; for people who made little, paying over that few dollars a month cemented organizational loyalty (SEIU Local 880 n.d.). In the early years of the organization, Kelleher explains,

"We didn't wait for the employer to formally recognize us, but forced the employer to deal with us without official recognition." It was the members that made it a union, not the state (Kelleher 2005, 27, 51). Now that it is a much bigger union, seeking to represent a wider range of health-care workers, it is returning to that orientation. For example, it has intensified campaigns to organize hospital workers. At this point, Kelleher says, "We think we can win more without going through NLRB certification"—as home-care workers once did (Kelleher 2005).

The unions are returning to those tactics while simultaneously reorienting particular institutionalized gains of collective bargaining. Most importantly, they are leveraging guaranteed training programs into deep and broad worker education. In Illinois, California, and Connecticut, public home-care workers' contracts with the state created a mandatory union-run orientation and training program. In addition to the specific allotment of time for training all new careworkers, it also specifies that consumers have to participate for some amount of time. The goal has been to make these programs increasingly capacious. Beyond basic skills preparation, it goes over what is in the union contract, what workers' rights are, what the boundaries are, and what workers can say no to.

This is still a fight, and union reps make sure workers have a reason to fight for the union. In Illinois, Republican governor Bruce Rauner keeps trying to eliminate union training time and state funding for it. (In fact, the *Janus* case was financed by Rauner and the Liberty Justice Center, which have tight financial ties; Rauner flew to Washington, D.C., to attend the oral arguments in the case before the Supreme Court.) Having secured this training time, these unions have been tooling up to prepare for the post-*Janus* era of the open shop. They have been extending the training by a half-hour for political education. As workers leave, union leaders speak with them about paying dues directly, including through direct bank transfer—thus going through the state will not be necessary. These discussions insist that the union, and all that it makes possible economically, politically, and socially, are rooted in fundamental rights. "These are rights we have. We have a right to a union and a right to act collectively in the state. They [anti-union forces] are taking away your rights and we can't let that happen." The union has widely distributed a "Recommit to Your Union" pledge, which includes a section called "What Will You Do to Fight for Your Rights?," asking members to check off a list of actions they will take, from signing letters and petitions; to attending union meetings, press conferences, and rallies; to engaging in civil disobedience (SEIU Healthcare-Illinois, Indiana, Missouri, Kansas 2018).

Training now emphasizes that it is within workers' rights to fight when terms and conditions of employment contracts seem to be violated. Public-sector unions from Washington and Oregon to Wisconsin and Connecticut are finding that when the slightest irritant arises, workers are quick to find fault with the union, call up the union representative, and ask to be withdrawn from the union. To counter this tendency, 1199 New England home-care officials explained, they are retraining organizers and stewards on how to lead a shop fight—to take on coercive bosses, to demand timely fair payment, to fight for consistency in hours, and to fight when due process is denied. The goal is explicitly "to build a fighting organization," affirms Norma Martinez, formerly with Oregon's public-sector Local 503 and now a lead organizer with 1199 New England's Home Care Division, "but this takes concerted training." The union is doing intensive education to make workers clearly aware of the systemic threats they are facing—"inoculation conversations"—and preparing the union to confront these threats. "We are building power," the education programs emphasize (Martinez 2018).

Beyond inoculation, however, home-care organizers, staff, and rank-and-file leaders state clearly, this is the time to build a vision. SEIU 1199 New England (1199 NE) has taken an additional step by creating rank-and-file workers' education sessions and the Home Care Leadership Academy. "We want workers to understand where their power comes from," says Puya Gerami, 1199 NE education director. They are no longer speaking the ameliorative language of the AFL-CIO about protecting the "middle class" and "the middle-class paycheck." This is now about the ruling class versus the working class. "We're building an organization that can take on the power of the ruling class," as Gerami puts it. What is a union for? Education programs emphasize that all of us have to sell our labor to a boss and that the boss has control over it. The only way to counter the control and expropriation of one's time and body on the cheap is through collective solidarity and action. The increasing difficulties and perpetual insecurity experienced by care workers are linked to the privatization of public responsibilities and austerity budgets (Gerami 2018). The new conversation insists that the union must be a fighting machine to take this on but also must gather other stakeholders into an alliance that can pressure the state on such exploitation. The union is the organization that can bring low-income workers together with people who need health care, elder care, child care, rehabilitation, living space, and control of their time, to articulate a vision of a healthy, vital, and thriving community through greater equity, social justice, and social investment.

To prepare and engage workers in that process, 1199 NE launched a Home Care Leadership Academy in spring 2018. The program cultivates rank-and-file leaders—of different ages, ethnicities, and immigrant backgrounds—and then brings them in for an eight-month program of deep education aimed at long-term change. Drawing in a diverse group of workers from around the region, the program has two dimensions: political education and skills training. The political education curriculum includes units on labor history, structural racism, intersectionality, the legislative process, the war on unions, and understanding of economic inequality. Skill building runs the gamut from public speaking to mapping networks, facilitating a meeting, and conducting one-on-one recruiting conversations. Between class-based sessions, members apply what they are learning in the field by presenting at a union meeting, recruiting a fellow member to a union activity, telling members about the contract won in April 2018, and recording their ideas for subsequent rounds of "train-the-trainers" (Gerami, e-mail message to the author, July 7, 2018). In the era of the open shop, members not only have to be clear-eyed about why they belong to the union but also have to be prepared to step up and run their own organizations.

The Meaning of Public Work and the Future of American Labor

Public-sector unionism has long meant redefining work and rights for many low-wage workers, especially women. The jobs of school custodians, cafeteria workers, hospital orderlies, and teachers had been stigmatized, associated with dirt, refuse, bodies, welfare, and dependence. From their inception, the nation's basic labor laws—the National Labor Relations Act; the Social Security Act; and the Fair Labor Standards Act, which regulates maximum hours, minimum wages, and overtime compensation—excluded service workers in public agencies. Enacted in 1938, the Fair Labor Standards Act still did not cover state and local workers by the early 1970s. Prior to the 1960s and 1970s, public-worker organizations lacked legal rights. They had no right to bargain, arbitrate disputes, or strike. Government workers could be fired simply for joining a union. Public workers labored under conditions that resembled those of involuntary servitude. Public-sector unionism fundamentally changed the status of these jobs. As workers who have historically made demands for high-quality public services and fair procedures, public workers opened more pressure points within the political process for public claims on the state. They helped reformulate economic and political citizenship.

The recent campaigns by conservative Republican governors to strip public workers of bargaining rights and the litigation strategy draw from the same deep wells of antiunionism, but they also draw on disdain for the work itself and for those who do it—the taint of dependency as something that is feminized and racialized. Without the vital movement of care workers and their web of social alliances, we end up with care on the cheap, pitting workers against recipients; hardly a stable solution to the mounting demand for long-term care at home. By ignoring realities on the ground, we succumb to the racialized and gendered anxieties of the past rather than seriously attempting to meet the pressing social needs of the present and future. Establishing the legitimacy of care as productive, necessary labor—a real job—would recognize the realities of both our aging society and our service economy and thereby advance the long-overdue work of updating labor standards and collective representation for the workplaces of a new century. Because of their closeness to the consequences of austerity budgets, privatization of public services and institutions, and the struggles of people who do not have means, care workers can help lead the class struggle for social equality in new ways.

Without collective form and collective action, workers would have no free speech on the job: that was the fundamental recognition of the New Deal. Conservative jurists and thinkers have now sought to cast workers as political agents or citizens only in the narrowest of individual terms. The notion that the collective power, voice, and authority of the union subvert the political rights and voice of the individual has been at the core of the "right-to-work" campaign since the 1940s. Today's jurisprudence holds that not only is the First Amendment a right solely of individuals in isolation but also that it is not a right to be exercised within the realm of work. With the *Janus* case, the Supreme Court drew a hard line between employment, where individuals can allegedly negotiate individually and directly with the employer (no matter the scale or structure), and the political realm, where individuals exercise free speech and franchise. Deliberately masking the power relations of employment, it resuscitates several pre–New Deal fictions: that an individual can "negotiate" directly with the boss; that employers are not coercive, only unions are; that industrial relations are a private, not a public, concern; and that the prerogatives of private property are so broad that they foreclose freedom of assembly (Janus v. AFSCME). In her dissenting opinion, Justice Elena Kagan, explicitly reminding us that states are employers, pointedly avers that in *Abood* the Court "understood that expression (really, who would not?) was intimately tied to the workplace and employment relationship. The speech was about 'working conditions, pay, discipline, promotions, leave, vacations, and terminations . . . the speech occurred (almost always) in the workplace; and the speech was directed (at least mainly) to the employer." Therefore, Abood "was meant not to undermine but to protect democratic governance—including over the role of public-sector unions" (Janus v. AFSCME, Justice Kagan dissenting, 12–13, 26–28). At a time when the deficits in political and economic democracy grow deeper and more entwined, unions will have to elevate freedom of association and freedom of assembly to generate new forms of democratic participation throughout our polity.

References

Beland, Daniel, and Brian Gran, eds. 2008. *Public and Private Social Policy: Health and Pension Policies in a New Era.* New York: Palgrave Macmillan.

Boris, Eileen, and Jennifer Klein. 2007. "We Were the Invisible Workforce': Unionizing Home Care," in *The Sex of Class: Women Transforming American Labor*, ed. Dorothy Sue Cobble. Ithaca: ILR Press, 177–193.

Boris, Eileen, and Jennifer Klein. 2010. "Not Really a Worker: Home Based Unions Challenged in Court." *Labor Notes*, October 19. http://www.labornotes.org/2010 /10/'not-really-worker'-home-based-unions-challenged-court.

Boris, Eileen, and Jennifer Klein. 2012. *Caring for America: Home Health Workers in the Shadow of the Welfare State.* New York: Oxford University Press.

Boris, Eileen, and Jennifer Klein. 2014. "Reducing Labor to Love." *The Nation*, July 2. https://www.thenation.com/article/after-harris-v-quinn-state-our-unions/.

Boris, Eileen, Jennifer Klein, Joel Rogers, Joshua Freeman, and Jane McAlevey. 2014. "After Harris v. Quinn: The State of Our Unions." *The Nation*, July 2. http://www .thenation.com/article/180478/after-harris-v-quinn-state-our-unions#.Brooks, Fred P. 2005. "New Turf for Organizing: Family Child Care Providers." *Labor Studies Journal* 29(4): 51–52.

Burbridge, Lyn C. 1993. "The Labor Market for Home Care Workers: Demand, Supply, and Institutional Barriers." *The Gerontologist* 33(1): 41–46.

Craig Clough. 2015. "Supreme Court to Hear Case of Teachers vs. CTA Over Union Dues," LA Report, June 30. http://laschoolreport.com/supreme-court-to-hear -case-of-teachers-vs-cta-over-union-dues/.

Crown, William, Dennis Ahlburg, and Margaret MacAdam. 1995. "The Demographic and Employment Characteristics of Home Care Aides: A Comparison with Nursing Home Aides, Hospital Aides, and Other Workers." *The Gerontologist* 35(2): 163–169.

Dawson, Steven, and Rick Surpin. 2005. *Direct Care Health Workers: The Unnecessary Crisis in Long-Term Care.* Report submitted by the Paraprofessional Health Care Institute to Aspen Institute, January, 11–12. http://www.paraprofessional.org /publications/Aspen.pdf.

Eidelson, Joshua. 2015. "The Teacher Who Would Gut Unions: Rebecca Friedrichs's Challenge to Mandatory Fees Could Reduce Labor's Political Clout." *Businessweek*, November 5.

Freedom Foundation. 2018. "About." https://www.freedomfoundation.com/about/.

Gerami, Puya. 2018. Interview by the author, February 21, New Haven, CT.

Greenhouse, Steven. 2016. "The Door-to-Door Union Killers: Rightwing Foundation Takes Labor Fight to the Streets." *The Guardian*, US edition, March 10. https:// www.theguardian.com/us-news/2016/mar/10/union-killers-freedom -foundation.

Harris et. al v. Quinn, Governor of Illinois, et. al, 573, U.S.__ (2014).

Howes, Candace, Carrie Leana, and Kristin Smith. 2012. "Paid Care Work." In *For Love and Money: Care Provision in the United States*, edited by Nancy Folbre. New York: Russell Sage Foundation, 65–91.

Janus v. American Federation of State, County, & Municipal Employees, Council 31, 585, U.S.__ (2018).

Kelleher, Keith. 1985. "ACORN Organizing and Chicago Homecare Workers." *Labor Research Review* 1, no 80, 32-45.

Kelleher, Keith. 2005. "A History of SEIU Local 880." Unpublished manuscript.

Kelleher, Keith. 2017. "The Janus Case: Kill Shot for Unions or 'Shot in the Arm?'" *Huffington Post*, November 28. https://www.huffingtonpost.com/entry/the-janus -case-kill-shot-for-unions-or-shot-in_us_5a1da40de4b0e6631c44bbcc.

Kelleher, Keith. 2018. Interview with the author, February 26.

Martinez, Norma. 2018. Interview by the author, February 21, New Haven, CT.

McCartin, Joseph A., and Jean-Christian Vinel. 2012. "Compulsory Unionism: Sylvester Petro and the Career of an Anti-union Idea, 1957–1987." In *The American Right and US Labor: Politics, Ideology, and Imagination*, edited by Nelson Lichtenstein and Elizabeth Tandy Shermer. Philadelphia: University of Pennsylvania Press, 226–251.

The Nation. 2014. "After Harris v. Quinn: The State of Our Unions," *The Nation*, July 2.

Rogers, Joel. 2014. "How Harris v. Quinn and Burrell v. Hobby Lobby Turned the First Amendment into a Weapon." *The Nation*, July 2. http://www.thenation.com /article/180478/after-harris-v-quinn-state-our-unions#.

Savage, David G. 2015. "Supreme Court to Hear California Teachers' Suit—A 'Life or Death' Case For Unions." *Los Angeles Times*, June 30. http://latimes.com/nation /la-na-supreme-court-teachers-unions-california-20150630-story.html.

Schwartz, Deborah. 2018. Interview by the author, February 21, New Haven, CT.

SEIU Healthcare-Illinois, Indiana, Missouri, Kansas. 2015. "REBUKED: Court Gives Low-Wage Home Healthcare Workers Major Victory against Another Gov. Rauner Attack," November 30. http://www.seiuhcilin.org/2015/11/30/rebuked -court-gives-low-wage-home-healthcare-workers-major-victory-against-another -gov-rauner-attack/.

SEIU Healthcare-Illinois, Indiana, Missouri, Kansas. 2018. "Recommit to Your Union." https://act.seiu.org/onlineactions/KVhcfu7JUEOHeFXgk6iGNA2.

SEIU Local 880. n.d. (c. 1986). "Discount Foundation Application Summary," 1. SEIU Local 880 Records, M2001-162; M2003-072. Madison: Wisconsin Historical Society.

Tait, Vanessa. 2005. *Poor Workers' Unions Rebuilding Labor from Below*. Boston: South End Press.

US Bureau of Labor Statistics. 2008a. "Personal and Home Care Aides." *Occupational Employment and Wages*, May. http://bls.gov/oes/2008/may399021.

US Bureau of Labor Statistics, . 2008b. "Home Health Aides." *Occupational Employment and Wages*, May. http://bls.gov/oes/2008/311011/.

US Bureau of Labor Statistics. 2011. "Home Health Aides and Personal and Home Care Aides." In *Occupational Outlook Handbook*, 2010–2011 edition, 4–5. US Department of Labor. http://data.bls.gov/cgi-bin/print.pl/oco/ocos326.htm.

Winslow, Samantha. 2017. "Bracing for Right to Work, Public Sector Unions Up the Ante." *Labor Notes*, October 27.

FIGHTING AND DEFEATING
THE CHARTER SCHOOL AGENDA

Kyla Walters

Teachers, labor unions, and community groups mobilized in an all-out battle over the fate of Massachusetts public education in 2016. Question 2 proposed a dramatic increase in the number of charter schools. If passed, this measure would have "lifted the cap" and eliminated the maximum number of charters permitted. This change could have affected every district in the state, not just the lower-performing, urban districts where most existing charter schools operate. In a decade, it was possible that 120 new charters would open across the state. Such an expansion would have completely reshaped the state's public school system.

Question 2 brought seemingly esoteric debates over education privatization into the public sphere. Deciding whether to lift the cap raised fundamental questions about the proper role of government and competitive markets in public education. The Walton Education Coalition, an organization that fervently supports charter schools, commissioned a postelection report on Question 2. According to this analysis, the battle "marked an important flash point for education reform broadly and for charters in particular" as a "test case" of how to effectively champion school choice (Plaut, Kuefler, and Graziano 2017, 1).

The Yes on 2 campaign expected that their unmatched funding and political support would decimate the opposition (Plaut, Kuefler, and Graziano 2017). In the end, the pro-expansion campaign received pledges of $18 million from the business community in January 2016; an endorsement and campaign participation from Charlie Baker, the most popular governor in the country; and support from the *Boston Globe*, the state's most prominent newspaper (O'Sullivan 2016; Scharfenberg 2016a, 2016b). Support for the measure also had a 25 percent lead in the polls in April 2016 (Western New England University Polling Institute 2016). Yet the teachers' unions led the opposition in a historic campaign that flipped the vote and won a decisive victory of 62 percent to 38 percent.

In this chapter, I analyze the 2016 Massachusetts charter school expansion battle based on 84 interviews with participants on both sides of the issue. I examine the key elements of the opposition's campaign: money, internal union dynamics, an interracial coalition, and on-the-ground organizing. I then focus on how teachers' unions successfully organized their members into effective campaign messengers to win against all odds.

Charter Schools and the School Choice Agenda

Charter schools are publicly funded and privately operated organizations, some of which are for-profit. They are exempt from some of the state and local regulations governing other public schools, reflecting the original stated purpose of charters as laboratories for educational innovation. Most charter schools, including those in Massachusetts, receive taxpayer funding for each student that opts out of the "traditional" district-run public school to attend a charter. This funding formula means that the money follows each individual pupil, leading to large financial losses for district schools.

Forty-four states, Washington, D.C., Puerto Rico, and Guam have passed charter school legislation since 1991. With nearly three million students attending charters in fall 2015 (National Center for Education Statistics 2018), these schools are the country's most widespread type of public school choice. Public school choice takes various forms, including education savings accounts, vouchers, and charter schools, as well as inter- and intradistrict transfers. Each maintains (at least some) public funding while introducing elements of "choice" so that students may leave their residence-assigned district school. Private school choice refers to students attending tuition-based independent (or "private") schools without taxpayer funding. One key argument undergirding school choice arrangements is that consumers should drive enrollment because it will enhance competition between schools (and districts) and thereby improve the quality of educational experiences and outcomes.

Proponents often laud school choice generally, and charter schools specifically, as crucial civil rights issues that provide youths of color and poor youths with access to valuable opportunities. Yet scholars complicate the claim that charters are superior to district schools. Charter school academic outcomes vary widely; on average, these schools perform about as well as their district counterparts

(Berends 2015). Other studies of charter enrollment also find resegregation effects (Frankenberg, Siegel-Hawley, and Wang 2011; Garcia 2008). Thus, charters do not comprehensively increase racial and economic equality. In recent years, the National Association for the Advancement of Colored People (NAACP) has adopted an increasingly cautionary stance toward school choice policies that redirect resources from the already underfunded district schools. The NAACP passed a resolution calling for a national moratorium on charter school expansion in 2016, as did the Black Lives Matter movement.

Critics regard charter schools as a part of the education privatization agenda that seeks to disrupt the so-called government monopoly on publicly financed K-12 schooling. The charter school sector includes various organizations, such as schools, nonprofit advocacy groups, education management companies, and conservative think tanks. For example, the American Legislative Exchange Council offers model state legislation to establish charter schools and to amend existing laws to permit rapid growth and unfetter charter school access to public funds for capital expenses, such as real estate. This sector aims to open more charter schools and increase their enrollments. Much like other school choice initiatives mentioned here, charters inject competition into the publicly funded education system while shifting control to private organizations that employ mostly nonunionized educators.

Massachusetts Charter Schools

Massachusetts is one of twenty states that cap charter school expansion. These rules regulate the charter sector so that it does not supplant other public schooling options. Legislators have altered the state's caps on charter schools three times. The first change, passed in 1997, doubled the number of charters allowed (to fifty) and established two kinds: Horace Mann charters, which are special in-district schools whose educators remain within the teachers' union; and Commonwealth charters, which function like independent school districts, are exempt from the local bargaining unit, and were the subject of the 2016 ballot question. In 2000, legislators increased the maximum number of charters to 120 (72 Commonwealth and 48 Horace Mann). Ten years later, lawmakers passed the most recent cap lift, doubling the allowed net district spending in specific low-performing districts.

Seventy-eight charter schools operated during the 2016–2017 academic year, including sixty-nine Commonwealth and nine Horace Mann. During this year, charter schools in Massachusetts diverted $450 million from district schools. Teachers' unions have become staunch opponents of charter schools because these schools move vital resources from district schools and into a privately controlled, largely nonunion sector. Teachers' unions are the mainstay of resistance against charter expansion and other privatization measures, both nationally and in Massachusetts.

Across the country, as in Massachusetts, charter schools enroll a greater percentage of students of color than they do white students. Charter enrollment composes 4.5 percent of the state's total public school enrollment. Comparing charter schools to the state's schools as a whole, it is clear that charters enroll a disproportionately high rate of black (29.9 percent vs. 8.9 percent) and Latinx (31.7 percent vs. 19.4 percent) students (Massachusetts Department of Elementary and Secondary Education 2017). Conversely, 96 percent of public school teachers in Massachusetts identify as non-Hispanic white (National Center for Education Statistics n.d.). This mismatch exacerbates racial tensions between teachers' unions and the charter school organizations, which claim to advance civil rights. It also means that the mostly white teachers' unions in Massachusetts have to engage carefully with voters of color and race-conscious arguments.

Battle over the Charter School Cap

Charter school supporters attempted to persuade the Massachusetts legislature to lift the cap again in 2015–2016, but lawmakers failed to act. Advocates then pursued a ballot referendum to dramatically expand the number of charter schools. Question 2 on the November 2016 ballot proposed permitting the state board of education—the sole charter authorizer in Massachusetts—to grant twelve new charters annually, with no upper limit. If the state received more than twelve quality applications, then applicants seeking to work in districts that performed in the bottom quarter of all districts in the previous two years would get preference (Massachusetts Office of the Secretary of the Commonwealth 2016).

Question 2 became the most expensive ballot referendum in Massachusetts history. Together, advocates and opponents spent more than $41 million (Massachusetts Office of Campaign and Political Finance 2017). The pro-expansion forces poured more than $26 million into the fight. Great Schools Massachusetts was the lead organization in support of the ballot question, spending $21.5 million on their efforts. They relied on so-called dark money, failing to disclose the identities of donors who contributed 70 percent of these funds; after the election, the state campaign monitors forced them to disclose donors and pay a fine (Levenson 2017). This money bankrolled an advertisement-heavy campaign that touted charter schools as enhancing racial equity in education.

Teachers' unions and public education allies opposed the ballot initiative. The opposition to Question 2 was directed by the Massachusetts Teachers Association

(MTA) as the largest teachers' union in the state, with more than 110,000 members. They joined ranks with the Boston Teachers Union (BTU), which represents more than 10,000 educators, and the American Federation of Teachers Massachusetts, which has about 5,000 non-BTU members. The No on 2 campaign developed three talking points as their basic framing: (1) charter schools drain funds from district schools, (2) charter schools undermine local control and accountability, and (3) charter schools create a separate and unequal education system. Though teachers' unions and other donors spent over $15 million to oppose Question 2, they were significantly outspent.

Influential Factors in the Campaign

I argue that what shaped the defeat of the Massachusetts charter school expansion ballot referendum was not simply money, but the teachers' unions' willingness to fight using grassroots organizing tactics and building an interracial coalition. One especially crucial element was the role of thousands of teachers who served as what I call "everyday spokespeople." Before developing this idea, I briefly consider three other factors that were necessary to the campaign's success: financial support, internal dynamics in the MTA, and the campaign's interracial coalition.

Money

The No on 2 campaign leaders could not hope to match the deep pockets of the pro-expansion forces. Still, the unions spent $15 million to defeat the initiative (Massachusetts Office of Campaign and Political Finance 2017). This money paid for campaign materials, television advertisements, t-shirts, bumper stickers, buttons, mailers, lawn signs, and trifold handouts. It also funded salaries of people to conduct focus groups, do polling, create advertisements, train and recruit volunteers, coordinate public events, and perform voter outreach.

Teachers' unions functioned as the campaign's major financial backers. The MTA contributed more than $8.4 million dollars, over half the total that was spent on No on 2. The BTU pitched in almost $350,000. The American Federation of Teachers of Massachusetts gave about $775,000. Both national teachers' unions donated significant sums: $5.4 from the National Education Association and $1.4 million from the American Federation of Teachers. Other labor unions also funded the campaign, including local units of teachers' unions and noneducator unions across the state. Hundreds of individuals also made small contributions.

Internal Union Dynamics

Becoming the opposition's biggest financial supporter entailed serious debates and challenges within the MTA. At the union's annual convention in May 2016, delegates debated whether and to what extent the union should throw its weight behind an effort to defeat Question 2. They ultimately voted to allocate $9.2 million of the union's reserves to the fight. Using the union's reserves prevented raising dues, which would have adversely impacted members with lower incomes.

The MTA's internal political struggles stretch back in time. Two years before the Question 2 campaign, the MTA underwent a dramatic, but partial, transformation. Delegates unexpectedly elected a rank-and-file outsider as president in 2014. Barbara Madeloni helped to lead a progressive caucus called Educators for a Democratic Union (EDU), looking to empower members to resist corporate-backed education policies. Yet the group that EDU members call the "Old Guard" remained in firm control of the board of directors. If this group had maintained more complete control, it is highly unlikely that the MTA would have fought Question 2, much less engaged in a member-driven strategy to defeat the measure.

Before 2014, the MTA had emphasized that teachers are professionals who should participate in creating the laws that affect their schools. However, for many years, the MTA compromised about policies that impacted teachers' working conditions. The union ceded some control over curriculum, seniority, high-stakes testing, and other issues that shape the education Massachusetts public school students receive, especially in the districts that serve more low-income youths. Will, a longtime MTA member I interviewed, said that the pre-2014 leaders were not committed to organizing members in political activities that helped teachers empower themselves to protest policies that would undermine public education. Although "there was lip service paid to it, [and] there was the appearance of" a commitment to organizing, Will found that former MTA president Paul Toner and "some of his predecessors very much tried to keep the power with himself, the executive director of the organization, [and] some like-minded members of the executive committee."

Under Madeloni's leadership, the MTA's 2016 summer conference strove to stimulate members' willingness to canvass on Question 2. This exercise exemplified the union's internal strife, as resistance toward the No on 2 campaign's organizing strategy became apparent. EDU urged members to get involved, offering opportunities to try canvassing. "We brought people together to go out and canvass and do that," Madeloni (2016a) explained, "and if you see who was where when, the Old Guard did not participate in the canvassing."

It was not only the central organization that experienced pushback and shaped the Question 2 campaign. Some locals successfully galvanized member participation, whereas others ignored the effort until late in the campaign, once it had become clear that the union was going to win. Despite these tensions, the MTA reached a new height of member engagement during the 2016 election season as a result of the union's partial transformation under Madeloni.

Interracial Coalition

Building an interracial coalition was the campaign's third critical factor. In March 2016, leaders from the teachers' union and community gathered before the statehouse to publicly announce their joint fight against charter school expansion. Juan Cofield, president of the New England Area Conference of the NAACP, spoke alongside BTU and MTA leaders (Cofield 2015). Together they introduced the Save Our Public Schools coalition, which grew out of two burgeoning labor and community groups: the Boston Education Justice Alliance and the Massachusetts Education Justice Alliance.

Several organizations dedicated to racial equality committed to No on 2. Cofield, who served as the coalition's steering committee chair, created the "Save Our Public Schools" slogan and penned the "no" opinion printed in the ballot booklet. At least eleven organizations working on racial justice endorsed the campaign, in addition to all thirteen local NAACP branches in Massachusetts and Black Lives Matter in Cambridge. Given that the yes side framed their concerns around racial justice and school choice as a civil right, the No on 2 side would have been vulnerable to assertions of racism if teachers' unions had been unable or unwilling to create a meaningful alliance with Black, Latinx, Asian, and other communities of color. The participation of the Boston Education Justice Alliance, a parent and community group that is led by and includes many Bostonians of color, along with Boston high school student-activists, meant that people talking to voters about rejecting Question 2 were anchored in the neighborhoods and networks where charter schools are particularly popular.

Support for the No on 2 coalition spread across Massachusetts. The Save Our Public Schools endorsement list features 155 elected officials, including both US senators, six (out of nine) US representatives, numerous mayors, and state senators and representatives. Elected leadership councils (e.g., city and town councils) in twenty-two municipalities passed resolutions to endorse the campaign. More than 130 organizations also recommended rejecting the ballot item, ranging from labor unions and advocacy organizations to education-focused groups, such as the Massachusetts Congress of Parents and Teachers (also known as the Massachusetts State PTA). Coalition members brought organizational capacity to contact voters, as well as symbolic elements to help refute the pro-expansion side's arguments that tried to pigeonhole the No on 2 campaign as representing self-interested, mostly white teachers.

A staggering 212 (out of 316) school committees passed resolutions opposing Question 2. Though these resolutions were not formally part of the Save Our Public Schools coalition's campaign, the MTA organized efforts to encourage school committees to oppose the initiative. Tracy Novick, a staff member of the Massachusetts Association of School Committees, sensed that these resolutions buttressed the campaign's messaging, saying, "In the communities where the teachers' union went to the school committee or there were school committee members who joined in with the parents' group . . . the message was much more effective because . . . management and the union were agreeing that this [charter school expansion proposal] was a problem" (Novick 2016). Across the state, activists and elected leaders worked to get school committees to explicitly oppose Question 2.

Everyday Spokespeople

Organizing members to engage voters in one-on-one conversations was the cornerstone of the campaign. Teachers' unions activated their members as trusted and persuasive messengers. Rather than only mobilizing a select few individuals groomed to represent the campaign during large-scale public events, the teachers' unions chose also to organize from the bottom up. This involved trusting, informing, and training thousands of rank-and-file members as "everyday spokespeople," a term I use to refer to the people who became campaign messengers, drawing on their status as educators and their own personal experiences of working in the Massachusetts district public schools. Teachers were especially influential in this capacity since they are highly skilled communicators and empathizers. As individuals, they are trustworthy and respected.

James exemplifies everyday spokespeople. A teacher and leader in his local, James performed various campaign tasks, from knocking on doors to informing and encouraging his colleagues to participate. Unlike the campaign to expand charter schools, which relied heavily on television ads, the No on 2 campaign pursued discussions with the public. "You can't have a conversation with a commercial," James responded when I asked him why canvassing is more effective than advertising. He then explained that an ad is unidirectional: "You can't ask it questions. You can certainly do that when you're having a face-to-face conversation. You can give people literature if they ask for it. You can provide them with examples. You answer questions they have. . . . Most importantly, you can personalize it." He applied the skills he has honed as an educator to pursue genuine-feeling interactions with the likely voters he canvassed. Teachers have an ideal skill set for organizing through dyadic conversations. Voters who had questions or lacked clarity on the issue were able to consult with educators, who were prepared and well-spoken canvassers.

Bill Brown, a librarian, detailed going door to door. He remarked on the open-mindedness with which many residents received him, as he told voters, "Nobody is paying me to be here. I'm doing it because I feel really passionate about public schools." "Most people do," he continued, "Plus, you tell them you're a teacher. . . . Once you tell somebody you're a teacher, they associate you with their local teacher because you're three dimensional. . . . Then all of a sudden, they trust you immediately and they'll have a nice conversation with you. That's great. They respect teachers." Bill's experience highlights the potential persuasive clout that teachers possess. Canvassing provided an opportunity to elevate educators as every-day spokespeople, giving voters a "three-dimensional" reminder that teachers are real people. They evoke trust, respect, and a sense of expertise in matters concerning education policy decisions and their real-life, daily consequences. Teachers thus possess a reputable standing with many community members. Going door to door offered chances for teachers to initiate one-on-one discussions where they may have realized their legitimacy as educators.

Informing and Training Members

Informing and exciting teachers' union members was the first step in recruiting educators to become everyday spokespeople. Leslie, a BTU member, nodded to the complexity around energizing teachers as political messengers: "People didn't necessarily trust the unions but the number one people they trusted were teach-ers." Based on polling data, campaign leaders identified teachers as best able to articulate the campaign's framing of the core issue, draw on their own experiences as educators, and offer embodied credibility to No on 2. The unions pushed for-ward with their work to simultaneously inform and engage teachers as everyday spokespeople. Leslie recalled that BTU field organizers "visited so many schools to give presentations to teachers to make sure teachers were informed, because if they are going to be our best messengers, they needed to have the facts straight, too." Teachers responded to this call. They required some training to feel competent about the issue while also exercising autonomy in their capacity as well-spoken and seasoned educators who had firsthand and secondhand experiences of the damage that charter school expansion can cause.

Training efforts were threefold. First, the campaign developed literature with key facts. For example, they created and distributed glossy yellow, blue, and red trifold handouts that succinctly explained the campaign's three main talking points. These helped inform teachers, giving them a clear sense of why they should reject a dramatic expansion of charter schools and providing clear arguments for them to use when talking to voters. Second, teachers required encouragement to balance using the prepared arguments and evidence but without reciting a script. Instead, teachers needed to speak conversationally to connect with people, drawing on their insights as educators and community members. Third, the campaign trained people on what it is like to go door to door and to phone bank. While teachers are experienced and comfortable communicating, they needed to be prepared for the fact that canvassing and phone banking meant that they would be at the mercy of the likely voters they attempted to engage. Rather than having the authority granted to them within the classroom, teachers had to recognize the power that their audience would have over the interaction—and the likelihood that some people would refuse them and order them away.

In addition to this training, several structural preconditions enabled teachers' success as everyday spokespeople. The campaign purchased data about the electorate through the proprietary Voter Activation Network. Among other things, the campaign used this database to divide areas into walkable "turfs" of neighborhoods. The Hub Dialer tool made phone banking fast and simple, displaying the likely voter's information and telling the caller the exact amount of money the voter's municipality recently spent on charter schools.

Experiencing the Campaign

Throughout the campaign, door-to-door canvassing remained the highest-priority task. This activity allowed the campaign to hold face-to-face conversations with voters they might not reach otherwise. The common experience that informants expressed during my interviews was how inspirational this work felt. As Will, the retired MTA teacher quoted earlier, noted, "Canvassing allows for genuine conversations." He saw his canvassing on Question 2 as personally rewarding and politically successful in changing people's stance. Will emphasized that these conversations can take time, explaining, "I went into people's homes and sat like we're sitting now and spent twenty minutes talking to people. That included, in my rap, an acknowledgment that any parent is going to do what they think is best for their child." Connecting on a personal level is a crucial aspect of persuasive canvassing.

For Will, this style entails a recognition that people reach their positions on issues through self-evaluation of their needs, interests, and beliefs. He explicitly identified himself as both a teacher and a parent who followed the same course of action, trying "to look at whatever's best" for his own kids. Will argued that these interactions represent "a degree of sophisticated canvassing and interacting with people, where I'm not just relying on a script. . . . You acknowledge some-body's personal circumstance, but then ask them to think about, Now, who's been left behind? So, I'm not fighting the fact that your nephew is in a charter school, and I hope they're doing well. . . . But your nephew left, took money with him, and now there are many more kids that are left behind, now at a disadvan-tage. And we need to build a world in which we're thinking about everybody." Will's adept movement from acknowledgment of his audience's current position to the core political issue at stake in his framing of Question 2 is rhetorically powerful. Teachers embodied their respected status as three-dimensional, empa-thetic beings. Everyday spokespeople are relatable and effective political messen-gers who connect with their audience from their numerous positions as parents, residents, taxpayers, and educators.

An essential aspect of educational practice is to create relationships, listen, rec-ognize bodily and verbal cues, and plainly state the points needed to raise aware-ness and move a person's thinking in the desired direction. Leslie, a BTU activist, identified Saul Alinsky's approach to community-based organizing that priori-tizes listening and building relationships. She regards listening as "the number one skill of an organizer." Like the MTA, the BTU held a summer organizing con-ference where "the number one thing we hammer[ed] home is a one-to-one conversation. You should be listening 70 percent of the time, and not talking. You need to hear about what people care about to know what they'll be moved to ac-tion for." Attentive listening takes practice and intentionality. Teachers are thus ideally positioned to be effective organizers and everyday spokespeople.

Activists learned to counter claims by those favoring charter school expansion with either data about draining funds or personal experiences that highlighted their status and knowledge base as educators. These discussions demonstrated how teachers are three-dimensional experts who care deeply about how their stu-dents fare and how well their schools operate. Quinn, a Boston teacher, special-izes in educating English-language learners, a student subgroup that is dispro-portionately underserved by the city's charter schools. She reflected on sharing her insider knowledge while canvassing: "I found [myself] speaking from my own experience and not so much the financial [information provided to teachers, which the campaign leaders had encouraged them to stress]. Although I agree with all the financial bigger-policy stuff, just talking about the specific students I serve and how they are not served in charter schools was a big one." Public school ad-vocates, including teachers like Quinn, highlighted various disparities between charter and district schools during campaign outreach. One concern was how nearly all district schools accept all students, including those the charters "coach out," students who have special needs, and students who are acquiring English-language skills. Teachers observe students reentering their classrooms upon leaving charters each year. They spoke to voters about this pattern, drawing directly from their lived experience.

Some teachers consciously prepared for this outreach, arming themselves with policy knowledge so that they were comfortable articulating the campaign's big ideas. Although being an everyday spokesperson does not require this level of policy understanding, it showcases the specific qualities that teachers bring to political organizing. Detailing her preparation as "a research project" to "understand the whole history of it" and speak lucidly about charter expansion, Linda Hanson cobbled together a timeline to learn when and why the state legislature adjusted the charter school caps. A local MTA leader and career educator, she indicated the importance of her autodidactic practice in activating herself as an everyday spokesperson and organizing the members of her local. Hanson reasoned that "to be leaders in this [campaign], we have to be able to speak very articulately about it." To her, doing so was essential to involving educators in the campaign because teachers want to make their own decisions. Thus, organizers needed to "lay the case out really logically, really factually . . . and let them come to their own conclusions. I think that was really important. I do think all the educating that went on, to me, that's always the key. That's the thing you really need to do . . . understand an issue from all sides and then be able to boil it down to a couple bullet points that are fairly easily explained" (Hanson 2016). Informing teachers not only allows them to better convince other people to oppose Question 2 but also enables them to more fully own their position on the issue. I argue that teachers were effective spokespeople because they possessed relevant experiences of the public schools and had also mastered the skills of learning about a topic well enough to teach it to others.

Linda Hanson, for example, demonstrated the effectiveness of her communication skills of listening and customizing a message for each individual with whom she spoke, saying, "Every person that I talked to, I felt like had a different approach to what they cared about. . . . I think that's what informed my canvassing." She never began by telling people, "Here's why I think you should vote no." As she put it, "I always said who I am, where I live, what I do: 'I'm walking around talking to people today about Question 2. Have you heard about it?' That gave me my first clue. 'Do you have any questions about it?' Each time you're like picking up clues to see what direction you're going to go in with them" (Hanson 2016). Based on their relationship to the public schools, as parents, grandparents, alumni, and/or taxpayers, the voters Linda met cared about many different things—from funding and local control to issues at a neighborhood school. She found that "part of the success in convincing them was just really figuring out where they were coming from and what they cared about," which corresponds to the community-organizing principle of elevating the person whom the organizer seeks to move.

From this point in the interaction, Linda employed the knowledge she had accumulated for this campaign to tailor a persuasive message.

Limits and Other Types of Participation

According to Barbara Madeloni, the teachers' unions activated their members fairly well. Although "within the MTA, we engaged more members than we've ever engaged . . . we still didn't engage nearly enough of them . . . not in the sort of hard work" of canvassing and phone banking (Madeloni 2016b). Although I did not interview anyone who refused to participate in these tasks or only did so once, it is clear from various sources that member engagement in campaign activities varied greatly. Moreover, it was difficult for the unions to measure all the kinds of outreach that members performed. Madeloni explained, "The number of people we can count, because we got their name when they showed up to do something, is more than we've ever had, but smaller than [we] would like. . . . But the number of people who felt themselves to be a part of something really powerful—that was their union—I think was broad" (Madeloni 2016b). This distinction between forms of participation illuminates the multipronged organization of efforts to defeat the ballot referendum. The ways that the MTA recorded involvement skewed the dataset such that member participation appears to be a lesser factor. Yet what is counted by the union omits multiple activities that bear political weight, namely one-on-one conversations with family and friends.

Questions of whether union members drove this campaign continued for months after the election. In March 2017, someone leaked an internal MTA document debriefing Question 2 activities to The 74 Million, a national anti-union, pro-education-privatization media organization. The revealed report provides certain details of the campaign's work, including the participation rates of members, which the union had previously kept private. MTA staffers Dan Callahan and Charmaine Champagne acknowledged the challenge of accurately collecting data on all member participation, noting, "On the face of it, only about one percent [roughly 1,110] of our members engaged in MTA-run volunteer activities" (Callahan and Champagne 2017, 2). They identified member involvement as widespread but difficult to correctly capture, underscoring the campaign's success at organizing a large swath of educators.

Although the leak attempted to unmask the unions' victory as relatively unimpressive given "the small number of members who volunteered" (Antonucci 2017), the fact that far more than 1,100 MTA members participated in the campaign speaks to the organizing that the largest teachers' union in Massachusetts accomplished. This figure is an underestimate, given the difficulty of tracking everyone who worked in their local unions on the campaign; those who had conversations with colleagues to push them to get involved and vote no; and those who talked about Question 2 with parents, with their spouses and neighbors, in the grocery checkout line, and via their social media accounts. Such coverage of the campaign fails to consider how and why all these educators were stimulated to speak out about rejecting this dramatic charter school expansion proposal. The postcampaign analysis that the Walton Education Coalition commissioned found that "personal conversations with friends, family, and neighbors who were teachers ultimately convinced many voters to oppose" the ballot measure (Plaut, Kuefler, and Graziano 2017, 6). They reported that 34 percent of Massachusetts parents and 32 percent of No voters talked to teachers about Question 2, arguing that the "less robust ground game and mobilization effort by Yes on 2" was unable to "counter the personal conversations driven by No voters" and the teachers' unions (Plaut, Kuefler, and Graziano 2017, 6).

Within the workplace, some locals held educational training and discussion sessions, called "ten-minute meetings." Louisa, a leader in her local MTA union, with decades of teaching experience, said, "We're encouraging one-on-one conversations whenever possible in the lunch room, at recess, on a Saturday if you run into somebody. [We're] trying to get people information. And I think the best way to do that is really through conversation." She saw political organizing as reaching beyond the immediate campaign to help teachers "realize they have more power than they think they do . . . because if they recognize their power we can accomplish quite a bit. We can get the conditions that we want in our schools."

There were also everyday spokespeople who talked to voters but did not knock on doors or phone bank. Getting members to engage their social networks was another potent tactic and form of rank-and-file involvement. The union's "Talk to 20" campaign exemplified the aim to have teachers act as everyday spokespeople. James, a teacher and local MTA leader, commented that during work conversations he and other leaders would emphasize doing something to participate. "For most people, what they were willing to do is just to have the conversation [and] find twenty people," he stated, "Convince their own family, their extended family—that they were definitely willing to do." During meetings with teachers and other unionized school personnel, union activists highlighted members' existing relationships and community ties as assets to the campaign. In straightforward and complimentary tones, James asked members who "work jobs outside of school . . . 'Can you put some of these buttons on display or see if [you can put] a sign in the window at the restaurant that you work at?'" Union leaders recognized their members' time constraints, making them appreciate members doing what they could—even if that meant only speaking with a handful of people.

Especially given the barrage of policy changes that increasingly impose on teachers' time in recent years, organizers had to identify how teachers could participate in manageable but still influential ways.

The MTA's Talk to 20 campaign played an important role in mobilizing teachers' extant social networks. Union activists like Mary Cummings, a speech pathologist and MTA Senate District Coordinator, emphasized this tactic at a Save Our Public Schools forum in Lexington. From talking to their hairdressers to chatting up security guards at the airport, organizers urged educators and their allies to engage in various campaign-related interactions, both planned and spontaneous, to champion their cause. Teachers also spoke to their extended families, neighbors, and friends. MTA retiree Bill Dooling did just this. While enjoying coffee with a friend, he mentioned charter school funding. His friend "was jolted" upon learning that the money left the district, responding, "What do you mean? That the money can leave the town without the town having any say? That doesn't seem right."

The MTA also recognized such widespread participation: "We knew that our members were informally getting the word out about the campaign by talking with family, friends, and neighbors. During phone banking, we all had many calls in which people told us they would vote no because their children, spouse, or friends were teachers" (Callahan and Champagne 2017, 2). How the union officially records participation and how critics use such data to diminish the campaign's grassroots success undercut the fact that teachers reached a new height of political engagement. The union did not successfully engage all its members, or even half, but they directly involved a small percentage of members and had the general support of another chunk of them to defeat Question 2. This means that empowering even a relatively small number of rank-and-file members as everyday spokespeople can achieve big wins.

Conclusion

Question 2 became a historic campaign, marking a major victory for teachers' unions and their coalition partners who engaged in the hard work of on-the-ground organizing. The opposition flipped the original polling numbers; voters across Massachusetts rejected the ballot question by twenty-four points. Only 15 towns voted for the resolution, 2 towns had tied results, and the remaining 351 municipalities defeated the question (Massachusetts Office of the Secretary of the Commonwealth n.d.). One MTA staff organizer remarked that this "huge victory" bears the potential of continued organizing to resist the right-wing agenda because it shows teachers' union members how they can positively influence political contests.

The Massachusetts teachers' unions and the Save Our Public Schools interracial coalition fashioned the core message that teachers helped deliver through political narratives about the need to reject dramatic expansion of charter schools. The campaign provided their messengers with three talking points: lost funding, lack of transparency, and unequal education. Data were readily available to support each of these points. Teachers coupled these talking points with their own experiences, and those of their colleagues, when speaking to voters and people in their networks about the potential harmful effects of passing Question 2.

Teachers possess key qualities that make them effective everyday spokespeople. They are eloquent, skilled at digesting information and explaining new ideas, and comfortable in dialogue. Teachers tend to be great listeners and reputable community members. They are sometimes vilified by politicians and the media. Teachers are also in every community in the state. Like nurses, educators occupy a woman-dominated and mostly white profession. The public sees teachers as trustworthy (Brenan 2017), leading to a willingness to talk to and believe them.

During spring 2018, teachers became everyday spokespeople on the national scene. They executed groundbreaking strikes and walkouts in West Virginia, Oklahoma, Arizona, Colorado, Kentucky, and North Carolina to protest their stagnant wages and cuts to public employee benefits, as well as the persistent underfunding of public schools that causes ballooning class sizes and narrowed curricular offerings. Sharing their stories of juggling multiple jobs and selling plasma to make ends meet, educators worked to dispel narratives about teachers being overpaid and uninvested in the communities they serve. Although this #RedforEd movement did not secure all the demands that teachers' unions asserted, they did win pay increases in several states. This union-based upsurge highlights the power of organizing rank-and-file teachers to affect policy.

Potential everyday spokespeople exist among every group of workers. Future research and activism should explore the conditions needed for everyday spokespeople to emerge and become effective. Teachers have a stacked deck: respected and nonthreatening occupations; lives dedicated to talking to people; training in knowledge acquisition; a sense that they matter; and a geographic distribution across the state, not just concentrated around one employer. Other groups might have some but not all of these attributes. They might have others that give their message more power. Unions should trust their members and elevate them as everyday spokespeople.

However, organizing rank-and-file members into everyday spokespeople was not the sole factor that led to this victory. Union commitment to fighting charter school expansion was the first crucial piece of creating a substantial resistance effort. Their nominal support transformed into political might when the teachers' unions—and other unions—contributed financially to this cause. The No on 2 campaign collected millions of dollars from teachers' unions, enabling campaign leaders to purchase expertise from a public affairs firm, hire experienced activists to train volunteers and participate in field activities, and buy access to the Voter Activation Network dataset, as well as craft and place advertisements to counter the pro-expansion campaign.

Union funding helped signal labor's commitment to this fight. Ongoing conversations between leaders of the teachers' unions and those of community organizations led to a new public education coalition. Community engagement efforts, including establishing an interracial coalition, increased the campaign's legitimacy and helped offset attacks claiming that racial animus motivated the unions' stance opposing charter school expansion. Therefore, a key lesson from this successful campaign is that labor union activism must be multipronged to combine strong organizational supports, shared decision making within community alliances, and on-the-ground organizing of workers.

References

Antonucci, Mike. 2017. "Analysis: Internal Documents Show Few Union Members Volunteered for Massachusetts Anti-charter Campaign." The 74 Million, March 14. https://www.the74million.org/article/analysis-internal-doc-few-union -members-volunteered-for-mass-anti-charter-campaign/.

Berends, Mark. 2015. "Sociology and School Choice: What We Know after Two Decades of Charter Schools." *Annual Review of Sociology* 41:1–22.

Brenan, Megan. 2017. "Nurses Keep Healthy Lead as Most Honest, Ethical Profession." Gallup, December 26. https://news.gallup.com/poll/224639/nurses-keep-healthy -lead-honest-ethical-profession.aspx.

Callahan, Dan, and Charmaine Champagne. 2017. "Report on No on 2 Campaign Staff Debriefs." Massachusetts Teachers Association. https://www.scribd.com /document/341885302/NoOn2-Campaign-Debrief#.

Cofield, Juan M. 2015. Testimony before the Massachusetts Legislative Joint Committee on Education, October 13. http://www.citizensforpublicschools.org/wp-content /uploads/2015/10/Juan-Cofield-Charter-Schools-Testimony-10-13-15.pdf.

Frankenberg, Erica, Genevieve Siegel-Hawley, and Jia Wang. 2011. "Choice without Equity: Charter School Segregation." *Education Policy Analysis Archives* 19(1): 1–96.

Garcia, David R. 2008. "The Impact of School Choice on Racial Segregation in Charter Schools." *Educational Policy* 22(6): 805–829.

Hanson, Linda. 2016. Interview by the author, December 10.

Levenson, Michael. 2017. "Pro-charter School Group Pays State's Largest Campaign Finance Penalty." *Boston Globe*, September 11.

Madeloni, Barbara. 2016a. Interview by the author, November 22.

Madeloni, Barbara. 2016b. Interview by the author, November 26.

Massachusetts Department of Elementary and Secondary Education. 2017. "Charter School Fact Sheet, Directory, and Application History. Massachusetts Charter Schools: About Charter Schools." http://www.doe.mass.edu/charter/about.html.

Massachusetts Office of Campaign and Political Finance. 2017. "Ballot Question Committees Break Spending Records in 2016." http://files.ocpf.us/pdf/releases/bq2016.pdf.

Massachusetts Office of the Secretary of the Commonwealth. 2016. "Information for Voters: 2016 Ballot Questions." Boston, MA.

Massachusetts Office of the Secretary of the Commonwealth. n.d. "Question 2 Results." http://electionstats.state.ma.us/ballot_questions/view/2739/.

National Center for Education Statistics. 2018. "Public Charter School Enrollment." https://nces.ed.gov/programs/coe/indicator_cgb.asp.

National Center for Education Statistics. n.d. "Table 1. Total number of public school teachers and percentage of distribution of school teachers, by race/ethnicity and state: 2011–12." https://nces.ed.gov/surveys/sass/tables/sass1112_2013314_t1s_001.asp.

Novick, Tracy. 2016. Interview by the author, December 9.

O'Sullivan, Jim. 2016. "Charter School Advocates Launch $18 Million Effort." *Boston Globe*, January 11. https://www.bostonglobe.com/metro/2016/01/11/charter-school-advocates-launch-million-campaign/3Z0jyljnQxWvVUBo2GBsrK/story.html.

Plaut, Jeff, Angela Kueffler, and Robin Graziano. 2017. "Question 2: What Happened and What Happens Next?" https://www.documentcloud.org/documents/4442316-WaltonQuestion2Full.html.

Scharfenberg, David. 2016a. "Bitter Fight Brewing over Mass. Charter School Expansion." *Boston Globe*, February 29. https://www.bostonglobe.com/metro/2016/02/28/bitter-fight-brewing-over-charter-school-expansion/JYgbiybS4YHqiHJgZ0vCGK/story.html.

Scharfenberg, David. 2016b. "Baker Affirms Support for Question 2 in TV Ad." *Boston Globe*, October 25. https://www.bostonglobe.com/news/politics/2016/10/25/baker-appear-pro-charter-school/8Gi49pn1vSoAYO3qlVwDlI/story.html.

Western New England University Polling Institute. 2016. "Charter School Expansion Now Trails in Mass Survey." October 5. https://www1.wne.edu/news/2016/10/poll-mass-referendums.cfm.

Acknowledgments

Our classrooms and hallways were buzzing after Trump was elected president in 2016. Everyone wanted to talk. How did this happen and what did it mean for the labor movement? What was likely to change as a result of the election? How should unions and worker centers organize?

As faculty of the University of Massachusetts Amherst Labor Center, we wanted to create an intellectual space to explore these questions, so we reached out to some leading scholars and asked them to compile their best thinking about where we are and where we need to be heading. On a snowy weekend in March, we brought people together and held a conference to discuss the future of the labor movement in this political moment of Trump and the rise of the right wing. Despite the snow, it was standing room only. Participants included Labor Center alumni from around the country, UMass students, faculty, community members, and a large showing of labor leaders and rank-and-file workers from across Massachusetts and New England.

The debates were fierce and lively. While we did not always agree on the best path forward, we did agree that coming together to discuss these issues is critical. This volume aims to extend these debates to a broader public, with analyses authored by leading labor scholars and public intellectuals.

We have many people to thank for this volume. Like much in life, it has been a collective effort. The long-standing support of the labor movement has been essential. You have shaped the questions and enabled the conversations to take place. There are too many individuals to list, but we are grateful to the Labor Center Advisory Boards (past and present), our colleagues who facilitated panel sessions and discussions at the conference, the Labor Centers at UMass Boston, Dartmouth, and Lowell, the Massachusetts AFL-CIO, the UMass Amherst Sociology Department, and the UMass administration.

The project was funded by the Massachusetts legislature and administered by the University of Massachusetts President's Office as part of the Future of Work in Massachusetts program. We are grateful for their support.

Our students contributed to this project in many ways. Hours of classroom debates helped inform the topics we covered. The energy and enthusiasm of the Labor Center students, past and present, inspires us to tackle projects like this.

Fran Benson and her team at Cornell University Press have moved mountains to enable a timely release. We thank them, as well as the anonymous reviewers, for their helpful feedback and encouragement. We also appreciate the excellent copy editing of Karen Freund.

The work of several Labor Center staff members made this project possible, including Tessa Stuart, Julie Rosier, and Ben Brucato. The Labor Center's new director, Cedric de Leon, has been very supportive and generous in seeing this book through its last stages.

We thank the thirteen chapter authors who contributed to this volume. Having all of you together in the same room, making connections between your individual work and the larger debates in the field, was a true honor. We have enjoyed working with you and appreciate your patience with our short deadlines.

We dedicate this book to our co-worker and co-conspirator, Dan Clawson. Dan worked tirelessly to bring this volume together, just as he worked on so many other projects. In his scholarship and activism, Dan always fought for workers, unions, and social justice. We honor you and we will continue the fight.

We will end by thanking the many folks around the country fighting for economic and social justice. May this collection be useful to you in the struggle.

In solidarity, the editors, who contributed equally:
Jasmine Kerrissey
Eve Weinbaum
Clare Hammonds
Tom Juravich
Dan Clawson

Biographies

Dan Clawson is professor of sociology at the University of Massachusetts, Amherst, and author of *The Next Upsurge: Labor and the New Social Movements* and other books.

Donald Cohen is the founder and executive director of In the Public Interest, a national center focused on privatization and responsible contracting, and is author of the book *Dismantling Democracy: The Forty-Year Attack on Government and the Long Game for the Common Good.*

Bill Fletcher Jr. has held a number of top positions in the labor movement, is a former president of TransAfrica Forum, and is a public intellectual. He is the author of *Solidarity Divided: The Crisis in Organized Labor and a New Path toward Social Justice* as well as the detective novel *The Man Who Fell from the Sky.*

Shannon Gleeson is associate professor at the Cornell University School of Industrial and Labor Relations and author of the book *Precarious Claims: The Promise and Failure of Workplace Protections in the United States.*

Clare Hammonds is faculty of labor studies at the University of Massachusetts, Amherst. She conducts and supports applied research and the labor extension program and also serves as the Labor Center's graduate program director.

Sarah Jaffe is an independent journalist covering labor, economic justice, social movements, politics, gender, and pop culture. Her work frequently appears in national outlets, and she is cohost of *Dissent* magazine's *Belabored* podcast.

Cedric Johnson is associate professor of African American studies and political science at the University of Illinois at Chicago and author of the book *Revolutionaries to Race Leaders: Black Power and the Making of African American Politics.*

Tom Juravich is professor of labor studies and sociology at the University of Massachusetts, Amherst, and author of *At the Altar of the Bottom Line: The Degradation of Work in the 21st Century* and other books.

Jasmine Kerrissey is assistant professor of labor studies and sociology at the University of Massachusetts, Amherst. Her research on labor unions has appeared in journals such as *American Sociological Review* and *Social Forces.*

Jennifer Klein is professor of history at Yale University. She has won multiple awards for her books, including the book *Caring for America: Home Health Workers in the Shadow of the Welfare State*, coauthored with Eileen Boris.

Gordon Lafer is professor at the University of Oregon's Labor Education and Research Center and author of the book *The One Percent Solution: How Corporations Are Remaking America One State at a Time*.

Josè La Luz is a labor activist and public intellectual who advocates for worker rights in the United States and Puerto Rico.

Nancy MacLean is professor of history and public policy at Duke University and author of the award-winning book *Democracy in Chains: The Deep History of the Radical Right's Stealth Plan for America*.

MaryBe McMillan is president of the North Carolina state AFL-CIO and holds a PhD in sociology.

Jon Shelton is associate professor of history at the University of Wisconsin, Green Bay, and author of the book *Teacher Strike! Public Education and the Making of a New American Political Order*.

Lara Skinner is associate director of The Worker Institute at Cornell University and chair of its Labor Leading on Climate Initiative.

Kyla Walters is assistant professor of sociology at Sonoma State University. Her research focuses on work, unions, and social movements.

Eve Weinbaum is associate professor of labor studies and sociology at the University of Massachusetts, Amherst, and union president of the Massachusetts Society of Professors. She is author of *To Move a Mountain: Fighting the Global Economy in Appalachia*.

Index

www.ingramcontent.com/pod-product-compliance
Lightning Source LLC
Chambersburg PA
CBHW030356270326
41926CB00009B/1125